THE YUGO

The Rise and Fall of
the Worst Car in History

JASON VUIC

Hill and Wang
A division of Farrar, Straus and Giroux
New York

Hill and Wang
A division of Farrar, Straus and Giroux
18 West 18th Street, New York 10011

First edition, 2010

Grateful acknowledgment is made for permission to reprint the following material:
Lyrics to "Jugo 45" by Zabranjeno Pusenje, reprinted by permission of Dario Vitez,
and lyrics to "The Bricklin" by Charlie Russell, reprinted by permission of Charlie
Russell.

Library of Congress Cataloging-in-Publication Data
Vuic, Jason, 1972–
    The Yugo : the rise and fall of the worst car in history / Jason
Vuic.—1st ed.
        p.   cm.
    Includes bibliographical references and index.
    ISBN 978-0-8090-9895-8
        1. Zastava automobile—History.   2. Automobiles, Foreign—United States.
3. Automobiles—Yugoslavia—History.   I. Title.

TL215.Z32V58 2009
629.222'2—dc22

                                                                    2009025612

Designed by Jonathan D. Lippincott

www.fsgbooks.com

P1

For Nancy and the Gerb

Contents

THE YUGO

Introduction

Q: What do you call the passengers in a Yugo?
A: Shock absorbers.

The artist Kevin O'Callaghan builds really big things—really big, really poppy, really visual things, like a giant pair of glasses for the singer Elton John or TV and movie sets for A&E, ABC, and the kids' network Nickelodeon. O'Callaghan is a master of "3-D illustration," and teaches a course on the subject at the prestigious School of Visual Arts in Manhattan.[1] Each year he sponsors several student shows. For one, titled "The Next Best . . . Ding!," O'Callaghan gave each student a vintage typewriter and asked the class "to reinterpret" the machine in a different way. "I've always been interested in useless items and giving them other uses," said O'Callaghan, whose students turned fifty decrepit typewriters into beautiful works of art.[2] They were functional too. There was a gumball machine, a meat slicer, a Kleenex dispenser, an aquarium, a blender, a shoe-shine kit, a snow globe, a pay phone, even a Corona-matic-cum-waffle iron that made keyboard-shaped waffles. O'Callaghan's other student shows have included chairs, beds, clocks, carousels, chessboards, and versions of the famed "Moon Man" from MTV.[3]

But O'Callaghan's most popular show, bar none, was on the Yugo, the failed car from Yugoslavia. "I was driving around one day and saw some kids playing stickball," he said, "and they were using a Yugo as the backstop." O'Callaghan stopped and asked them about it. " 'Does your father know you're doing this?' [And the kids] said 'Yeah, it's a piece of junk.' "[4] As O'Callaghan drove away, he had an idea: his next show, scheduled for the main foyer of New York's Grand Central Terminal, would involve the Yugo. "The Yugo was like the little engine that couldn't," said O'Callaghan. "It was the worst-designed product of all time. [So, in holding a show,] we wanted to give the Yugo a new life other than the one [it was designed for]."[5] But for that, O'Callaghan needed Yugos, dozens and dozens of Yugos. He placed an ad in several New York newspapers under the caption "Yugos Wanted Dead or Alive." He received seventy-nine calls in three days, and bought thirty-nine relatively un-dented Yugos for $92 apiece.[6]

Then his students went to work. They transformed the automobiles into truly eye-popping displays that one magazine called "witty, playful, [and] brilliant . . . impeccably crafted and technically amazing."[7] Like the Yugo Easter Island head, the Yugo Zippo, and the Yugo baby grand. There was also a Yugo accordion, a Yugo subway car, photo booth, toaster, telephone, diner, shower, movie theater, and a cozy Yugo fireplace complete with a deer head. There was a Yugo barbecue, a Yugo confessional, and a Yugo port-a-potty with the license plate GOT2GO. The crowds loved it. In May 1995, literally thousands of people took in the exhibit, which then traveled to more than twenty cities, including Montreal. It was featured on NPR, CNN, NBC, CBS, and in newspaper and TV reports from as far away as Croatia. The *National Enquirer* even covered it. "We've gotten a better reception than we ever expected," said Celia Landegger, the creator of the Yugo baby grand. "We're all just blown away. Every day we're amazed [at] how many people have heard of it."[8]

"Squeezing Lemons to Make Art," read a *Washington Post* headline. "Sad Little Cars Given New Life as Sculpture," said *The Dallas Morning News*. In all, several dozen newspapers and magazines reviewed the exhibit, giving it high praise for its creativity, sense of humor, and optimism. The reviews also agreed that the Yugo, the tiny, unassuming $3,990 import, was a "hopelessly degenerate hunk of trash."[9] For just a sampling: "The Yugo is to cars what Milli Vanilli is to rock n' roll" (*Chicago Tribune*); it was "the auto industry's greatest fumble" (*St. Louis Post-Dispatch*); the "scourge of interstates everywhere" (*Daily News* [Los Angeles]); "the Rodney Dangerfield of cars" (*People*).[10] As *The Buffalo News* put it: "Nobody has sympathy for the Yugo. Only bad dreams. Junkyards won't take them. Dogs never chased them. No Yugo was reported stolen, because no owner wanted it back. [And when Kevin] O'Callaghan picked up one for his [art exhibit], he got it for nothing plus a spaghetti dinner."[11]

But was the Yugo *that* bad? Can any car, even a bad car, be a "hopelessly degenerate hunk of trash"? Why was the Yugo so reviled? Even today, a simple Google search of the terms "Yugo" and "worst car" receives more than twenty thousand hits. In 2000, listeners of the popular National Public Radio program *Car Talk* voted the Yugo "the Worst Car of the Millennium."[12] According to Yahoo! Answers it is "the worst car ever sold in the U.S."[13] Ditto at rateitall.com, bestandworst.com, and automotoportal.com.[14] In 2008, readers of the AAA magazine *Via* ranked the Yugo the worst car ever and a 2007 Hagerty Insurance poll declared the Yugo the second ugliest car in history.[15] It was second in Richard Porter's book *Crap Cars* and was named by Time.com and Forbes.com as one of the worst cars of all time.[16] The Yugo appears in Eric Peters's book *Automotive Atrocities*, in Craig Cheetham's book *The World's Worst Cars*, and in Giles Chapman's book *The Worst Cars Ever Sold*.[17] The Yugo even has an entry in the online Urban Dictionary—collector of such useful terms as *dope*, *snap*, and *dawg*—that reads simply: "the world's worst car."[18]

Comedians use the Yugo for their jokes. "President [George H. W.] Bush again denied that the U.S. is in a recession," quipped Jay Leno. "I don't know if people believed him. After his speech [he] returned to the airport in [a] presidential limo [named] Yugo One."[19] Singers sing songs about it. There's "My Bloody Yugo" by the Legendary Jim Ruiz Group (a slick bossa nova ditty), there's "I Drive a Yugo" by the Left Wing Fascists (a kind of alt-punk number), there's "I'll Stay Yugo" by the Belgian electronica group OwlMusik, and then there's Paul Shanklin's satirical ballad "In a Yugo."[20] Writers parody the car in books such as *Florida Roadkill* by Tim Dorsey; in television shows such as *Moonlighting*, *The Simpsons*, and *Saturday Night Live*; and in movies such as *Dragnet*, *Bowfinger*, *Drowning Mona*, *Nick and Norah's Infinite Playlist*, and *Die Hard III*. Advertisers spoof the Yugo in commercials for Yahoo! and Midas, kids destroy the Yugo in games such as *Grand Theft Auto IV* and *Carmageddon II: Carpocalypse Now*, and university professors study the car's importer, Yugo America Inc., in order to show students how *not* to run a business.[21]

In short, the Yugo is an icon. "People made fun of the Edsel," wrote one author, "Ford's $400 million mistake . . . [but] at least the Edsel worked . . . The dreadful Yugo, on the other hand, was both hard to view on a full stomach and an out-and-out vile little car that stretched the most generous usage of [the terms] 'shoddy' and 'slapped together.' The car was less reliable than . . . a Halliburton financial disclosure . . . [and] will likely hold in perpetual ignominy the title of 'Worst Car Ever Sold to the American Public.' "[22] Strong words, but what do we know about the Yugo? Who imported it? Who made it? And why? One would think that such an iconic automobile would have a story behind it, a tale, but what most Americans know are the jokes: How do you make a Yugo go faster? Use a tow truck. How do you double the value of your Yugo? Fill the gas tank. What's included in every Yugo owner's manual? A bus schedule.

But what Americans don't know, for instance, is that it was the fastest-selling first-year European import in U.S. history. Or that when the Yugo went on sale in America, there were lines at some dealerships ten deep. Or that Yugo dealers once sold 1,050 cars in a single day. Or that Chrysler once offered to buy the company, or that its CEO, Malcolm Bricklin, was the first person to bring Subaru to the United States. What Americans do know is that the Yugo was bad, really bad, but relatively few people have ever seen one. The company sold, at most, 150,000 cars between 1985 and 1992. Since then, their numbers have dwindled to perhaps 1,000 working Yugos. (And that's generous: as of 1999 there were more than seventeen million registered vehicles in Florida, but just one registered Yugo.)[23]

So was the Yugo *that* bad? Yes . . . by almost any measure. It was cheap, poorly built, somewhat unsafe in a crash, prone to breakdowns, and dirty emissions-wise, and for such a small automobile its gas mileage was poor. In 1986, *Consumer Reports* wrote that it was better to buy a good used car than a new Yugo. That same year the Yugo ranked thirty-three out of thirty-three in a J.D. Power and Associates consumer satisfaction survey, and in a series of 5-mile-per-hour crash tests conducted by the Insurance Institute for Highway

Safety (IIHS), it sustained a whopping $2,197 in damage, more than twenty-three other cars. In 1987 it topped both the Massachusetts and New York state Lemon Indexes, and in 1988, in the midst of a *Motor Trend* magazine road test, the Yugo GVX broke down. The Yugo was also last in a North Carolina emissions test and last in a *Car Book* survey of resale values, and in a report published by the IIHS the Yugo had the eighth highest death rate of any 1984–88 model-year automobile on the highway between 1985 and 1989. So, yes, the Yugo was bad.

But was it the worst car in history? No. Any ranking is subjective, but as a rule if an automobile passes U.S. safety and emissions tests it is a *relatively* decent car. Not necessarily a good car or a reliable car, but one that has met certain basic, presale standards that are among the toughest in the world. Said one Peugeot executive, whose company left America in 1991, "There were considerable changes [we had to comply with]. Emissions systems, injection equipment, [and] on-board diagnostics are all different on U.S. vehicles . . . and [they] must be reinforced for crash requirements and fuel-system integrity . . . It [simply] has to be done."[24] One Mercedes manager estimated "that the company sold 15 percent of its cars in the U.S., [but] had 50 percent of [its] engineers working on U.S. emissions problems."[25] The standards were that tight. Thus, there's a reason why Russian Ladas and Samaras aren't sold here, or why Indian Tatas or Malaysian Protons or Chinese Dongfengs haven't captured the American market (though, in the case of Chinese cars, this may indeed happen).

For my vote, the worst car ever sold in America was the Subaru 360, a car so light it was exempt from federal safety regulations and was considered a covered motorcycle (see Chapter Two). It had forward-opening "suicide doors," burned a quart of outboard motor oil every 260 miles, and had front and rear bumpers that were several inches lower than those of any car on the road. *Consumer Reports* rated it "not acceptable." Then there was the super-mini BMW Isetta, which in the 1950s was banned from California's freeway system for being too small and too slow, and the three-wheeled Messerschmitt (yes, of German Luftwaffe fame), which sat two passengers in tandem, had a handlebar instead of a steering wheel, had no reverse gear, and started with a pull chord. (You may have seen it in the film *The Addams Family*, where it was driven, fittingly enough, by Cousin Itt.) So no, the Yugo wasn't the worst car in history, not by a long shot.

What the Yugo was was a dated automobile, even in 1985. The car was based on the Fiat 127 and the Fiat 128, both utilitarian subcompacts conceived in the 1960s. Thus, the Yugo was incredibly spartan: the original GV model came only with a stick shift. It had no radio, no air-conditioning, no air bags, and no tachometer; its windows were hand cranked, of course, and it lacked even a glove compartment. "To understand [the Yugo], you've got to look at it strictly in terms of fundamental transportation," wrote *Car and Driver*. "[It is a] cheap, no-frills appliance."[26] The Yugo was cheap. At $3,990, it was the least expensive new car in America. (With dealer financing, a new Yugo cost just $99 a month). It was pitched as a generic people's car; a new Volkswagen; in the words of the man principally behind its introduction to America, Malcolm Bricklin, "a nineteen-cent hamburger with meat."[27] In the fall of 1985, people flocked to buy it. Hundreds bought Yugos sight unseen. Though a dull little car built in communist Yugoslavia, the Yugo was a hit—no, a mania, something the Associated Press called a "Yugo-mania." It didn't last. Critics panned the car for its poor quality. Sales dipped, Bricklin sold the company, and Yugo America went bankrupt in 1992.

That should have been it, but by then the Yugo was firmly ensconced as the worst car in history, a car that Americans love to hate. It's true. We hate the Yugo. The Brits hate it too. (In 1996, British TV journalist Jeremy Clarkson called the Yugo "a hateful, hateful car," and destroyed one sorry example with a shell from a Chieftain tank.)[28] The question is: Why? Why are bad cars pop icons, and why is the Yugo the greatest bad-car pop icon of all time? The answer is in this book. The Yugo story is in this book. It is the sad, sometimes funny, and altogether fascinating tale of how entrepreneur Malcolm Bricklin brought the Yugo to the United States. It is a short history of the worst car in history.

1

Yugo Girls!

Q: How do you double the value of your Yugo?
A: Fill the gas tank.

The original idea to sell the Yugo in America came from California entrepreneur Miroslav Kefurt, who in March 1984 imported three Yugo 45s for display at the Los Angeles AutoExpo. Slight of build yet long in personality, Kefurt was a character. He had come to Los Angeles in 1969 from Prague, Czechoslovakia, where he and his father sold used cars. The Kefurts specialized in one model, the Fiat 600, which they sold in one color: red. "It wasn't that Czech car buyers were demanding red Fiat 600s," remembers Kefurt, "it was because private car dealing was illegal."[1] Technically, Czech citizens could sell their cars only after their odometers had reached 5,000 kilometers. But buying and selling used cars in quantity, as a business, was against the law. Thus, there were no used car lots in communist Czechoslovakia. Buyers simply found their cars through word of mouth or ordered new cars directly from Czechoslovakia's two main auto producers, Skoda and Tatra.

However, like all Soviet bloc countries, Czechoslovakia had government waiting lists for new cars. To buy a Tatra 613, for instance, car buyers paid full price in advance, then waited six months to a year for delivery. The buyer had no say over the car's color or interior, and received no warranty of any kind.[2] "That was one of the flaws of a communist country," states Kefurt. "Somebody in the government would make a decision of how much of anything could be exported, imported, manufactured, or sold . . . It was the same thing with cars. The government didn't make enough new cars, so a black market developed for used ones . . . But since it was illegal for people to deal in used cars as a business, my father had to be careful. That's why he bought the same make and model [the Fiat 600] over and over, then drove the cars for five thousand kilometers before selling them at a profit. Nobody could tell these were all different cars. It was good business."[3]

Kefurt's father was a tour guide by profession, which meant he could acquire new Fiat 600s during business trips to northern Italy. He would buy a car, drive it back to Czechoslovakia, then bribe a guard at the border. "Bribes always worked in those days," remembers Kefurt. "You could bribe anyone for anything."[4] His father bought three or four Fiats per year, and each family member had a Fiat registered to them. The goal was to put 5,000 kilometers on each car, a daunting task for the Kefurts, considering the poor roads and lack of interstates in Czechoslovakia. In 1967, for instance, the Central Intelligence Agency estimated that Czechoslovakia had 46,000 kilometers of roads, of which only 10,000 kilometers were paved. By contrast, the United States had over 3 million kilometers of roads, of which 1 million were paved.[5] That was when Kefurt's father had an idea. He and his son would race their Fiats in local road rallies to burn the 5,000 kilometers.

Kefurt began racing at age fourteen; at sixteen, he placed in one of Czechoslovakia's main road rallies and was well on his way to becoming a professional driver. But in 1969 Kefurt decided to leave Czechoslovakia to live with an uncle in the United States. Through various family connections he secured an exit visa and began working at his uncle's restaurant in West Hollywood, California. Kefurt arrived in the United States in 1969, the same year as Woodstock, the launching of Apollo 10, and the first troop withdrawals from Vietnam. As a student at Hollywood High he found most of his friends owned muscle cars: Pontiac Firebirds and Plymouth Barracudas. They were a far cry from Kefurt's Fiat 600.

One day while walking along Santa Monica Boulevard, Kefurt passed a Honda motorcycle dealership, which had just displayed the company's first-ever imported automobile in its showroom window, a tiny two-door sedan known as the 600. By almost any measure, the Honda 600 was a midget. At a length of 125 inches, the 600 was nearly three feet shorter than the Volkswagen Beetle. At 1,355 pounds, it also weighed 500 pounds less than the Beetle. In addition, the Honda 600 had a four-speed manual transmission, a unibody steel construction, and reached a top speed of 80 miles per hour. The price: $1,275. Kefurt was in love. "Compared to the Fiat 600," he states, "the Honda 600 was a rocket."[6]

Like many small-car enthusiasts, Kefurt favored the 600's handling to that of larger and more powerful muscle cars. He eventually bought other 600s and opened a business fixing the cars for Hollywood-area owners. Though Honda stopped selling the 600 in 1972, in the early 1980s Kefurt discovered that people were willing to spend thousands of dollars to restore their tiny 600s. The car had a real following, so much so that Kefurt developed a profitable Honda 600 business and was known locally as a small-car guru. He drove and tested not only Hondas but also any other small car he could find. In 1982 Kefurt read that socialist Yugoslavia was producing a new two-door hatchback based on the Fiat 127 and with a 903cc, 45-horsepower engine.

Known as the Yugo 45, the car was cheap (by American standards) and, in Kefurt's words, "an import opportunity just waiting to happen."[7] The Yugoslavs planned to export the car to Great Britain in mid-1983 but had no such plans for the United States.[8] Therefore, in the summer of 1982 Kefurt hopped into his Honda 600 and drove to the Yugoslav consulate in San Francisco. At the time, socialist Yugoslavia had consulates in California, Illinois, New York, Ohio, and Pennsylvania, as well as a sprawling embassy complex in Washington, D.C.[9] In San Francisco, Kefurt met with an official commercial attaché who assisted him in contacting the Yugoslav auto manufacturer Crvena Zastava, the maker of the Yugo 45. Located ninety minutes south of Belgrade in Kragujevac, Serbia, Crvena Zastava had been established in 1953 in a failing armaments plant in the city center.

The name Crvena Zastava means Red Flag in Serbo-Croatian, as in the red flag of communism. In later years the Yugo 45 would send up a different red flag among Western consumers. According to economic historian Michael Palairet, the car "was badly built, like all

Zastava's cars, and bottlenecks of every kind limited output."[10] Although in 1962 Zastava teamed with Italian car manufacturer Fiat to build a new $30 million factory on the outskirts of Kragujevac, by the 1980s its facilities were outdated.[11] According to one observer, "By US, Japanese and Western European standards, the Zastava works are a throwback to the Dark Ages—a Diego Rivera mural choreographed live. Noisy, smoky, and in many places poorly lit, the facilities teem with workers . . . OSHA [the U.S. Occupational Safety and Health Administration] would have a field day here."[12] Zastava also lacked many of the production standards then common in the West, which was the direct result of being the only true car manufacturer in a protected market.

Kefurt had never been to Kragujevac. He also had no experience with Zastava's low-quality motorcars. But he knew that the Yugo 45 was essentially a Fiat, a car sold in the United States in one form or another since 1957. Even though Fiat had announced that because of poor sales it was leaving the American market, Kefurt believed that he could "keep" Fiat in the United States by importing the Yugo.[13] For that, however, he needed a license, so with the help of the Yugoslav commercial attaché in San Francisco, in 1982 Kefurt sent a telex to Yugoslavia's state-run export company Genex. Short for General Export, Genex was socialist Yugoslavia's main trading house, whose job it was to sell consumer goods and other commodities for over 1,200 domestic firms. In 1982, Genex did $4 billion in business. The company had offices in some seventy countries and in 1986 introduced McDonald's to Yugoslavia.[14]

Genex put Kefurt in touch with Zastava, but officials there were skeptical that consumers in the United States would buy Yugos. Remembers Kefurt, "They told me that Americans wanted V-8s, that Americans wanted air-conditioning and automatics and that Zastava just didn't make them."[15] Nevertheless, Kefurt was determined. He pestered Zastava until late 1983, when the company awarded him Yugo 45 distribution rights for the state of California. There were no contracts, no negotiations, and no paperwork. In fact, Kefurt's Yugo license, if it could be called a license, was a one-page telex. It stated that beginning with the 1985 model year, Zastava would provide Kefurt with five thousand cars annually. The telex said nothing of price.

What is more, Zastava offered no guarantees and demanded that Kefurt pay for each car up front.

License in hand, in November 1983 Kefurt ordered three Yugo 45s from Kragujevac. They cost a grand total of $7,200 and were shipped to Los Angeles in a forty-foot container that arrived in March 1984. Kefurt was beside himself. He'd spent less than ten grand and was now owner, president, and CEO of YugoCars, Inc., the official distributor of Yugo 45 automobiles from Yugoslavia.[16] Kefurt knew it was a long shot, that most Americans wanted V-8s, and air-conditioning, and automatic transmissions. But timing was on his side. Just two months earlier Yugoslavia had hosted the XIV Winter Olympiad in Sarajevo and ABC had given the Games over sixty-three hours of television coverage.[17] There were Sarajevo placemats at McDonald's, Sarajevo postage stamps from the U.S. Postal Service, even a thermos and bowl set from Campbell's, the "official soups" of the 1984 Winter Olympics.

Night after night, reporters praised Yugoslavia for its efficiency. The Yugoslavs have done "everything capitalists say socialists can't do," exclaimed one.[18] Buses "run frequently and on time . . . Messages are delivered quickly . . . [and arriving American journalists are] whisked to their village, assigned porters, and shown to [their] rooms . . . Skeptics said [Yugoslavia] couldn't handle a modern Games. Well, wherever Marshall Tito is these days . . . he must be smiling. What the Yugoslavs have pulled off is a tribute to the virtues of nonaligned socialism."[19] The Sarajevo Games closed on February 19, 1984, and were described by Juan Antonio Samaranch, the International Olympic Committee president, as "the best organized Winter Games in the history of the Olympic Movement."[20]

Next up: Los Angeles. As Kefurt waited for his first shipment of Yugos to arrive in California, Los Angeles readied itself for the 1984 Summer Games. The Games' chief organizer, Peter Ueberroth, actually "wondered aloud whether Los Angeles would be able to muster the [same sort of] enthusiasm that Sarajevo had" in supporting its Olympics, then praised Yugoslavia for being one of only three communist countries then planning to attend.[21] (The others were China and Romania.) Since early May, a group of fourteen communist countries led by the Soviet Union had been boycotting the Games because, as the Soviets claimed, the U.S. government had failed "to guarantee the safety of Soviet athletes" in Los Angeles or "squelch the activities of private anti-Soviet groups in California."[22]

The Soviets alleged that CIA operatives were planning to give psychotropic drugs to Russian athletes in order to "trick" them into defecting, and had "infiltrated members of terrorist and extremist [groups]" into Ueberroth's organizing committee.[23] Ueberroth was livid. If the Soviet Union and its allies failed to make it to Los Angeles, over half of the world's "world champions" would be absent.[24] It'll be a "second-rate competition," said one official, "really no competition at all. [It'll be like a] Pan Am Games with Asians and Africans . . . I mean, what kind of Olympics [is] that?"[25] To ABC, the Games would be a bore, a profit-killing, audience-shrinking bore, which is why, in its contract with Ueberroth, it had stipulated that if the Soviet Union chose to boycott the Olympics, Ueberroth's organizing committee would refund the network upwards of $90 million in fees.[26]

Although Ueberroth and ABC settled on a much lower figure, as of May 1984, Los Angeles needed a boost, something to remind viewers that America's first summer Olympics in over fifty years wouldn't just be competitive, it'd be watchable—in industry terms, "good TV." As it stood, ABC planned over 180 hours of coverage through two full weeks, nearly thirteen hours a day. For months, it had been charging companies as much as $260,000 for a thirty-second spot and had already sold over $428 million in airtime.[27] "If ratings turn out to be less than expected," wrote *The Wall Street Journal*, "advertisers may ask ABC for compensation in the form of credits," maybe even refunds.[28] Thus, when China, Romania, and Yugoslavia defied the Soviet boycott and sent teams to the Olympics, they were quickly dubbed Los Angeles's "great Red hopes."[29]

The Yugoslavs called the boycott deplorable and, in mid-May 1984, announced they were sending their largest Olympic team ever: 223 athletes competing in 19 different sports. As one Yugoslav coach put it, "We didn't discuss the boycott at all. [And] why should we? We are an independent country, and we do what we feel is right. We will not be told what to do by the Soviet Union, or anybody else."[30] Yugoslavia had been independent of Moscow since 1948 when its leader, Josip Broz Tito, announced he was pulling the country out of the Soviet bloc. In the coming decades, Yugoslavia maintained good (if not close) relations with both superpowers, but refused to ally itself with either. By 1984 its foreign trade was almost equally distributed between East and West.[31] Yugoslavs drank Coke, wore blue jeans, did business with American firms such as Dow Chemical and Westinghouse, and traded their farm produce for Soviet oil. They "liked to play both sides equally," said one former diplomat. "They could really straddle the fence."[32]

Yugoslavia was neutral politically, and since it had already competed in the 1980 Moscow Olympics, which the Americans had boycotted, it saw no reason to boycott the 1984 Games. "Sports are meant to be liberated from all political influence," said Ahmed Karabegovic, a Yugoslav Olympic official from Bosnia. And besides, "where the Olympics are concerned, the most important element is business."[33] The Yugoslavs had learned that lesson in Sarajevo, where they'd made, by some estimates, at least $20 million.[34] They wouldn't make anything in L.A. They were only participants. But the Yugoslavs hoped that their anti-boycott stance, so praised in the press, would be a good form of "company" PR. And in fact it was. At the Games' opening ceremonies, the Yugoslav team entered the Los Angeles Coliseum to thunderous applause, second only to the Americans'.[35]

Yugoslav officials no doubt hoped that Americans' goodwill toward Yugoslavia would mean that they'd buy, for instance, Yugoslav wines (such as Avia, which Coke distributed) and Yugoslav tools, furniture, and textiles. Who knows? Maybe even cars. At least that's what Kefurt hoped. But then his Yugos arrived. They were red, white, and blue. They had yellow French headlights, tartan interiors, and retread tires. They were three of the worst cars Kefurt had ever seen. "I almost cried," he says. "Before then I had only seen pictures and the pictures were nice but now we can't start things. The doors don't lock. The windows don't go up and down. Then I find paperwork in one of the cars saying that these three were factory rejects. They were supposed to go to France, but there were so many problems with them, the French sent them back!"[36] Kefurt and his mechanic spent the next three weeks making the cars presentable. To the red Yugo, Kefurt added a sunroof, mag alloy wheels, and a "super-duper" stereo system, which he claims cost more than the car. He also took the red Yugo to Olson Laboratories in nearby Fullerton, California, where it underwent a series of emissions tests required by the state's Air Resources Board (CARB).

The CARB set strict emissions standards for all new automobiles sold in California, which the Yugo promptly failed. The car performed poorly on its tests because it continued to use an antiquated carburetor. Thus, to sell Yugos in the United States, Kefurt faced a choice: he could equip the car with a cleaner carburetor, or he could replace the Yugo's carburetion system with electronic fuel injection.[37] Either way, he needed help from Zastava. "The carburetion was bad," remembers Kefurt. "So it was my decision to have a fuel-injected car. The fuel injection designed by Bosch in those days was fantastic, but Zastava wasn't interested. I realized then that these guys didn't want a successful car."[38]

Undeterred, Kefurt made plans for the Los Angeles AutoExpo. He printed up Yugo 45 brochures, signs, and promotional literature, then recruited his wife and four teenage models to wear tight Yugo 45 T-shirts and miniskirts and attend the Expo as his "Yugo Girls." The Expo took place in June 1984 in the Los Angeles Convention Center. Kefurt's display included his red, white, and blue Yugos, a plain, unadorned table, and folding chairs for his Yugo Girls. For some reason the Expo's organizers had given Kefurt a premium display space next to the main entrance and directly opposite Mercedes-Benz. As a result, thousands of people visited Kefurt's Yugo exhibit, where his five Yugo Girls were a hit. By show's end, they had distributed four hundred Yugo T-shirts and twenty thousand Yugo brochures, and had taken forty-two $100 deposits on back-ordered automobiles. To demonstrate the Yugo's toughness, Kefurt spoke to potential buyers while standing on the car's roof. When at one point he dented the roof, he jumped down, reached inside, and popped out the dent out with a loud *Thwop!* "Go try that at Mercedes-Benz," he said, "and see what they tell ya! Go stand on a Mercedes!"[39]

Eventually Kefurt's Yugo exhibit drew the attention of Paul Dean, a reporter for the *Los Angeles Times*. "When the Big Three and the European Eleven and the Oriental Six go to car shows," wrote Dean, "it's a million-dollar bazaar of revolving neon and Simonized gloss beneath sequins . . . Then there's the Yugo 45 and Miroslav Kefurt. His booth is five folding chairs around a rented table and no potted chrysanthemums because they cost extra. The models, female, are Kefurt's secretary and her Sun Valley friends uniformed in company T-shirts and red miniskirts. And the models, vehicular, are sedans made in Yugoslavia from a decade-old body design around an engine that's been in production for 27 years."[40]

Dean's depiction of the cars themselves was direct—some might say brutal. Likening them to Spam cans with orange tartan interiors only the color-blind could love, he offered the opinion that their bumpers "wouldn't smother a collision with a bowling ball."[41]

However, to Dean, the Yugo wasn't all bad. Its low price and its Fiat-built engine were in his words "a pretty hefty combination," while the beauty of the Yugo, wrote Dean, was in its "plainness." The Yugo is "simple, utilitarian, [and] honest. It performs the way it looks, and that look tells [you] exactly what it was built to be . . . a commuter car." Quoting Kefurt, Dean then compared the Yugo to the Ford Model T, the Volkswagen Beetle, and the Citroën DV2, giving it high praise as an inexpensive people's car, a reminder of when automobiles "were for transportation, not status," when "turbo-charging was for airplanes and racecars," and when "lifting the hood revealed an engine, not electronic plumbing."

Although most likely Dean had never driven a Yugo—and although he had no idea that one of Kefurt's three floor models had broken down en route to the AutoExpo—he portrayed the Yugo as a dependable foreign car and allowed Kefurt to pontificate on the Yugo's supposed virtues. "It comes with no surprises," stated Kefurt. "Everything fits, everything works, and it's designed to last 15 years." Moreover, the Yugo "comes with a 10-year or 100,000-mile warranty . . . If anything major goes wrong with the engine you bring the car in and we change the engine because to us that's the cheapest way."[42]

Of course, the Yugo had no warranty: Kefurt's entire contract with Zastava was that one-page telex awarding him five thousand cars per year. Zastava expected cash in advance. The contract made no promises to Kefurt and offered no guarantees of any kind. Thus, like any good salesman, Kefurt was telling buyers what they wanted to hear: that the Yugo was a smart, economical car "for people tired of model changes and [tired of] planned obsolescence."[43] And, at $4,500, the Yugo would be the least expensive new car sold in the United States. In 1984 the average compact car cost $9,113, with the cheapest car being the Chevrolet Sprint at $5,151. According to the Hertz Corporation, in 1984 the average cost to own and run a compact car in the United States had reached an all-time high, amounting to 45.67 cents per mile. That figure was 5.5 percent higher than in 1983, and 172 percent higher than in 1972. The bottom line, reported Hertz, was that even small cars were expensive and that during the past twelve years motorists had been "driving less, keeping cars longer, and buying smaller vehicles with fewer options."[44]

Known as "econo-boxes," these vehicles were almost exclusively Japanese. In 1980, six Japanese companies exported over 1.8 million cars to the United States, a staggering 27 percent of the American market.[45] On average, Japanese cars were cheaper, better built, and more fuel-efficient than their U.S. counterparts were. In 1980, for example, only one American-designed car, the Chevrolet Chevette, had a fuel efficiency rating of more than twenty-five miles per gallon.[46] By contrast, eleven Japanese cars did, with eight Japanese cars averaging more than thirty miles per gallon.[47] In addition, nearly 50 percent of Detroit engineers queried in 1979 believed that Japanese cars were the highest-quality cars sold in the United States. (In the same poll, American cars received just 27 percent, while German cars received 23 percent).[48]

Interest in smaller, more efficient cars had been growing in the United States since the mid-1960s, but exploded with the twin world oil crises of 1973 and 1979. In both instances, the Organization of Petroleum Exporting Countries increased the price of crude oil, causing U.S. gasoline prices to jump from 39 cents per gallon in 1973 to $1.38 per gallon in 1979.[49] Consumers reacted by buying cheap econo-box imports. In 1980, a record 2.3 million Americans purchased some $13 billion in foreign-made automobiles. That same year, import sales jumped 21 percent, while sales of domestic cars plummeted 11 percent, to their lowest level since 1961.[50]

The result was a wave of red ink for American automakers. In 1980, General Motors recorded its first loss in modern history

($762.5 million). Ford lost $1.5 billion, Chrysler a staggering $1.7 billion, which at that time was the largest twelve-month operating loss in American corporate history.[51] Decreased auto sales naturally meant layoffs, the kind not seen in Detroit since the days of the Great Depression. At least one-third of Detroit's automotive workforce was on "indefinite layoff" in 1980, an estimated 210,000 workers.[52]

The situation grew so bleak that many in the United States began calling for congressional action limiting the importation of foreign (specifically Japanese) cars. However, before Congress could respond, in early 1981 the Japanese Ministry for International Trade and Industry announced a "voluntary export restraint" (VER), which in effect was a self-imposed quota on auto exports to the United States. The quota for 1981 was set at 1.68 million cars, divided among each Japanese automaker in proportion to its 1979 sales. The VER "was intended to halt the growth of Japan's share of US car sales," wrote one economist, "and to provide the United States with time to catch up with the Japanese in producing smaller, more fuel-efficient cars." But "rather than improving our competitive advantage, the VER encouraged the Japanese to begin producing larger, more expensive cars."[53] The goal was higher profit per unit.

Thus, instead of boxy econo-cars, Japanese manufacturers started to build luxury sedans such as the Nissan Maxima and the Honda Accord LX. In 1982, the Accord LX model featured such standard items as velour upholstery, electronic warning system, tachometer, remote trunk release, and intermittent wipers. The 1982 Accord LX was also 2.8 inches wider than the 1981 model and cost over 20 percent more. Likewise, in 1982 Nissan renamed its Datsun 810 model the Maxima and raised its base price from $8,329 to over $11,000.

Although Honda, Toyota, and Nissan continued to sell cars in the mid-$5,000 range, by 1984–85 they had more or less vacated the econo-box market. The push for upscale automobiles meant that even the tiny Honda Civic, heretofore the gold standard of subcompact cars, had the same wheelbase in 1984 as the midsize Honda Accord.[54] Gone were the days of shoe-box automobiles and gone, too, were mega-cheap Japanese cars. "At the moment," stated one industry observer, "there really aren't any $5,000 cars . . . [available] in the United States because the profit margins on those kinds of cars are little, or nonexistent."[55] But as Miroslav Kefurt discovered in July 1984, the Yugo 45 was profitable—or rather, potentially profitable—provided, of course, that U.S. car buyers wanted Fiat hybrids made by Zastava.

Odds are they didn't, but if the Los Angeles AutoExpo was any indication, the Yugo was interesting. For not only had Kefurt taken $4,200 in deposits, he'd also received inquiries from close to a dozen dealers interested in selling the Yugo. Like Kefurt, the dealers realized that a niche market existed in the United States for import minicars priced at under $5,000. In neighboring Canada, for instance, the Hyundai Motor Company of Korea had sold more than 2,200 subcompact Pony models in the first three months of 1984.[56] At $4,530, the Pony soon became the most successful first-year import ever sold in Canada, "a warm-up," wrote *The Wall Street Journal*, "for what Hyundai sees as its real battle in the U.S."[57] Although Hyundai scrapped the Pony before exporting a new car stateside in 1986 (known as the Excel), the company's Canadian venture proved that cheap, outmoded automobiles could sell well in North America, and for a profit at that.

2

The Habitual Entrepreneur

Q: How do you make a Yugo go faster?
A: Use a tow truck.

As of May 1984, few people in the world had had more experience with cheap, outmoded automobiles than Malcolm Bricklin. In 1968, Bricklin had cofounded Subaru of America and had imported a 10-foot-long, 965-pound Japanese car known as the 360. Priced at $1,297, the diminutive 360 was so structurally unsound that *Consumer Reports* rated it "not acceptable."[1] In 1983, Bricklin's International Automobile Importers sold Pininfarina Spiders and Bertone X1/9s, smallish Italian sports cars originally designed in the 1960s. The cars, which both had engines made by Fiat, sold poorly in the United States and motivated Bricklin to search for another vehicle. As fate would have it, the vehicle he found was the Yugo.

Born on March 9, 1939, in Philadelphia, Pennsylvania, Malcolm Bricklin was, in business school parlance, a "habitual entrepreneur."[2] In 1958, at the age of nineteen, he dropped out of college to work for his father's building supply business in Orlando, Florida. Bored with life and uninterested in working a forty-hour-a-week job, Bricklin had an idea: he would parlay his experience in the building supply business to sell franchises in Handyman America Inc., a chain of hardware stores backed by corporate advertising, computer-based inventory, and a central warehouse. The problem was that in 1962, the year Bricklin came up with the idea and began selling his Handyman franchises, he owned just a handful of stores. He did not have a warehouse.

"Bricklin's adventures in business," wrote one author, "for all their twists and turns," had "a pattern to them. Everything he touched turned to franchises . . . Franchises are promotions. They are an idea sold for a fee. [They became] almost a reflex action with him: think of an idea and franchise it."[3] In the case of Handyman America Inc., Bricklin's franchise fee was $15,000. Although later he claimed to have had 147 stores under license (which he didn't; Bricklin reportedly had sixteen maximum), he found that no matter how many franchises he sold, he still couldn't afford a warehouse.[4] And Bricklin needed a warehouse to make the plan work: as part of the $15,000 franchise fee, Handyman America Inc. agreed to supply merchandise to each Handyman store.

To raise money for a Handyman warehouse, Bricklin expanded his franchise system to include territorial licenses in which buyers would have the exclusive right to sell Handyman franchises in specific regions, such as the Midwest. The territorial franchise fee was $250,000. According to H. A. Fredericks and Allan Chambers, authors of the 1977 book *Bricklin*, in mid-1964 Bricklin used fraudulent asset figures to dupe three California businessmen into making a $95,000 down payment on a territorial Handyman license for the western United States.[5] Apparently, Bricklin told the men that Handyman America Inc. had assets of $868,000, including $75,000 in cash, when the company in fact had few assets to speak of. Bricklin used the same technique to attract additional investors in Florida and New Jersey respectively, telling one man that Handyman America Inc. expected to sell a whopping ten thousand franchises by the end of the decade.[6] According to Fredericks and Chambers, this was all pie in the sky, for Handyman wasn't a company, it was a sales pitch, an idea—to its investors, a fraudulent scheme.

Needless to say, in spring 1965 Handyman America Inc. went bankrupt. The company listed debts of $864,510, assets of $237,906, and just sixteen stores.[7] Fourteen of these stores were in Orlando, although Bricklin would later claim to have founded a "nationwide" chain of hardware stores. In fact, in 1965 the only thing "nationwide" about Handyman America Inc. was its chain of jilted investors. These investors sued Handyman in court in California, Florida, and New Jersey, claiming Bricklin had tricked them into buying franchises and/or territorial licenses through the use of cooked books. The court ruled in favor of Bricklin's investors just prior to the Handyman bankruptcy.

Twenty-six and broke but completely undeterred, Bricklin left Orlando in mid-1965 to become president and CEO of a one-man consulting firm in Philadelphia. Although he and his wife rented a very modest apartment in the city, Bricklin often told people that he had sold his Handyman interests for $1 million *after taxes.* "For the first time in my life," reminisced Bricklin in 1974, "I was scared. Until then, everything I had done I'd done without money. Now it was my money, and if I made a mistake, it was gone. And I was a millionaire—but if I spent one dollar, I wasn't anymore."[8] But Handyman investors told a different story. When asked to comment on Bricklin's claim that he had sold Handyman America Inc. for $1 million, the investor W. Quealy Walker of Sea Isle, Georgia, exclaimed: "I'm the one he was supposed to sell out to, so I ought to know. He did not make one nickel when he got out of Handyman. *A million dollars!* That's the biggest damn fool lie I ever heard."[9]

Whatever the case, in 1965 Bricklin gave up his Handyman aspirations and attempted to sell Italian-made jukeboxes (known as Cine Boxes) that played music and videos at the same time.[10] At one point he traveled to Italy to negotiate sole distribution rights with the Cine Box's manufacturer. Those negotiations failed, but Bricklin secured a meeting with officials from Innocenti, a Milan-based company that produced Lambretta scooters. "After I sold out the Handyman franchises," remembers Bricklin, "I came back to Philly and opened up a consulting firm. The way I did this was by saying, I'm now a consulting firm. I went to Italy and met the people who ran the Innocenti company. Their Lambretta scooters [were] big there but they never went over here and as a result they had a shitload of unsold scooters in New York. I told them my consulting firm would be glad to get rid of them all. Certainly they were interested. So I said I wanted $5,000 a week to unload them. I figured they'd choke on that . . . [but when] they said fine, I near crapped myself."[11]

True to his word, Bricklin sold Innocenti's entire American inventory, hustling back and forth between Philadelphia and New York in a rented Rolls-Royce. Whether or not Bricklin made any real money with Innocenti is debatable, but in 1967 he began selling a second scooter known as the Rabbit, a product of Fuji Heavy Industries of Japan. Fuji was the parent company of Subaru, which in May 1966 had introduced the 1000 Super Deluxe, a four-cylinder, front-wheel-drive subcompact that was a hit among Japanese consumers. Bricklin believed the 1000 Super Deluxe could sell in the United States if only he could import it; however, the bosses at Subaru were unwilling to make the necessary safety modifications required by the U.S. government.[12] Undaunted, Bricklin began researching these regulations. He found that under Federal Motor Vehicle Safety Standards, any vehicle weighing under 1,000 pounds was officially exempt.[13] Be it four-wheeled, two-wheeled, three-wheeled, it didn't matter. If it weighed less than 1,000 pounds, it was—to U.S. regulators—the same as a motorcycle.

Unfortunately for Bricklin, the 1000 Super Deluxe weighed some 1,500 pounds. Therefore, in order to import Subarus to the United States and avoid costly repairs, Bricklin needed to downsize. And downsize he did, to the 965-pound Subaru 360, a car that "bore a striking resemblance to a ladybug."[14] The 360 was short, stout, and goofy. In the words of one author: "It was . . . wretched. Its headlights sat recessed inside cylinders that looked like late-model stovepipes, on two sides of a distended hood that resembled an anteater's snout. The rolling pitch of the front fenders, which continued across the sides of the stubby car all the way to its attenuated rear, made the sedan look as if it had the mumps."[15] According to *Car and Driver,* the Subaru 360 was one of the ugliest cars in history, in its characterization "the most bulbous bubble ever to putt-putt."[16]

But the 360 *was* an automobile. It had an air-cooled, rear-mounted engine. It sat four people, had a top speed of 55 miles per hour, and got an impressive 66 miles per gallon.[17] The 360 was also cheap. Very cheap. Bricklin could purchase Subaru 360s in Japan and ship them to the United States for approximately $650 apiece. All he needed now was a contract. The problem, however, was that few if anyone at Subaru believed that selling cars in the United States was possible. Although a sizable manufacturer, Subaru's rival Nissan had had only limited success in the United States with its Datsun Bluebird series, purchased for the most part by California hippies and foreign-born Japanese. Honda had yet to try the American market, while even Toyota had failed to see any real success in the United States until it introduced the Corona model in 1966.

Thus, it was with very low expectations that Subaru awarded Malcolm Bricklin an exclusive four-year distribution contract in 1968. The contract obligated Bricklin and partner Harvey Lamm to purchase two thousand cars the first year, with an increase of one thousand cars per year through 1971. Subaru could cancel the agreement if either America or Japan changed its import or export regulations, if "circumstances" made participation by either party "physically or financially infeasible or extremely difficult," or if Subaru quit producing the 360.[18] To sell the 360, in February 1968 Bricklin and Lamm incorporated a new company known as Subaru of America. Bricklin's investment was $50,000, Lamm's investment $25,000, far less than the $1.3 million in capital they needed to import two thousand Subarus. Their plan was to sell the Subaru 360 wholesale to a network of independent dealers throughout the United States, who in turn would offer the car for $1,297. Their slogan: "The Subaru 360 . . . Cheap and Ugly Does It!"

Dealers would pay a $1,000 franchise fee, receiving signs, brochures, and other promotional literature while paying approximately $950 per car. Soon eighty dealers signed on. For Bricklin and Lamm, though, the dealers weren't enough. They needed to raise over $1 million in capital just to honor their contract, so they did what most companies do: they sold shares—three hundred thousand shares on the Philadelphia Stock Exchange—and by late spring 1968 they had raised the million bucks.[19] Now they needed a headquarters. Bricklin chose a site just outside Philadelphia in Pennsauken, New Jersey, where he built a massive structure complete with a helipad. "The entire place," wrote one observer, looked "like a gigantic Wizard of Oz put-on."[20] It had an atrium, a Japanese waterfall, a collection of bonsai trees, a goldfish aquarium, and a sculpture made of loose Subaru parts.[21]

The coup de grâce, however, was Bricklin's office, "a push-button-remote-control-automatic-all-in-one-007-fantasy chamber," wrote one historian. "Its imposing, ten-foot-tall oak doors swung open without visible human intervention when Mal[colm] pressed a button on the underside of his palette-shaped, Formica-topped desk. Other buttons caused half a dozen miniature television sets to rise from beneath the desk, and still other buttons allowed Mal to view activities, courtesy of hidden cameras, in every part of his Jersey empire." Lamm's office was notable for its desk too. He had had it covered—all of it, including the top—in animal fur.[22]

Although it can never be said that the Subaru 360 was a popular car, Bricklin and Lamm sold enough of them in 1968–69 to borrow even more money from creditors and to float additional shares. Bricklin used the funds to obtain a private plane and also an apartment and yacht in California, where he began spending his time. He also added elaborate murals of geishas and sumo wrestlers to the parts department of Subaru's headquarters. "Taste is one thing," wrote a reporter from *Philadelphia* magazine, "effect is another. Whether you liked it or didn't, Malcolm Bricklin's Subaru office served its purpose: it got you talking about Malcolm Bricklin. Whether this was any way to run an auto distributorship is another thing."[23] Bricklin's lavish spending certainly did draw attention, but it belied the fact that he and Harvey Lamm were in debt to their ears. As of April 1969, Subaru of America had "a negative cash flow of $750,000," sales were nonexistent, and almost inexplicably Bricklin and Lamm had signed a new contract with Fuji calling for a minimum purchase of ten thousand vehicles per year for the next thirteen years.[24]

If this wasn't enough, that same month disaster struck when *Consumer Reports* issued its "Annual Auto Issue," in which it panned the 360. In the magazine's table of contents, *Consumer Reports* wrote unequivocally: "The Subaru 360 (Not Acceptable)." In test after test, the tiny car failed to meet even minimal standards. It took 37.5 seconds to go from 0 to 50, a full 23 seconds slower (!) than the already very slow Volkswagen Beetle.[25] In its 30-mile-per-hour collision test with an American auto, reviewers found that the car was "shockingly deficient structural[ly]" and that its bumpers were "virtually useless against anything more formidable than a watermelon." To *Consumer Reports*, the 360 was "unacceptably hazardous," and it "was a pleasure," wrote its reviewers, "to squirm out of the [car], slam the door and walk away."[26]

The *Consumer Reports* review of the 360 nearly put Subaru of

America out of business. By late February 1970, SOA had lost almost $4 million, and even though Bricklin repeatedly insisted that the 360 "had been the safest car on the road in Japan in its 10-year history," no one believed him.[27] Soon Malcolm had more than two thousand rusticating cars in inventory, and bankruptcy was in sight. "Say you had 2,000 four-wheel fishbowls," wrote one observer, "no distributors for these fishbowls, a negative cash flow, a reputation for not paying your debts, not a line of credit anywhere around, and a habit of living very high: what would you do? Some folks might ship straight out to Borneo. Malcolm Bricklin merely hustled harder." First, he and Lamm traveled to Tokyo, where they kicked and screamed and pleaded with Fuji to give them something—anything—better than the 360. Fuji grudgingly agreed and in 1970 authorized Subaru of America to begin selling the FF1-Star series of front-wheel-drive sedans and station wagons that were a forerunner of today's successful Subaru cars.[28]

Although the FF1-Star series was a major upgrade from the abominable 360, Subaru of America still needed money. Lots of money. Bricklin attempted to attract investors by appointing a big-name auto man to serve on Subaru's board. The man he chose was S. E. "Bunky" Knudsen, a former president of Ford who had left the company in 1969. Bricklin intended to approach Knudsen with a truly harebrained scheme of merging Subaru of America with the ailing American Motor Company with Knudsen as chairman of the board and Bricklin as president. Bricklin had virtually no money and no track record, and as of 1970 his total automobile experience was the importation and sale of several thousand Subaru 360s deemed too unsafe to drive. Nevertheless, in a demonstration of true moxie, Bricklin met with Knudsen at his home in suburban Detroit after landing a helicopter on Knudsen's lawn. The deal never went through.[29]

Bricklin then set his sights on another scheme known as Fas-Track International, Inc. "Once behind the wheel," read Bricklin's FasTrack brochure, "you rev up the throaty engine while waving a salute to the crowd in the grandstands. The authentic Christmas tree starter lights begin blinking . . . and with wheels spinning behind the roaring engine, you're off on one of the most thrilling rides of your life!"[30] As Bricklin pitched it, FasTrack was to be (what else but) a national franchise of go-kart tracks in which investors would pay $25,000 for ten modified 360s, twenty helmets and racing uniforms, lighting, and a fence. Investors needed their own land and resources to build a track, but were promised an annual net profit of over $135,000 for just twenty-seven hours of operation per week.

So excited was Bricklin by FasTrack that he built his own miniature track outside of Subaru's Pennsauken headquarters. In 1971, he even introduced a FasTrack spin-off called FasTrack Leisure Land, Inc., a proposed chain of resort hotels where guests could relax and race go-karts. FasTrack itself had few investors, although FasTrack Leisure Land, Inc., drew the attention of a Florida real estate developer named Leon Stern. In early 1971, Stern agreed to a partnership with Malcolm Bricklin, by which Stern gave Bricklin a resort property in the Poconos in exchange for $1.25 million in FasTrack Leisure Land shares as well as $1,000 a week in salary. In effect, Stern had sold the resort to Bricklin for a sizable chunk of FasTrack Leisure Land, while as a new FasTrack employee it was Stern's job to scour the country in search of new resort sites and investors.

However, once Bricklin gained control of Stern's property, he used it to borrow large sums from various Pennsylvania banks, which he then invested in other non-FasTrack-related projects.[31] (Stern eventually sued Bricklin for breach of contract and was awarded $2.39 million in damages by a federal court in 1974.)[32] One such project was Goodway Printing, a Philadelphia company owned by Donald and Beryl Wolk that was listed on the American Stock Exchange (Amex). The Wolks had had difficulties in recent years meeting the minimum net worth requirements set forth by Amex for all of its listed companies. In 1971 the minimum net worth requirement was $3 million, of which the Wolks were $500,000 short. Thus, it was Bricklin's plan to invest the $400,000 he had received from Stern's resort property into Goodway Printing. Bricklin also planned to attract additional investors through—what else?—the franchising of Goodway Copy Centers, a forerunner of today's Kinko's.[33]

"Malcolm was interested in Goodway Printing," claims Bricklin's friend and onetime accountant Ira Edelson, "because it could be [used as] a vehicle for raising substantial sums for his FasTrack venture while at the same time aiding Goodway Printing in improving its financial condition."[34] Put simply, Bricklin planned to borrow money in the name of Goodway to invest in a go-kart venture that would somehow earn enough money to repay Goodway while earning a profit. Although at one point Bricklin swooped in via helicopter to close the deal, the Wolk brothers were either lucky enough or smart enough to fend him off. "We are very happy," stated Beryl Wolk in 1975, "to no longer be associated with Malcolm Bricklin."[35]

Nevertheless, Bricklin did find an investor to save Subaru of America: the wealthy Koffman family of Binghamton, New York. In 1971 the Koffmans took control of some 36 percent of the company. In exchange they paid off numerous Subaru loans and backed new letters of credit. Their one condition: Bricklin had to go. As a parting gift, Bricklin received a three-year consulting contract worth $120,000, relief from a $40,000 personal debt to Subaru, and legal ownership of FasTrack. FasTrack was reportedly worth $978,000, but its real value was zero. Its assets included 454 aging Subaru 360 sedans, 391 Subaru 360 trucks and minivans, and 55 other vehicles of little or no value.[36] Thus, it was in June 1971 that Subaru of America parted ways with its cofounder Malcolm Bricklin. Some thirty-five years later, in 2006, it sold more than two hundred thousand cars in a single year.[37]

3

A Canadian Sports Car?

In June 1971, Malcolm Bricklin moved to his next project, General Vehicle Inc., through which he was planning to build a state-of-the-art acrylic-bodied sports car with gull-wing doors known as the Bricklin. Since early 1971, Bricklin had been working on an elaborate prototype, which included a Chrysler six-cylinder engine and Datsun rear suspension, as well as a mishmash of Opel, Chevrolet, and Toyota parts. The car had been conceptualized by Bricklin but was physically designed by a custom car shop in Newport Beach, California. It was completed in late 1972. Meanwhile, Bricklin had heard that French automaker Renault was planning to close its plant in Saint-Bruno-de-Montarville, Quebec, so he approached the Quebec government with a deal: he would build his new automobile at Saint-Bruno if Quebec would give him the Renault plant as well as approximately $7 million in seed money. In return, the citizens of Quebec would take a 40 percent stake in the company. Quebec said no. By then Bricklin had made other Canadian connections and sometime in February 1973 opened a new round of negotiations with the government of New Brunswick.

A small, economically depressed province in eastern Canada, New Brunswick was badly in need of industry, so much so that its lead development agency, Multiplex, quickly jumped at the idea. In March 1973, Bricklin met with Multiplex officials in Montreal, where he outlined an ambitious plan: with help from the New Brunswick government, he would begin producing cars in September 1973, a mere six months hence. He planned to sell ten thousand cars the first year, eighteen thousand cars the second year, twenty-seven thousand cars the third year, thirty thousand cars the fourth year, and thirty-two thousand cars in year five. All he needed from New Brunswick was a plant and $5.5 million.[1] Bricklin had no capital; he had never designed a car, let alone manufactured a car. And worse yet, the $5.5 million he was asking of New Brunswick was, to put it mildly, chump change. Bricklin could have asked for a hundred times that amount and still been short of the estimated $2 billion it took in the 1970s to truly compete with Detroit and to enter the manufacturing game.[2]

But money was only half of Bricklin's worries. He still had a small problem with the car: it wasn't ready. His prototype envisioned a six-cylinder, 2,200-pound automobile with an exterior surface of thermoformed, colored acrylic backed by fiberglass. The acrylic would be corrosionproof and impregnated with color rather than painted. As of March 1971, however, the only full-size car in the world with an acrylic finish was Bricklin's prototype. That prototype had been painstakingly built by hand, costing tens of thousands of dollars and hundreds of man-hours. To bring it to full production, Bricklin now needed specially constructed molds, presses, tools, and human expertise that New Brunswick authorities thought he already had. Thus, when Multiplex officials prepared their first report on the Bricklin project, they erroneously assumed that General Vehicle Inc. was ready to produce cars. It wasn't.[3]

The company still wasn't ready three months later, when in June 1973 New Brunswick premier Richard Hatfield announced that the province would provide Bricklin with $6.5 million in start-up funds and a $2.88 million loan guarantee and that it would purchase 51 percent of Bricklin Canada Ltd. stock.[4] (Bricklin Canada Ltd. was a new company incorporated in New Brunswick, and was separate from General Vehicle Inc.) "Sure it's a high-risk venture," stated Hatfield. "It's time that someone in Canada took a chance. We Canadians are very conservative. The last time we took a real risk, it was on the Canadian Pacific Railway—and it worked!"[5] Comparing the Bricklin project to a transcontinental railroad was blather even Bricklin could appreciate, for if Bricklin knew anything at all, it was the power of the sales pitch. Since spring 1973 he had worked fever-ishly to line up dozens of car dealers at $5,000 a pop, though few if any of these dealers had ever seen the car.

That summer Bricklin also employed the New York advertising firm Lois Holland Callaway, which worked up an entire media cam-paign of print and television ads.[6] The firm pitched the car as the "Bricklin Safety Vehicle" (or "SV-1" for short), emphasizing the car's dent-resistant body and other protective features. That the SV-1 was obviously not a "safety vehicle" was the least of Bricklin's concerns; more immediate was the fact that, because he went into production with a very rough prototype, the SV-1 was doomed from the start. No one knew, for instance, if the SV-1's acrylic finish would bond properly with its fiberglass base. It wouldn't. No one knew why the car's gull-wing doors leaked, or how—at 170 pounds each—they'd go up and down easily.[7] The doors were eventually hooked to a tog-gle switch on the SV-1's dash, which meant that if the battery went dead, occupants had to exit the car through a hatchback in the rear.

"If I knew then what I know now about building an automobile," stated Bricklin in 1974, "I would never have made the Bricklin . . . There's a great advantage to ignorance. If you see all the pitfalls, all the problems in one big lump before you, you just don't do it."[8] How-ever, in June 1973, with some $9 million in hand and another $1 million coming from the First Pennsylvania Bank, Bricklin wasn't so contrite. In fact, he was garish. He took to wearing denim jeans, silver and turquoise jewelry, Indian beads, a big belt buckle, pointed cowboy boots, a straw rodeo hat, and a wide leather belt with MAL-COLM spelled out in silver studs. In July, Bricklin also moved his of-fices from Philadelphia to Scottsdale, Arizona, where, according to one journalist, he went Western "all the way."[9]

Why Bricklin moved to Arizona in July 1973 is a mystery, con-sidering that General Vehicle Inc. had just signed its agreement with New Brunswick and was expected to begin building cars in St. John, the capital, that September. Apparently, Bricklin believed that his "Director of Canadian Operations," a former Renault executive named Jean de Villers, could transform the SV-1 from rough proto-type to finished production model in less than three months, then oversee its assembly in St. John. By August it was clear to everyone that he couldn't. Still lacking a production model, in February 1974 Bricklin unveiled an SV-1 prototype at a gala event at the Riviera Hotel in Las Vegas. He planned the event to take place next to the annual convention of the National Automobile Dealers Association, which was also in Las Vegas, hiring the professional race-car driver Bobby Unser and the actor and amateur racer Paul Newman to peddle the car.[10]

Bricklin's second opening took place in New York City in a special ballroom of the famed Four Seasons restaurant. He had rented the room for $50,000 and, with the help of a Beverly Hills PR firm, had personally invited an impressive list of business and community leaders, journalists, car dealers, car enthusiasts, and representatives from the government of New Brunswick and the First Pennsylvania Bank. Bricklin wore a white bell-bottomed leisure suit and a loud patterned shirt, and after a few introductory remarks he pulled the covering off an ivory SV-1. As the crowd applauded, Bricklin's father, Albert, ascended the stage with a red-hot branding iron in the shape of a stylized *B*. "I name this car," exclaimed Albert as he singed the SV-1's fender, "the Bricklin." The crowd cheered its approval as Bricklin calmly explained that because of the SV-1's space-age acrylic finish, the brand could be buffed out. Behind Bricklin, the legendary Broadway composer Sammy Cahn provided entertainment.[11] Bricklin was in his element. He walked through the crowd, shaking hands, taking compliments, and assuring people that the SV-1 would be in production by September.[12]

"Remember Preston Tucker?" asked *Playboy* magazine. "Right after World War Two, Tucker attempted the impossible—taking on Detroit's Big Three with what was heralded as a revolutionary new automobile, the Tucker Torpedo. As it turned out, it *was* impossible; the Tucker was torpedoed almost before it was launched. Now, more than a quarter century later, 35-year-old Malcolm Bricklin, a fast-revving entrepreneur, . . . is going to take a crack at it . . . Will Mal Bricklin make it? Well, Preston Tucker may be forgotten, but does the name Henry Ford ring a bell?"[13]

In August 1974, the first Bricklin SV-1 came off the assembly line. According to one estimate, it had cost over $50,000 to produce, far more than the $7,490 price tag it was supposed to have. Eventually, in the fall of 1974, Bricklin's St. John production team succeeded in assembling new cars at a rate of two per hour. To get to this point Bricklin had spent $15.4 million, including $12.2 million in operational expenses and $3.15 million in parts.[14] But of the first one hundred cars produced, few were ready for sale. Many had body panels that were scratched, warped, or wavy; others had misaligned dashboards or crooked visors, while virtually every SV-1 had doors that leaked. "We had so many problems with leaks," stated Bill Marsh, a Ford dealer from Newton, Pennsylvania, that "we seriously considered drilling holes in the floor to let the water out . . ."[15] Dealers, who months earlier had clamored for a Bricklin franchise, wrote *The Wall Street Journal*, "took one look [at the car] and asked for their money back. The workmanship left much to be desired."[16]

However, in late 1974 Bricklin had more important things to worry about than quality control. For one thing, he was broke. Both Bricklin Canada Ltd. and General Vehicle Inc. were on the verge of bankruptcy. Since August, more than a hundred assembly-line workers at Bricklin's St. John plant had been working just half days, while the plant's owner threatened to evict Bricklin for violating the terms of his lease. Inches from insolvency, Bricklin used his ace in the hole: Richard Hatfield. The sanguine premier had insisted on featuring the SV-1 as a central component in his November 1974 campaign. Hatfield drove from speech to speech throughout New Brunswick in an orange SV-1, drawing large crowds and assuring voters that the Bricklin would be a success.[17]

Politically boxed in, Hatfield provided Bricklin with a $1 million loan, in addition to a $2 million "shareholders' loan" that he had floated Bricklin in October. Then on November 6 Hatfield agreed to buy Bricklin's St. John plant for $1.54 million. By this point, New Brunswick owned 67 percent of Bricklin Canada Ltd. and was, oddly enough, both tenant *and* landlord of the plant in St. John. "That car is going to sell," stated Hatfield optimistically. "Bricklin is assured of an excellent market. Already it has orders for forty thousand cars and the arrangement announced today enables the province to share fully in its success."[18] The only problem was that by November 1974 Bricklin hadn't had any success. He had produced a grand total of 180 cars, the majority of which had been shipped to northeastern showrooms *without locks*. The parts hadn't arrived.[19]

By June, Bricklin Canada Ltd. had produced and shipped more

than 1,800 vehicles. Their quality, by most accounts, was atrocious. What is more, production costs on the first 1,800 vehicles were running at $13,500 per car, although in 1975 Bricklin was charging his dealers just $9,388 per car, a loss of over $4,100 each. As Hatfield would later learn, Bricklin was also transferring cars from Bricklin Canada Ltd. to General Vehicle Inc., Bricklin's stateside company, for the paltry sum of $5,400 per car, which meant that New Brunswick wasn't just losing money on the Bricklin, it was losing money *to* Bricklin.[20] In terms of salary, the government of New Brunswick paid Malcolm Bricklin $120,000 a year. His father, Albert, made $60,000; his mother, Gertrude, $30,000; his sister, Barbara Jonas, $37,000; while Bricklin's uncle Ben, a onetime Handyman investor, made $18,000. Also on the payroll at $24,000 a year was Michael Avery, a specialist in personal motivation who appeared in company records as "Assistant to the Chairman."[21]

In mid-1975, Hatfield's economic minister would slash executive salaries and force Bricklin to pay more for imported cars, but it wasn't enough. The Bricklin was a bust. "Things look very, very bad," Bricklin told the Associated Press in late September 1975. "We need $4 million to $5 million in immediate funds."[22] By early October, Bricklin was asking Hatfield for $15 million in new funds while claiming to have American investors who were willing to put up an additional $10 million, but only if Bricklin "could operate without political [i.e., Canadian] interference."[23] But Bricklin *had* operated without interference—political, pecuniary, or otherwise. That was the problem: his company had never been audited. The firm hired to audit Bricklin Canada Ltd. couldn't find the company's records. They were incomplete, missing, or scattered in boxes in five offices in two countries, a managerial mess.[24]

Thus, by the fall of 1975, even Richard Hatfield could see that the Bricklin was doomed. The premier had won his election by tying himself to what in 1973–74 was an exciting new car. By 1975 that same car was a national joke. In fact, the seventeenth most popular song that year on Canada's country one hundred was "The Bricklin" by the satirist Charlie Russell. "O' the Bricklin, O' the Bricklin," crooned Russell. "Is it just another Edsel wait an' see. We'll let the Yankees try it, an' hope to God they'll buy it. Let it be, dear Lord, let it be!"[25]

But Bricklin, whose can-do attitude sometimes bordered on the bizarre, wasn't ready to give up. Through the summer of 1975 he busied himself with plans for a second automobile called the Bricklin Chairman, a luxury sedan similar to the Ford LTD. He even declared that in spite of the company's problems, it still had a backlog of orders and that Bricklin Canada was, in his words, "gonna make it!"[26] In reality, it wasn't. On September 24, 1974, New Brunswick pulled the plug. "Although the government had always believed that the potential advantages of the project were worth the financial risk taken," said Premier Hatfield, "we have also known from the beginning that there was a point beyond which the government should not, on its own, risk additional government funds on this one project. That point has been reached."[27] Two days later Bricklin Canada Ltd. was placed in receivership.

Bricklin responded by issuing a press release in which he claimed that Bricklin Canada Ltd. was still in business but experiencing a "temporary shutdown." The reason, he insisted, was that the First Pennsylvania Bank and the government of New Brunswick had failed "to agree on a method" of providing the company with a new $10 million loan. "We have received literally thousands of telephone calls from people who shared our dream, wanting to help in any way possible during the present crisis. Even children, whose identification with the Bricklin was so strong, they offered their allowances to insure there would be a Bricklin when they got old enough to drive."[28] Bricklin then told the press: "Right now, it's a 50-50 tossup whether we'll get back in business. If we don't, I'll be personally wiped out and it will wipe out more than 1,000 people who have put their hearts into this project."[29]

Bricklin was in denial. At an October news conference in Toronto, he said that he would continue producing the SV-1 even if he had to roll up his sleeves and work on the assembly line himself. The only problem was that by mid-November 1975 there were no assembly lines. The assets of Bricklin Canada Ltd., including cars, tools, and pneumatic presses, had been sold at auction. Then in December 1975 Bricklin declared bankruptcy. At a hearing in Phoenix, Bricklin claimed personal debts of $32.3 million. He owed $23 million to New Brunswick, $6 million to the First Pennsylvania Bank, $2.75 million to Leon Stern, the jilted FasTrack investor, and $200,000 to the Koffman family, the late purchasers of Subaru. In terms of personal assets, Bricklin claimed just $2,000 but stated in court that the name *Bricklin* was "a personal attribute not subject to the use or sale by the bankruptcy Trustee."[30] Put simply: Bricklin believed that his very name had value, a clear indication that no matter how far Bricklin was down, he was never out.

4

Walkin' Down a London Street

Q: Why don't Yugos sustain much damage in a front-end collision?
A: The tow truck takes the impact.

Over the next seven years, Malcolm Bricklin faded from the national spotlight. He attempted for a time to build and market a "revolutionary" twelve-cylinder rotary engine known as the Bricklin-Turner Rotary Vee, but had little success. He then ran a go-kart track, promoted soul singers, and tried to scare up investors willing to back his next great adventure, the production of a new Bricklin car.[1] This time Bricklin wished to go upscale, in the $75,000 range, more expensive than a Mercedes but close in price to a Rolls-Royce. "Unfortunately the failed Bricklin SV-1 venture was a great impediment," remembers Bricklin accountant Ira Edelson. "Although Malcolm was greatly respected in the automobile industry for his knowledge and organizational ability, his bankruptcy was an insurmountable impediment towards raising capital."[2] Bricklin made presentations to dozens of potential investors and even traveled to Turin, Italy, to meet with famed coach builders Sergio Pininfarina and Nuccio Bertone.

Although nothing came of the meetings and Bricklin's dream of building a new car died a slow death, in 1983 he used his Italian contacts to establish International Automobile Importers (IAI), a New York–based business that sold Pininfarina- and Bertone-built cars. Bricklin established IAI after a chance meeting with Tony Ciminera, a manager at *Road & Track*, who ran into Bricklin at the 1982 *Auto-*

motive News World Congress in Detroit. Ciminera had never met Bricklin but had been present at Bricklin's grand opening at the Four Seasons restaurant in 1974. By chance, Ciminera sat next to Bricklin at the congress luncheon. He was working for *Road & Track*, Ciminera told Bricklin, but had previously been a dealer and customer-relations manager at Fiat's North American operation. He had moved to *Road & Track* in 1982 when Fiat announced that, due to declining sales, it was leaving the American market. "It's a shame to hear they closed up and left the country," Ciminera remembers Bricklin telling him. "I always admired those two sports cars of theirs," the Spider and the X1/9.[3]

Fiat had been selling the Spider in the United States in one form or another since 1958; the X1/9 since 1973. Both were classic Italian sports cars. They were small—they had only two seats—quick but not fast, and technologically unsophisticated. The cars' engines and mechanical components were built by Fiat, but their bodies and interior upholsteries were built by Pininfarina and Bertone, respectively. As Ciminera told Bricklin: "You know, it's funny you say that because I happen to know the two coach builders, Mr. Pininfarina and Mr. Bertone." They "just so happen to feel the same way that you do . . . That the cars still have life in them and that they want to continue their sale in the U.S." Bricklin was "electrified." He said "What? Are you serious? I know them too. Let's go!" He grabbed Ciminera's arm and nearly dragged him outside. He told Ciminera to call the two coach builders and to tell them that he and Malcolm Bricklin wanted to import the cars. "So I did," says Ciminera, "and that was the start of it all."[4]

Soon Ciminera and Bricklin were in Turin sitting face-to-face with Sergio Pininfarina and Nuccio Bertone. Bricklin explained that, yes, he had gone bankrupt on the SV-1 but that his real talent wasn't in manufacturing; it was in importing. He'd founded Subaru of America, hadn't he? By 1982, Subaru of America was importing over twelve thousand cars per month—not per year but *per month.*[5] If Pininfarina and Bertone wanted to import cars to the United States, he told them, they should use someone with a proven track record, which in this case was Malcolm Bricklin. Thus, Pininfarina and Bertone "looked not so much at Bricklin's Bricklin exploits," wrote *Motor Trend*, but at "his earlier achievement in establishing Subaru of America. Assessed as a potential importer/distributor, Bricklin's credentials looked good to the Italians."[6] So in December 1982 a deal was struck. Bricklin was now the official importer of the Bertone X1/9 and the Pininfarina Spider, which was renamed the Azzurra.

All he needed now were investors. "I'm going to be calling all the people I know in Europe, the U.S., Asia, Hawaii," Ciminera quotes Bricklin as saying. "I'll just follow the sun, so to speak, and hit everybody I know that could possibly fund this project."[7] Bricklin eventually contacted Ira Edelson, a senior partner at the New York accounting firm of Goldstein Golub Kessler, whom he had known since his days at Subaru. Edelson was a reserved, wealthy, established personage, the polar opposite of Malcolm Bricklin. His clients were among the most powerful and respected men in New York, but for some reason Bricklin thrilled him. After their first meeting in 1971, Edelson had remained a close friend of Bricklin and had been at least a peripheral witness to Bricklin's FasTrack venture, his Goodway Printing venture, and his Bricklin SV-1 venture. He had also helped Bricklin with his failed luxury car venture in the 1970s. "I had many interesting clients," remembers Edelson, but "no one was as interesting as Malcolm."[8]

In 1983, Edelson attempted to assist Bricklin in his newest project, the establishment of IAI. "Malcolm returned from Italy and told me about the new venture," remembers Edelson. "Again the problem was raising capital . . . Malcolm told me that a backer of his from his Subaru days might be willing to invest some money. When we first went to see him, he said he was not interested. Malcolm was persistent and other meetings were arranged with this financier. Finally, [he] said to us: I'll invest $50,000 and I have five or six of my friends that will also invest $50,000 each, but only if you, Ira, are responsible for the financial matters."[9]

On the strength of this initial investment, Bricklin then lined up a series of seven regional distributors to sell the two cars.[10] The distributors were expected to purchase the cars from IAI using irrevocable letters of credit, which IAI would then use as collateral to secure its own letters of credit from the Merrill Lynch Bank of London. Once the cars were at sea and turned over to IAI, Merrill Lynch would then issue payment to the cars' manufacturers, Pininfarina and Bertone. IAI thus owned the automobiles only in transit; as soon as they arrived in the United States and were delivered to American dealers, they were no longer the property of IAI. As the official importer for Pininfarina and Bertone, however, IAI was responsible for warehousing spare parts, honoring warranties, troubleshooting, advertising, and maintaining close corporate links with the cars' manufacturers.

The IAI company office was in Manhattan, but it also maintained a separate warehouse facility in Montvale, New Jersey. Bricklin was president and chief executive officer; Tony Ciminera was vice president; and Ira Edelson, who had left his accounting firm, was the company's chief financial officer. In all, IAI hired close to forty employees, including a number of car men who had been with Fiat when it closed down. Many of these men, including Ciminera, had had years of experience with the two Fiat models and therefore had a precise idea of what needed to be changed before they were reimported to the United States. The cars had exceptionally good handling, for instance. However, their bodies were made of a skimpy sheet metal known primarily for rust. Worse yet was the cars' interior finish, which Bricklin hoped to correct by sending Tony Ciminera to Italy to assist with production on the Pininfarina and Bertone assembly lines.

"I went to Italy and lived there for two months," remembers Ciminera. "I worked every day on the line ... We made literally hundreds of changes to those cars."[11] Most of them "were very minor ... little detail changes, but cumulatively they added up ... When I was with Fiat, I used to tell them things that were wrong with the car ... and we could document it up the wazoo ... [but Fiat] wouldn't do it."[12] Ciminera's main changes aimed at smoothing out the cars' rough edges and bringing their more or less spartan interiors upscale. He made few if any alterations to the cars' drivetrains, as IAI had neither the time nor the money to induce Fiat to improve the engines. To both cars Ciminera added leather interiors, air-conditioning, electric windows, color-coordinated fabrics, AM/FM cassette stereos, and improved rustproofing, including a three-year warranty on the paint and a whopping seven-year warranty against rust perforation. The X1/9 even had Nuccio Bertone's signature emblazoned on the dashboard. "IAI is plainly serious," wrote one reviewer, "about making the car[s] as civilized and modern as anyone could reasonably expect."[13]

However, as the cars went on sale in the United States in August 1983, consumers could only scoff at their price: $16,995 for the Azzurra and a more moderate but still expensive $13,990 for the X1/9. Neither car was worth it. Nevertheless, Bricklin claimed in December 1983 that IAI was "doing extremely well" and "had already turned a profit."[14] This was technically true. According to Ira Edelson, IAI had made over a million dollars in its first quarter of operation, but the money had come from IAI's regional distributors, who had purchased the cars using irrevocable letters of credit. After three months of nearly nonexistent sales, these same distributors refused to purchase new cars without a sharp reduction in price, which Bertone and Pininfarina could not or would not give. "That's when I told Malcolm," remembers Edelson, "that we are 120 days from going out of business unless we find another car to import."[15]

Bricklin responded by locating Austin Rover, an automotive producer from Great Britain whose owner, British Leyland (BL), also manufactured the Jaguar. The financially strapped BL had recently announced that it was selling Jaguar, its leading export marque, to focus on Austin Rover. In the early 1980s, Austin Rover produced a range of cars that included the Austin Ambassador, the Austin Maestro, and the MG Metro, each of which, in Bricklin's estimation, was perfect for IAI.[16] But when a team of IAI executives, led by Bricklin, met with British Leyland in April 1984, the answer was no: BL had no interest in moving MG Metros or Jaguars or any other automobiles through Malcolm Bricklin.

It was at this point that fate intervened. As Bricklin and the other International Automobile Importers executives were exiting British Leyland's headquarters and walking down a London street, they spotted a Yugo 45. When Bricklin came home the next day he had Tony Ciminera look it up. "I was told that walking down the street in London someone in the group spotted a car parked on the street, a little car, and on the back of the car was written JUGO . . . When he [Bricklin] got home the next day he had me do some research on it, [so I went and looked it up]."[17] Ciminera found that the Jugo 45 was essentially a generic version of the Fiat 127 and Fiat 128 built under license by Crvena Zastava, a relatively large automotive company located in Yugoslavia. (In the Serbo-Croatian language the letter *j* is pronounced as a *y*, thus the word *Jugo* is pronounced *Yugo*.)

Ciminera also found that although the Yugo 45 had a small, somewhat dated engine, it otherwise had "all of the buzzwords," such as front-wheel drive, rack and pinion steering, disc brakes, and independent rear suspension. Ciminera told Bricklin that the Yugo 45 was no different than any other Fiat, it just happened to be produced in Yugoslavia. "I think we could really fix it up nicely," Ciminera told him. "The mechanicals are all Fiat . . . They've been used around the world" and "having worked for Fiat, I know that the drive transmission is in many of our cars, including the Bertone X1/9 . . . I think we could find some merit here."[18] Facing yet another bankruptcy and needing to import a new car as soon as possible, Bricklin was keenly interested. He had his IAI officials contact the Yugoslav commercial attaché in New York to begin searching for ways to meet, greet, and have a sit-down with Zastava.

Out of pure serendipity, about this time an IAI public relations officer named Jonas Halperin was having lunch in New York with a friend from Occidental Petroleum, the famed oil, gas, and fertilizer conglomerate headed by Armand Hammer. Halperin explained that IAI was cutting staff and would soon be out of business unless Bricklin or the other IAI executives found a car. Bricklin had been looking into a Yugoslav car, Halperin told him, some kind of Fiat-based model known as the Yugo 45. The friend said "Really?" and proceeded to tell Halperin that Occidental had just signed a huge deal with Yugoslavia, a ten-year trade-barter arrangement by which Occidental was to provide Yugoslavia with $400 million a year in oil, coal, and phosphates in exchange for Adriatic drilling rights, industrial products, and other Yugoslav commodities that Occidental would then sell for cash.[19] The Occidental-Yugoslav trade/barter agreement was one of many such agreements negotiated by Hammer during the 1970s and '80s.

Commonly known as countertrades, these agreements stemmed

from the fact that Yugoslavia and other East European nations were eager trading partners, but because their markets were closed and their finished goods of such low quality, they were perpetually short of cash. "They simply have no other means of generating exports or paying for imports," stated one economist. "They prefer cash transactions as much as the next country but are forced to use countertrade and barter."[20] As of 1981, the world countertrade market was estimated at $350 billion a year. It involved every product imaginable: blue jeans, soda pop, airplanes, computers, farm equipment, chemicals, soybeans, glassware, and, in one deal between McDonnell Douglas and Yugoslavia, canned hams. "I don't care what the product is," stated Jack B. Utley, the head of McDonnell Douglas's countertrade department, "as long as I can find a market for it and move it."[21]

Occidental CEO Armand Hammer, who was eighty-six years old in 1984, was perhaps the most prolific countertrader in history. Beginning in 1972 with a $3 billion oil-for-fertilizer agreement with the Soviet Union, by 1984 the flamboyant Hammer had inked over a dozen trade-barter agreements with the countries of Eastern Europe. Hammer had hunted with Romania's Ceaușescu ("a fine, warm-hearted man," he called him), supped with Poland's Gierek, and once given a copy of *Dr. Atkins' Diet Revolution* to Leonid Brezhnev.[22] Hammer's goal was nothing less than Russo-American détente through close personal relationships and bilateral trade. He was a walking, talking, East-West peace summit, a man who had known and traded with Lenin, and who had enjoyed what one journalist called "unparalleled entrée to the Communist world."[23]

But as it turned out, few of Hammer's trade-barter agreements ever came to anything. A $1.33 billion agreement signed with Poland in 1978, for example, went nowhere, as did a $53 million agreement with Romania in 1977 and a ten-year "cooperation agreement" with Bulgaria in 1979. "There's no question that these deals have been done solely because Hammer wants them to be done," said one Occidental director. "After he's gone, there won't be any more."[24] Most likely, Hammer continued to ink trades with Eastern Europe as a form of company PR. In 1972, for instance, the news of Occidental's Soviet agreement caused its stock price to jump 55 percent. Under the ticker symbol OXY, Occidental stock led the New York Stock Exchange's "most-active" list for an entire week. At one point, trading in OXY shares came to a stop because the stock exchange couldn't process that many "buy" orders.[25]

By February 1984, however, when Hammer announced his Yugoslav deal, virtually no one believed that Occidental could turn a profit by bartering with Yugoslavia. As it were, the Occidental-Yugoslav agreement called for the exchange of 35,000 barrels a day of light crude oil, which Occidental proposed to give Yugoslavia, as well as 3 million tons of metallurgical and steam coal per year. In exchange, the Yugoslavs would grant Occidental oil exploration rights for portions of the Adriatic as well as first dibs on various Yugoslav commodities and other finished goods, such as automobiles.[26] In calendar year 1983, the Yugoslav automotive industry had produced approximately 250,000 vehicles, including 210,000 passenger cars, 33,000 trucks and vans, and 4,000 buses.[27] Although a majority of these vehicles were produced for domestic consumption, in 1983 Yugoslavia exported a full 20 percent of its output, or 49,747 vehicles, to countries in Western and Eastern Europe, northern Africa, and the Middle East.[28]

Perhaps the best Yugoslav automobile was the Yugo 45 by Zastava, which officials hoped would sell in the West and thus interest Armand Hammer. But to swap oil and coal for Yugos, Hammer needed a buyer, a person brave enough or imprudent enough to pay hard currency for a communist car. The buyer he found was Malcolm Bricklin. Apparently Hammer heard that Bricklin was interested in the Yugo from his New York PR man. This led to a sit-down meeting in Belgrade in May 1984 comprised of Bricklin and other IAI officials and Alex Crossan, an Occidental executive who had helped negotiate the February 1984 agreement with Yugoslavia. Also present were officials from Genex, Yugoslavia's main trading house, and Zastava.

It is unclear what agreements were reached at the meeting, but there seems to have been a nonbinding Occidental-Zastava-IAI agreement of some kind. However, within weeks, Occidental exited the negotiations and withdrew from the Yugo project altogether. "Hammer wasn't very positive about the deal," states Ira Edelson, "because he knew he was depending on a company [IAI] that I'm

sure he checked out and found did not have much capital. His
$400 million a year was dependent on this small company making a
big success in this venture."[29] But while Armand Hammer probably
regarded Malcolm Bricklin as a risky trading partner, Bricklin saw
Zastava as his proverbial golden goose. Therefore, he insisted in May
1984 that Zastava and IAI continue their agreement without Occidental. The twist? Instead of bartering for new Yugos, IAI would pay
cash per car.

By then Bricklin was broke and again needed investors, but he
also faced an additional problem in Miroslav Kefurt, the California
entrepreneur who in June had shown two Yugo 45s at the Los Angeles AutoExpo. Officials at Zastava told Bricklin that Kefurt had a
five-thousand-car contract for the state of California. They would
give him exclusive distribution rights for the other forty-nine states,
they told him, but to sell cars in California he'd have to deal with
Kefurt. "Bricklin was coming back from Yugoslavia," remembers
Kefurt. "He had the stewardess of whatever airline he was on tell me
that *Malcolm Bricklin* was calling me from the air . . . trying to impress me. He made a big point of it so that I would know that he was
calling me from a plane."[30]

The two men agreed to meet at the Century Center Plaza Hotel
in downtown Los Angeles, where Bricklin rented a luxurious penthouse suite and invited Kefurt to lunch. "He musta spent a thousand
dollars on shrimp, crab, or whatever other stuff he imported," says
Kefurt. "I wasn't exactly poor myself and I'd seen fancy food before . . . but no one was eating. So I decided to pig out."[31] The Century Center meeting was pure Bricklin. He had hoped that by wining
and dining Kefurt, he could purchase the Yugo and its coveted distribution rights for a song. But the meeting ended without an agreement, only a promise that Kefurt would come to New York for a
second meeting at IAI. When Bricklin offered to pay for Kefurt's
plane ticket, however, Kefurt refused. He told Bricklin that he and
his wife were planning to drive to New York, a full forty-two hours,
in—yes, you guessed it—a Yugo.

En route, Kefurt's blue Yugo broke down three times. The car
had no air-conditioning, so the Kefurts were fried, blackened, and
charred by interior temperatures that reached, in Kefurt's estima-

tion, 120 degrees. According to Kefurt, the couple stopped often, drank buckets of water, and took to putting ice cubes in the car's front air intakes as a form of air-conditioning. When finally they arrived in New York, Bricklin negotiated with Kefurt at IAI's Manhattan headquarters for two and a half days. At one point, says Kefurt, Bricklin introduced him to an investor he was courting for IAI's Italian sports car project. Kefurt, Bricklin told the man, was "the head of our West Coast division." A few hours later he introduced Kefurt to another investor as his "market research manager for California," and still later as his "chief technical engineer." "Before the day was over I had like twelve different titles," says Kefurt. "With every person that showed up, I was somebody else."[32]

In the end, Kefurt agreed to sell Bricklin his California distribution rights for $50,000.[33] However, when Bricklin cut Kefurt a check, it was for $16,500. "I asked why and he said that he had some difficulties with this and that," says Kefurt, "so I called the bank and it turned out that that was all he had." Wisely, Kefurt took the money and flew home. Bricklin assured Kefurt that he'd pay him the remaining money and that he should be happy with $50,000. "Don't worry about the Yugo," Kefurt insists Bricklin told him. "We're only going to use it as a carrot to get more money from dealers before we go belly-up." Bricklin "was ready to go into bankruptcy," insists Kefurt. "This was his parting thing . . . that I should be happy I got $50,000 from him . . . I was in shock. I didn't know what to say."[34]

Eventually, Bricklin paid Kefurt the remaining $33,500. But IAI didn't go belly-up. It simply faded into the background as first Bertone, then Pininfarina, canceled their agreements with Malcolm Bricklin. Neither coach builder publicly blamed Bricklin for the failed IAI operation. The breakup was "a sad situation," said one Pininfarina rep: "A better job could have been done all the way around."[35] It didn't help, however, that since mid-1984 Bricklin had ignored his Italian imports to focus instead on the Yugo. According to Ira Edelson, in the summer of 1984 Bricklin used IAI funds to establish Yugo America Inc., the company that in August 1985 began importing the Yugo.

Yugo America's parent company was Bricklin Industries, which also owned IAI. Naturally, Bricklin himself owned Bricklin Industries, but BI's primary source of funding came not from Malcolm Bricklin but from the dealer-distribution network and investors of IAI. At one point Bricklin sold 350,000 shares of IAI at a dollar a share to John and Rebecca Bednarik. The Bednariks owned Mid-Atlantic International Imports of Accokeek, Maryland, and had invested the money in IAI in exchange for U.S. distribution rights for the Yugo. However, once Bricklin received the Bednariks' money, he allegedly diverted it from IAI's Bertone and Pininfarina projects and used it to secure Yugo distribution rights for himself.[36] By early 1985, Yugo America Inc. had twenty-one major investors, including Nordic American Bank and shipping magnate Per Arneberg. It issued 10 million shares, 5.1 million of which were owned by Bricklin and various members of the Bricklin family.[37]

The Bednariks received nothing. Bricklin merely took their money and stopped speaking to them. A few years later the couple sued Bricklin in federal court and were awarded $17 million in damages for breach of contract. The judgment forced Bricklin into his third bankruptcy in thirty years. In the summer of 1984, though, the Bednariks' money kept Bricklin in business. It allowed him to negotiate with Zastava, to buy Kefurt's distribution rights, and to jump unscathed from his moribund IAI project to the Yugo. In November 1984 he began signing dealers and in December received a $2 million infusion of capital from Nordic American Bank and Per Arneberg. "From that point on it was hell-bent," says Pete Mulhern, a technical services manager at IAI who in 1984 followed Bricklin to Yugo. "Malcolm wanted a car for the 1986 model year. I know he spoke to various people in the industry and they said, 'Seven months? No way. No way we can we make the Yugo a viable product in seven months! It's impossible!' But that wasn't good enough for Mr. Bricklin. His approach was, how about tomorrow?"[38]

With that, the Yugo began. From December 1984 to August 1985, a small team of Yugo America employees and consultants ventured to Kragujevac, Serbia, the home of Crvena Zastava, where they prepped the car for the U.S. market. Bricklin's goal was to import 35,000 cars the first year (1985), 76,000 cars the second year (1986), and a whopping 272,000 cars by 1990.[39] The numbers, of course, were unrealistic, but by early 1985 Bricklin was off and running. He and Yugo America president Bill Prior and IAI's former PR man, Jonas Halperin, began a three-man media blitz that earned the company an estimated $20 million in free publicity. When, in March 1985, Yugo America selected the New York PR firm of Rosenfeld, Sirowitz & Lawson to handle its print and TV advertising, even *that* was news.[40] Like the Bricklin SV-1, the Yugo was a hit—a premarket hit. Except this time Bricklin was banking that Americans wanted a low-priced car, rather than a safety-vehicle-cum-sports-car, and that at $3,990 he could give it to them.

5

The Serbian Detroit

Q: What do you call a Yugo with a flat tire?
A: Totaled.

Kragujevac, Serbia, is a small industrial town of about 150,000 people. Although Kragujevac is home to a major state university, a regional archive, five or six museums, a district court, and a successful theater, what truly defines the city is Zastava. In the mid-1980s, Zastava and its parent company, Zastava Group, employed some 35,000 workers, meaning one out of every four residents in Kragujevac worked for Zastava. Zastava Group was an industrial conglomerate that produced, among other things, cars, trucks, buses, pickups, automotive supplies and parts, machine tools, mining and manufacturing equipment, and arms.

Zastava itself had grown out of Serbia's first cannon factory, established in Kragujevac in 1853.[1] At the time, Serbia was an autonomous principality under the Ottoman Turks, an Asiatic people who had conquered the Serbs, who were Slavs, in the fourteenth and fifteenth centuries. By the mid-nineteenth century, however, the Turks had so little control over Serbia that the tiny principality was able to hoist its own flag, build its own state institutions, and equip a standing army. The Serb army used Zastava-made weaponry in 1878 when it liberated itself from the Turks, in 1885 when it fought Bulgaria, in 1912–13 when it fought Turkey and Bulgaria, and again during World War I.

The "Great War" began when a Serb terrorist named Gavrilo Princip assassinated the Austrian archduke Franz Ferdinand during a June 1914 visit to Bosnia. Princip had been backed, clandestinely, by a group of Serbian army officers in Belgrade who wished to punish Austria-Hungary for its annexation of Bosnia in 1908. The Serb officers considered Bosnia to be a Serbian land. At least, they considered it a Slavic land of Orthodox Serbs, Catholic Croats, and Bosnian Muslims, whom they wished to unify with neighboring Serbia. But instead of unifying Bosnia with Serbia or helping the Serbian cause in any real way, the assassination of Franz Ferdinand only prompted Austria-Hungary, an empire of 51 million, to declare war on Serbia, a kingdom of less than 5 million.

The war was a disaster for Serbia. By November 1915 the country had been completely overrun, its army and government were in exile, while the arms factory in Kragujevac was taken apart and shipped to Austria. Luckily for Serbia, though, in April 1917 America intervened. It intervened not to assist Serbia per se but to assist America's traditional allies, Britain and France, in their fight against Germany, which was Austria's ally. In the end, the presence of hundreds of thousands of fresh American troops on the Western Front forced Germany and Austria to surrender. This was in November 1918. Although tiny Serbia had to some extent caused World War I, in the postwar peace settlements signed at Paris it was awarded the Austro-Hungarian provinces of Slovenia, Bosnia, Croatia, and Vojvodina, which it merged under one government with a Serbian king.

The new country was called the Kingdom of the Serbs, Croats, and Slovenes. In 1929 it changed its name to Yugoslavia, meaning Land of the Southern Slavs. The country's two main ethnic groups, in terms of size and political power, were the Serbs and the Croats. The two groups had separate religions, separate state traditions, and separate conceptions of how Yugoslavia was to be. The Serbs, for example, wanted a centralized state with Belgrade as capital. They viewed Serbia as a Balkan Piedmont, playing the same historical role that the Italian province of Savoy did in unifying Italy. The Croats, on the other hand, favored a decentralized state and viewed Croatia as an autonomous equal. They wanted their own flag and their own bureaucracy, and wanted to cooperate with Serbia as part of a larger confederation.

The centralist-decentralist debate would remain with Yugoslavia for the next seventy years. But since the Serbs were the larger of the two groups and had considerably more power than the Croats, in 1921 they pushed through a centralist constitution giving the bulk of political authority to various Serbian parties in Belgrade. Thus began a period of political unrest in which Croatia's main political party boycotted parliament, in which Croatia's leading politician was imprisoned by the government and later shot by a Serbian rival, and in which a Croat terrorist organization killed Yugoslavia's Serbian king during a visit to France.

Even worse were Yugoslavia's external relations with neighboring states. By the late interwar period the country was surrounded by enemies, including Fascist Italy to the west, Nazi Germany and Hungary to the north, and Bulgaria to the east. Each of these countries wished to dismember Yugoslavia; therefore the Yugoslav government pursued a twofold approach. First, it would appease its neighbors diplomatically, such as in 1937 when it signed a non-aggression pact with Italy, and second it would arm itself as quickly and quietly as possible. During the 1930s, for instance, the Yugoslav arms factory in Kragujevac dramatically increased its production. Then known as the Military Technical Works, the factory employed some twelve thousand workers who made pistols, rifles, machine guns, mortars, hand grenades, and, beginning in 1940, a small line of Chevy trucks.[2]

The trucks were an early variation of the G-105 one-and-a-half-ton military vehicles that the U.S. government later sent to the Soviets during World War II. The trucks' engines were built in Detroit, but the vehicles themselves were assembled in Kragujevac under license from General Motors. The Military Technical Works had assembled trucks and buses before, but to this point no Yugoslav company had ever built a car. For one thing, cars were expensive to produce. They required, among other things, a truly mind-boggling list of very costly and imported machinery, such as conveyor belts, stamping and pressing machines, and lathes. A state-of-the-art fifty-acre French Citroën plant built at Javel in 1925 required 3,100 different pieces of machinery, most imported from the United States.[3]

A second impediment to Yugoslav car production was that interwar Yugoslavia had a dearth of domestic buyers. As of 1937, Yugoslavia's per capita national income was $80. By contrast, the average per capita national income for all twenty-four European countries was $200. It was $440 for Great Britain.[4] However, in most of Europe the average price of a small-size car in the 1930s was between $500 and $700. Even the famed Volkswagen, which had been built and subsidized by Nazi Germany, came in at about $400, far more than the average Yugoslav could afford.[5] A third impediment to Yugoslav car production was the country's lack of usable roads. In the late 1930s Yugoslavia had just over 26,000 miles of roads, more than Greece, Bulgaria, and Romania but still considerably less than Great Britain, which had over 179,000 miles of roads.[6] In addition, the great majority of all Yugoslav thoroughfares were finished with dirt or gravel, while the country lacked even a single highway or even one "automobile-only" road.

Whatever the case, in the late 1930s the government of Yugoslavia wasn't interested in automobiles. Its most pressing issue was Germany. Since 1939, the German dictator Adolf Hitler had been bullying Yugoslavia into joining his Tripartite Pact, which it did reluctantly in March 1941. The Yugoslav leader at that time was Prince Paul Karadjordjevic, who came to power in October 1934 after his cousin King Alexander had been assassinated in Marseilles. Paul had no stomach for the job and planned to rule Yugoslavia as "prince regent" until Alexander's son Peter, who was seventeen years old in 1941, came of age. But Paul's decision to align Yugoslavia with Hitler was unpopular with Yugoslavia's five million or so Serbs, who as part of the Kingdom of Serbia had fought Germany during World War I. Therefore, on March 27, 1941, only two days after Yugoslavia had joined the Tripartite Pact, a group of anti-German officers deposed Prince Paul and brought the young King Peter to power.

Hitler's response was swift and bloody. Known as "Operation Punishment," it included a three-day bombing of Belgrade that killed five to ten thousand people.[7] The operation was supported by a blitzkrieg invasion of some fifty-two Axis divisions, who destroyed the Yugoslav army and toppled its government in just twelve days. By mid-April 1941, Yugoslavia had ceased to exist. The Yugoslav province of Slovenia, for example, was divided into two roughly equal parts that were physically absorbed by Italy and Germany. Croatia became a Nazi puppet state administered by a Croatian fascist organization known as the Ustasha, while Serbia was placed under direct German control. In Kragujevac, the Military Technical Works was once again captured, disassembled, and shipped to enemy territory. All that remained in the factory was a truck repair shop and an assembly line for small arms.

Meanwhile, the citizens of Kragujevac, though staunchly anti-German, were in no position to resist. The German authorities who administered Serbia had concentrated their troops in city centers and along Yugoslavia's main transportation routes to guard their supply lines between Serbia and Greece. However, the Serbian hinterland was outside of German control and fell into the hands of two rival groups, the Chetniks and Partisans. The Chetniks were a collection of Serb nationalist detachments loyal to King Peter, who at the outbreak of war had fled Yugoslavia and settled in Great Britain. Their rivals the Partisans were the guerrilla arm of the Yugoslav Communist Party and were led by a professional revolutionary named Josip Broz Tito. The Chetniks and the Partisans were bitter rivals: from 1941 to 1945 they fought a civil war with each other and a guerrilla war with the occupying German army.

At one point in October 1941 the two groups briefly cooperated in an attack on a German battalion. In a brief firefight, they succeeded in killing ten German soldiers and wounding twenty-six others. Even though the attack took place outside Kragujevac, in retaliation German authorities ordered that for every German killed they would execute one hundred Kragujevac civilians; for every soldier wounded, they would execute fifty Kragujevac civilians, which they did between October 18 and 21, 1941. Among the 2,300 dead were several hundred teenage boys whom the Germans took from a local high school and shot by firing squad in a wooded area outside of town. As legend has it, the school's headmaster refused to leave his students and asked to accompany them to the execution site. When they began lining the boys up to be shot, the Germans told the headmaster to get out of the way, to which he supposedly retorted: "Go ahead and shoot. I am conducting my class."[8]

Such acts of genocide and of extreme almost inexplicable heroism were common in Yugoslavia, where during World War II over 1.7 million people, or 11 percent of the population, were killed.⁹ By comparison, the United States lost 405,399 men and women during World War II, less than 24 pecent of Yugoslav losses and only .31 percent of the American population as a whole.¹⁰ Although estimates vary, it is safe to assume that fully half of all Yugoslav casualties occurred at the hands of other Yugoslavs. In Croatia, Croat fascists killed Serbs, Gypsies, and Jews; in Bosnia, Serb Chetniks killed Muslims and Croats, while Muslim SS detachments killed Serbs, Croats, and Jews. Tito's Partisans, as it turned out, were the only Yugoslav combatants who preached antifascism *and* multiethnicity. As a result, their numbers rose from a mere 11,000 in 1941 to over 700,000 in 1945.¹¹

By war's end the Partisans were the single greatest force in Yugoslavia. They were also the most popular. In 1945 the country held open elections in which the monarchy was abolished and Yugoslavia became a socialist people's republic with Tito at the helm. Almost immediately, Tito's government began nationalizing property and making huge investments in heavy industry. In Kragujevac, for example, the Military Technical Works was rebuilt from the ground up. From late 1944 through the end of 1945 it was known as the "October 21 Works" in honor of the Kragujevac students and other civilians massacred by the Germans in 1941. For some unknown reason, the company again changed its name in early 1946 from the October 21 Works to the Crvena Zastava Works. Crvena Zastava meant Red Flag, as in the red flag of communism, and was an advertisement of sorts for Tito's communist regime.

By 1948–49, the Crvena Zastava Works had regained its position as one of the leading arms producers in Yugoslavia. Its government-approved plan for 1949 called for a minimum production of one hundred thousand rifles and one hundred thousand hand grenades.¹² But just as Zastava began production that year, the government abruptly decided to move most of the factory to Bosnia. The reason was that in June 1948, after a prolonged and very public dispute with the Soviet dictator Joseph Stalin, Tito decided to pull Yugoslavia out of the Soviet bloc. From that point forward, declared Tito, Yugoslavia was an independent state. It had its own right to govern its own affairs and could pursue, if it wanted to, its own unique path to communism. The United States praised Tito as a "maverick" and a "good communist," but Tito's advisers feared that the Red Army was planning to invade Yugoslavia to depose Tito and reestablish control. Therefore, the Yugoslav government shipped its most essential equipment to the mountains of Bosnia, where it could be better protected in the event of a Soviet invasion.

The invasion never happened, but since most of Zastava's arms production was now in Bosnia, the Kragujevac company needed something to produce. In spring 1953 it opened negotiations with Willys-Overland, the famed Toledo, Ohio, company that produced the Jeep.[13] As part of an extended test run, Zastava assembled more than 160 CJ-3A models, a close relative of the CJ-2A model used by the U.S. Army during World War II. However, the negotiations collapsed because Willys-Overland wanted 6 percent of profits but refused to send in its experts or to assist Zastava with setting up its assembly lines. The reason for this is unclear, but having failed with Jeep and still needing an automobile Zastava issued a public tender in August 1953.[14] It requested, among other things, full production rights—and not just rights of assembly—for either a Western European or an American-made automobile. The following companies replied: Fiat, Renault, Alfa Romeo, Rover, Austin, and Delahaye.[15]

Each company sent sample automobiles to Kragujevac, which were then tested by Zastava in October and November 1953. Zastava decided to award the contract to Fiat because the giant Italian automaker offered Zastava two different car models (the 1400 and 1900), a one-and-a-half-ton transport truck, a tractor, and a jeeplike military vehicle called the Campagnola.[16] The price: a mere 350 million lira ($560,000), which Zastava would pay for through future parts and machine purchases from Fiat. By almost any measure the deal was a steal. Zastava could pick and choose which automobiles it wished to produce and at what pace. It could produce, for example, a four-door 1400 sedan or a two-door 1900 coupe, or it could concentrate solely on the Campagnola, which the Yugoslav military wanted, now that the Willys-Overland negotiations had fallen through.

The contract between Zastava and Fiat was signed on August 12,

1954. Zastava's director at that time was a former Partisan war hero named Voja Radic. Apparently Radic was intelligent enough to sign with Fiat, but as a manager he was completely incapable of handling the Herculean task of building and assembling cars. Therefore, in 1955 Zastava replaced Radic with Prvoslav Rakovic, a onetime railway engineer whose "can-do" attitude was unique among communist apparatchiks.[17] Over the next twenty years, Rakovic would build one of the largest automotive companies in the world. "Although car making was not regarded as a priority area for funding in the building of socialism," wrote the economic historian Michael Palairet, "Rakovic worked single-mindedly to develop this small semi-mechanized operation into a fully fledged assembly plant."[18]

It was Rakovic who in August 1955 persuaded Fiat to sign a second deal with Zastava, in which the Italian carmaker agreed to invest an undisclosed sum into the construction of a new Zastava-owned factory in Kragujevac. The contract called for a production capability of 12,000 vehicles per year. In September 1957, Fiat extended the contract to include an additional 20,000 cars of the popular Fiat 600 line and in May 1959 agreed to invest a whopping $30 million into an expanded 150,000-car facility in Kragujevac.[19] Of course, Fiat was motivated by profit. Its management knew that, like all communist countries, Yugoslavia needed Western-made machinery to industrialize. But because its currency (the dinar) was a "soft" currency and had no convertible value outside of Yugoslavia, the country was broke.

Therefore, Fiat invested in Zastava in hopes that it would enter the Yugoslav market on the ground floor. As of 1954, there were only 11,290 private cars in all of Yugoslavia, a ratio of 1 to every 1,500 people.[20] Fiat assumed, quite reasonably, that Yugoslavia's domestic car market simply had to expand. And when it did, Fiat would be part owner of the only true production facility around. Through the 1950s Fiat pursued a similar strategy in both Argentina and Brazil as well as in the Soviet Union, where in 1965 it agreed to construct a 600,000-car facility in Stavropol-on-Volga, Russia. (That facility became known as the Volzhsky Avtomobilny Zavod, or VAZ, the famed producer of the Lada automobile.) "Profit margins on [Fiat's] deals with the Soviet Bloc," wrote The Times of London, "will inevitably be slim. But Fiat's main asset could well likely be state control . . . A paper deal involving long-term credits and the payment of fees or royalties over a long period of time and in goods rather than cash is most likely."[21]

It can be assumed, then, that Fiat's deal with Zastava in 1959 was similar to its 1965 deal with VAZ. Fiat provided start-up capital and licensing rights, and received a long-term combination of fees, royalties, guaranteed parts purchases, and bartered goods. In later years Zastava would use its cheap labor force to assemble automobile parts for Fiat, including shock absorbers, batteries, electrical equipment, and seats.[22] Implicit in the deal was the promise that no Zastava-made automobiles would be sold in markets where Fiats were sold, such as Italy. Thus, it was with great fanfare that on July 6, 1962, Zastava's new Kragujevac facility opened its doors.[23] Its main production model was the famed Fiat 600, the first rear-engined Fiat and the first true "people's car" produced in Yugoslavia. The two-door 600 had four seats and a four-cylinder 767cc engine, and was just over ten feet five inches long. At the time of its production, the Fiat 600 was one of the smallest, cheapest, most fuel-efficient cars in the world, and a perfect fit for Yugoslavia. Although Zastava renamed the 600 the Zastava 750, the public affectionately called it the Fica ("Fee-cha"), meaning "Little Fiat."[24]

6

Bricklin's Next Big Thing

Q: What do a Yugo and a ceiling fan have in common?
A: They both have the same motor.

Zastava began production of the Fica shortly after the company's second deal with Fiat in 1955. Between 1955 and 1985, Zastava produced over 923,000 Ficas, an astounding number considering that prior to 1955 Zastava had never made a car.[1] In addition, in 1961 Zastava also introduced the Fiat 1300/1500. Somewhat bigger than the Fica, it was primarily used for taxis, government vehicles, and police cars. The Fiat 1300/1500 was an early version of the Fiat 124 and 125, which were later produced by Poland's Passenger Car Factory (Fabryka Samochodow Osobowych, or FSO) as the Polski Fiat and by the Soviet VAZ factory as the Lada. Upon its introduction, the Fiat 1300/1500 offered what one British reviewer called a "zestful performance"; by most accounts it was a decent car.[2]

But whereas Fiat stopped producing the 1300/1500 model in 1967, Zastava churned out more than two hundred thousand of these increasingly aging cars before ending production in 1979. Likewise, Zastava manufactured the tiny 750 model (the Fica) until 1985, though Fiat itself had dropped the automobile sixteen years earlier in 1969. To the average car-crazed American, it would seem almost sacrilegious if a car company failed to introduce at least one "new" model each calendar year. Take the 2005 Toyota Camry, for instance. It was only slightly different than the 2004 Camry. Although U.S. car dealers marketed the 2005 model as being an improvement over the 2004, in reality it wasn't. The only real difference was that the

2005 model had redesigned headlamps and tail lamps, chrome door handles and a chrome gear-shifter base, and a new wheel cap. Otherwise, the mechanics—and appearance—were the same.[3]

The American automobile industry and in particular General Motors (GM) first introduced annual model changes in the 1920s. GM's competitor at that time was the Ford Motor Company, whose founder, Henry Ford, was insistent that his Model T should stay in production (year after year after year) unchanged. Ford's goal was to streamline his company's manufacturing process to reduce cost. He therefore introduced the world's first automotive assembly lines and implemented hundreds of new manufacturing techniques to produce automobiles that cost $850 in 1908 but just $300 in 1923.[4] At one point Ford reduced the price of his Model T by ordering his factory to use only black body paint, because black was cheaper and supposedly dried faster than other colors.

Ford would produce fifteen million Models Ts but slowly lost market share because he refused to adapt to, or even consider, consumer taste. Ford's "production-centered ethos," wrote one scholar, was "unwavering . . . he almost drove his company to ruin by continuing to build economical machines and to advertise them as just that—and only that."[5] By the 1920s, American car buyers were no longer interested in basic transportation. They wanted style, prestige, and status, something GM and its innovative president, Alfred P. Sloan, could offer them. Sloan insisted that GM should have a broad product line, a "car for every purse and purpose," a "Chevrolet for the hoi-polloi, [an] Oakland for the poor but proud, [an] Oldsmobile for the comfortable but discreet, [a] Buick for the striving, [and a] Cadillac for the rich."[6]

Sloan's strategy was to sell GM vehicles along what he called a "price stairway," with low-priced Chevys at the bottom end and expensive Cadillacs at the top end. In this way, GM models wouldn't compete with each other, and as customers aged and became more affluent, they could buy more expensive cars within the GM "family."[7] GM's product line also involved what to that point was the priciest PR campaign in history, one that pitched the automobile not as a mere product, as Ford did, but as a symbol of one's personal worth within American society. In addition to Sloan's "price stairway," the GM president also introduced "annual design changes," which were small, stylistic changes meant to entice or even fool consumers into thinking that this year's Cadillac Fleetwood was somehow better or more valuable than last's.

Price stairways and annual design changes have long been standard practices in the industry. In 2009, for instance, Ford's U.S. operation offered six cars, two "crossovers," five sport-utility vehicles, four trucks, and a van. These vehicles came in several dozen submodels, from the lowly Ford Focus sedan at $14,995 to the unbelievably gauche Ford Harley-Davidson Super Duty truck, which cost $45,790.[8] Needless to say, Ford provided its customers with literally hundreds of options, such as automatic or manual transmissions, cloth seats, leather seats, sports bucket seats, roof racks, mud flaps, spoilers, chrome grilles, and leather gearshift knobs as well as metal, aluminum, and/or alloy wheels.

In the 1960s Ford's production line was no less diverse. In 1969 Ford of Britain produced eight different cars.[9] Consumers could purchase the cars in two-, three-, four-door, and even hatchback submodels and choose from dozens of options. By contrast, the average Zastava buyer in 1969 had just two options: the four-door 1300/1500 model and the two-door Fica. They were given no choice as to the car's color or accoutrements, and often waited weeks or months for delivery. The former Yugoslavia was a socialist country and its economy was a planned economy whose focus was on industrialization, on using the country's meager resources to build key infrastructure such as factories, roads, bridges, railways, housing blocks, electric plants, and highways.

Therefore, the Yugoslav government felt that consumer goods, or more to the point consumer *preferences*, were frivolous. Fashionable clothes were frivolous. Children's toys were frivolous. Cosmetics were frivolous. Even toilet paper was frivolous. (Ask anyone who traveled to Yugoslavia in the 1950s and '60s and they'll mention the sandpaper-like qualities of Golub toilet paper.) It was because of Yugoslavia's centralized planning and, subsequently, its forced industrialization that by the 1960s the country's annual growth rate was one of the highest in the world.[10] But Yugoslavia, like most communist countries, did not invest its money wisely. Often it built surplus capacity in some sectors, such as in the military industry, while ignoring other sectors entirely. For political reasons, it also built many of its factories in poorer, remote regions such as Montenegro, where roads were bad and the workforce composed of unskilled, uneducated labor.[11]

The result was that Yugoslavia's poorer regions tended to drain money from its richer regions, which included Slovenia, Yugoslavia's wealthiest republic at 187 percent of per capita GMP; Croatia, its second-wealthiest republic at 127 percent of per capita GMP; and Serbia, the country's third-wealthiest republic at 96 percent of per capita GMP. By contrast, the poorer republics of Macedonia, Montenegro, and Bosnia were just 66 percent, 72 percent, and 67 percent of per capita GMP respectively. (The Albanian-populated but Serb-dominated province of Kosovo was even poorer at 32 percent!)[12] Even though Yugoslavia's total GMP grew some 6 percent per year during the 1960s and personal income of industrial workers by almost 7 percent, by the end of the decade Yugoslavia's trade deficit stood at $1 billion.[13]

To make up the difference and to sustain economic growth, in the early 1960s Yugoslavia began borrowing from Western banks. As a result, by 1969 Yugoslavia was $2 billion in debt.[14] However, to pay back its loans or even meet its interest payments Yugoslavia needed currency—hard currency—which it attempted to earn by doing what no communist country had ever done: it opened its borders. Beginning in 1965, Yugoslav citizens were permitted to leave the country and work (the government hoped) as seasonal guest workers in the booming economies of Sweden, Austria, and Germany. According to one study, in 1966 Yugoslavs made 3.3 million legal border crossings, a figure that rose to 6.9 million in 1967, 8.1 million in 1968, and 10.6 million in 1969. By comparison, in 1960, when the border was closed to out-migration, Yugoslavs entered or exited the country a mere 191,000 times, a nine-year difference of over 5,400 percent.[15] Open borders also meant that Western tourists could now enter Yugoslavia to visit its Adriatic coast.

In 1966, remittances from workers abroad and earnings from tourism netted Yugoslavia some $168 million. In 1970, that figure rose to $688 million and $930 million in 1971.[16] But by that point

Yugoslavia's foreign debt had nearly doubled (to $4 billion), while its trade deficit that year was a whopping $1.1 billion. Yugoslavia's only hope, then, was to stop borrowing, which it didn't do, and to export more goods—or at least *more valuable* goods—than it imported. Thus, Yugoslav companies were told by the government to export, export, export, which they did. By the mid-1970s, Yugoslav firms were selling a variety of goods on the world market, including footwear, textiles, furniture, chemicals, cooking oil, canned meats, kitchen appliances, and cars.

The cars, of course, came from Zastava, which in 1971 designed and built a new automobile called the 101. The Zastava 101 was based on the Fiat 128, a four-door, four-cylinder, 55-horsepower automobile with an 1100cc front-end engine. The Fiat 128 was by all accounts a good car. In 1970 a group of leading automobile magazines named it the "European Car of the Year." Britain's *Car* magazine called the 128 "the best 1100 saloon yet to come from any manufacturer, matching the competition point for point and outstripping most of it at every turn."[17] The distinguishing feature of the 128 was its intelligent use of unequal-length driveshafts, which enabled the car's engine to be placed directly beside the gearbox. That meant the Fiat 128 carried its 1100cc engine in a smaller, more compact package, which in turn meant more carriage space and room for passengers.

Although based on the 128 and designed with the help of Fiat engineers, the 101 was a poorly built car. In Serbo-Croatian, the Zastava 101 was called the *stojedan*, meaning "one hundred and one." But after buying and driving the car and finding its quality was atrocious, Yugoslav consumers dubbed it the *stojadin*, "one hundred troubles." However, the 101 gave Zastava what it wanted most: a relatively new car with newer technology that it could export. It sent the 101, for instance, to third-world countries such as Egypt and India, and began a massive exchange in 101 component parts with Poland and the Soviet Union.[18] Consequently, Zastava, Poland's FSO company, and Russia's VAZ company provided each other with economies of scale, the idea being that if one company mass-produced a given component for all three companies, the components themselves would be cheaper.

To encourage the component trade, the companies agreed to keep a running record of who produced what and to pay for their debts in finished automobiles. Therefore, by the mid-1970s Zastava's domestic lineup included the 750 (the Fica), the 1300/1500, the 101, the Polski Fiat 125p, and the Soviet Lada. All five automobiles appeared side by side in Yugoslav showrooms. In general, Zastava's new car showrooms were smaller than Ford or GM showrooms in the United States. They consisted, usually, of three to four rooms with large glass windows in key buildings in every city and town in Yugoslavia, some seventy in all. Above each storefront was a large sign with ZASTAVA in modern, neat script lettering. Unlike showrooms in the United States, however, the typical Zastava showroom did not keep cars in stock. Cars were ordered on credit and shipped directly from Kragujevac to the showroom.

In addition to its showrooms, Zastava also maintained close to one hundred repair shops throughout Yugoslavia. The shops were overseen by a "central service department" at the factory in Kragujevac, which ran its own repair shop and directed parts distribution to all shops nationwide. During the 1970s, the director of the central service department was a Serbian engineer named Toma Savic. Then in his early thirties, Savic had come to Zastava in 1969 fresh out of college and a two-year stint in the Yugoslav military. He had been given his position at a very young age by general manager Prvoslav Rakovic, whose very un-communist-like policy was to promote young talent to high company positions. Although Rakovic was sacked in 1974 and replaced by the former Serbian president Milenko Bojanic, Savic continued to climb. In 1981, he became "director of sales" at Zastava, and in early 1984 became one of three "deputy managers" below Bojanic's successor Srboljub Vasovic.[19]

In American terms, Savic was Zastava's executive vice president for marketing, worldwide export, and sales. He was young and talented and remembers his 1984 promotion as his big break, in which he was given direct responsibility for the Yugo. Designed in 1978 by Fiat and Zastava engineers at Fiat's design center in Turin, Italy, the Yugo was originally known as the Zastava 102. It was meant to be a two-door hatchback that would update the aging Fica and complement the larger 101, hence the name 102. The Yugo was based on the Fiat 127, which Fiat first built in 1971 and which earned "European Car of the Year" honors in 1972.[20] The Yugo had a 903cc, 45-horsepower engine and had a maximum speed of 96 miles per hour. In terms of its power train and chassis, the Yugo was identical to the 127, but its body shape and interior were different. As Savic recollects, Zastava gave two Yugo prototypes to then-president Tito as a present, although what the eighty-five-year-old dictator did with the cars is unknown.[21] By then Tito was in failing health and would die of heart complications in 1980.

Zastava began full-scale production of the Yugo on Friday, November 28, 1980. The company chose November 28 so that its first Yugo would roll off the assembly line on Saturday the twenty-ninth, the same day that communist Yugoslavia had been founded in 1945. Although the Yugo was meant to replace the Fica, Zastava decided to increase its production only gradually. In 1981, for instance, Zastava built 9,715 Yugos versus 52,867 Ficas. In 1982 it built 14,856 Yugos versus 37,989 Ficas. The Yugo surpassed the Fica in 1985, the Fica's last full year of production. When the 923,487th Fica rolled out of the factory, an era came to an end. Though tiny, underpowered, and undersized, in over thirty years of production the Fica had done the impossible: it had brought the automobile to Yugoslavia.

The hope, then, was that its replacement, the Yugo, would have a similarly long life and would somehow find its way into foreign markets. In 1981, Zastava exported two Yugos to Poland and in 1982 exported 724 Yugos to Belgium (19 cars), Holland (205 cars), and Greece (500 cars). In 1983, Zastava began selling the car in Great Britain, which is where Malcolm Bricklin discovered it in April 1984 while walking down a London street.[22] The car Bricklin discovered was the Yugo 45. Zastava had changed its name from 102 to Jugo, and then from Jugo with a *J* to Yugo with a *Y*. The number 45 stood for the car's horsepower. However, contrary to popular belief, the name Yugo had nothing to do with Yugoslavia. In Serbo-Croatian, the word *jug* means "south." Thus *Jugoslavija* means "Land of the Southern Slavs." However, a *jugo* is a southeasterly wind on the Adriatic.[23] Therefore, Zastava chose the name Jugo because German automaker Volkswagen had given two of its hatchbacks, the Scirocco and the Passat, similar wind-related names.

But this doesn't explain why Zastava changed the car's name from 102 to Jugo, and from Jugo with a *J* to Yugo with a *Y*. First, the car's original three-digit name, the 102, was copyright protected in Europe by French automaker Peugeot; in fact, all three-digit names with a zero in the middle were protected by Peugeot.[24] Therefore, if Zastava wanted to sell the 102 in Europe, and especially in France, it had to give the car a new name, i.e., "Jugo." But secondly, even though the word *jugo* meant a southerly wind in Serbo-Croatian, it didn't sound right or translate well into other languages. In English, the word *jugo* is gibberish, but it looks like *jug-o*, an impossibly bad moniker for a car. By the same token, the word *jugo* is pronounced "hugo" in Spanish, which means juice, as in *orange juice* (*jugo de naranja*) or even worse *gastrointestinal juice* (*jugo gástrico*). So to avoid confusion and to equate the automobile with the country of its origin, in 1980 Zastava chose the export name Yugo. Cars sold in Yugoslavia, of course, were still named Jugo.

Later, as the Yugo's fame grew, the company changed its name to Zastava Yugo. This was in 1985. From that point forward Yugo was the company's automotive marque, while the 101 and the Jugo 45 were given specific model names. The 101 became the Jugo Skala, for instance, while the Jugo 45 became the Jugo Koral, as in *sea coral*. In 1990, Zastava also introduced a four-door hatchback called the Jugo Florida, which later appeared in Great Britain as the Yugo Sana. As a whole, Zastava enjoyed moderate success in the United Kingdom. In 1983 it sold 1,115 Yugos in Britain, representing some 16.5 percent of the company's total Yugo exports. That number would rise to 3,746 in 1984 and 4,186 in 1985. The basic model in 1983 cost £2,749 (about $4,600), which was cheaper than the Ford Fiesta (£4,162, or $6,967) or the Honda Civic (£3,845, or $6,436).

Naturally, British consumers who bought the Yugo were attracted by its price, but the car did receive favorable if not glowing reviews in the British press. "British motorists considering whether to buy cars made in Eastern Europe," wrote *The Times* of London, "have had to weigh temptingly low prices against, in most cases, thoroughly old-fashioned designs and the likelihood of high depreciation. It has not been an easy choice to make. But the cars have gradually gotten better and the Yugo 45 from Yugoslavia, which goes on sale at the end of the month, is probably the best so far." *The Times* also noted that though the Yugo 45 was an outmoded automobile, because of its Fiat 127 bloodlines it possessed "a distinguished pedigree."[25] The only question was whether or not Zastava, in building a generic Fiat, could maintain the same assembly-line standards that Fiat could. Malcolm Bricklin concluded yes, but most British experts, including *The Times*'s automotive correspondent Peter Waymark, said no.

Bricklin was motivated to be optimistic. In the spring of 1984, his International Automobile Importers (IAI) had struck out with both the Pininfarina Spider and the Bertone X1/9. Bankruptcy was on the horizon. Thus, when Occidental Petroleum contacted Bricklin in 1984 about a possible trade-barter agreement involving the Yugo, Bricklin and other IAI officials raced to Belgrade in May 1984 for a sit-down meeting with representatives from Occidental, Zastava, and Genex (the Yugoslav export conglomerate) at Genex's Belgrade headquarters.

To that point, no IAI official had ever inspected the car. Most, including IAI vice president Tony Ciminera, had had years of experience with Fiat, but Yugo was another story. As Ciminera states: "We went down there [to the parking lot of the hotel] to see the cars. I had seen pictures, but this was the first time that I had actually seen the car . . . And I'm supposed to be the car guy, right? So I'm looking at it with a very critical eye. And I said, 'Ugh! This is really primitive! Shoddy.' And I opened up the hood and I opened up the trunk and I drove the car. I did all those things." Ciminera saw, with amazement, that his sample Yugo had rust spots in the trunk. "I said, 'Ahhh . . . Malcolm! This is not good. I don't know what these rust spots are or why they're there or how they got there, but they shouldn't be there!'"[26] Ciminera was floored. He had never seen anything like it, not from Bertone, not from Pininfarina, and especially not from Fiat. Rust in the *trunk*? Ciminera guessed that some Zastava worker had been grinding metal near the car and that metal dust had been trapped in the paint. Automaking 101: You paint cars in dust-free, sterile environments, in sealed rooms, which apparently Zastava didn't do. If this was Zastava's best product, Ciminera could only imagine what the factory looked like. He shuddered.

But Bricklin was unmoved. He told Ciminera to relax. They had a meeting to go to at Genex, then tomorrow they'd tour the factory in Kragujevac. Maybe then they'd figure out what the problem was. Bricklin's main concern wasn't the car per se, because he knew that Ciminera could fix it. Just a year earlier Ciminera had traveled to Turin, Italy, where he had made hundreds of changes to the Spider and the X1/9 and had prepped them for the American market. Bricklin assumed then that if Zastava agreed to export the Yugo, Ciminera would make similar changes in Kragujevac. His real concern was whether or not he could persuade a communist car company to sell its cars in the United States. This had been done only twice before. But Bricklin was up to the task. He went to the meeting at Genex full of enthusiasm and was determined to get the car.

Toma Savic remembers that although he and other officials from Zastava were excited by the meeting and wanted to export as many Yugos as possible, they were afraid that all Zastava would receive was oil. After all, the Yugoslav government hoped to exchange Adriatic drilling rights, industrial products, and other commodities for $400 million per year in Occidental oil. "That's where Genex came in," states Savic. "It had a specialized oil subsidiary [Inex] and could in theory give us hard currency for our cars . . . Like every other company in Yugoslavia, we needed cash. We were constantly purchasing raw and even finished materials on the open market: paint from PPG [Pittsburgh Plate Glass], glass from PPG or sometimes a French company, and steel from Austria and Germany. Fortunately for us, [sometime in June 1984] the Occidental portion of the deal fell through. So Occidental was out and so were the middlemen, but Bricklin still wanted the car."[27]

The four-way meeting in Belgrade ended on May 16, 1984, whereupon the participants, including Bricklin, Ciminera, IAI's chief financial officer Ira Edelson, and vice president Bill Prior, traveled to Kragujevac for a tour of the factory. There in local Serbian style they were treated to a sumptuous, alcohol-laden feast. "They met us very graciously," remembers Ciminera. "There was this beautiful luncheon and then a tour of the plant . . . The place was humongous. But it was also filthy. I mean, the floor was two inches thick with grease in the press shop! It was just black filth. And it was dimly lit but no one was wearing any safety goggles or helmets or gloves."[28] At one point Ciminera noticed the men in the press shop were stamping out pieces of sheet metal for hoods and doors. But once the pieces had been stamped, instead of carefully stacking the sheets and arranging them for later use, the men would physically toss them into a bin.

"I said, 'Malcolm, they're manhandling the sheet metal! It's got to be handled with kid gloves!' So later when the cars were being painted and assembled and brought down to ground level on an assembly line . . . I was shocked. I saw dents. These raw body shells had just left the oven and were coming along overhead, but because of the angle I could see them. They'd put damaged parts on a finished car . . . and no one was doing anything about it." In disgust, Ciminera turned to Bricklin and said, "Let's go. We're through. You can't change the culture of this place. It's impossible."[29]

But "Bricklin stopped me," remembers Ciminera, "and I'll never forget what he said. He told me that 'yeah, the car is ugly . . . but what we have here is a quality issue. We can fix that. But if you told me that the engine was horrible or that it had smoke coming out of it or that the bearings were rattling and that it'd take $15 [million] to $20 million to fix it . . . that'd be different. I'd agree with you. But it's a quality issue. Those dents wouldn't be there if we were running things. This place is a diamond in the rough.' So I started thinking . . . Maybe we could clean these floors. You can't just throw away a billion-dollar facility like this. So he convinced me. What we had here was a challenge . . . a doable challenge."[30] With that, Ciminera was aboard. When and if a deal went through, he would be the one to examine, analyze, and prep every square inch of the automobile to make it palatable to the U.S. market. This was no small job.

To assist Ciminera, it was decided at a second four-way meeting the afternoon of the factory tour that Zastava would send eight Yugos to the United States and that over the next month Ciminera would fax Zastava a list of changes. The only problem was that Zastava didn't have a fax. The company actually bought and installed a new fax machine while Ciminera was examining the cars. It was also decided that all four parties would sign a basic protocol calling for the barter of Yugo 45 automobiles for Occidental's petroleum-based products. The specific arrangements between IAI and Occidental, on the one hand, and Genex and Zastava on the other were left to negotiation.

This first four-way protocol was simply a memorandum of understanding. It did not bind the parties in any way. However, according to Ira Edelson, Bricklin insisted that even this first protocol include a special clause stating that "if for any reason the full deal fell apart, that portion of the deal which pertained to Zastava manufacturing the cars and the Bricklin organization purchasing the cars would remain operative."[31] Though inserted at the last minute, Bricklin's special clause is what linked IAI to Zastava and led, in the summer of 1984, to the creation of Yugo America Inc., the company that brought the Yugo to the United States. Bricklin was overjoyed. Soon he'd be selling, promoting, and pitching the Yugo like a man possessed. The Yugo was his next big thing.

7

The "Four-Meter Fax"

Q: How do you make a Yugo go from 0 to 60 in less than 15 seconds?
A: Push it off a cliff.

Bricklin's Yugo America Inc. was established in the summer of 1984 and included most of the key players from IAI. Bricklin was chairman of the board and chief executive officer, Ira Edelson was vice chairman of the board and chief financial officer, Bill Prior was president and chief operating officer, while Tony Ciminera was senior vice president of production and engineering. In all, stock in Yugo America amounted to ten million shares, over 51 percent of which was owned by the Bricklin family.[1] Edelson, Prior, and Ciminera each owned shares, as did seventeen other parties including the Nordic American Bank Corporation and the Fram Shipping Company, for a total of twenty-one separate investors. Nordic American and Fram purchased 1.5 million shares of Yugo America stock in December 1984 for $2 million.[2] Owned by Norwegian shipping magnate Per Arneberg, the Fram Shipping Company specialized in car transportation. Thus, as an investor in Yugo America, Arneberg was given an exclusive contract to ship Yugo automobiles from the port city of Bar in Montenegro to the United States.

Meanwhile, in June 1984, just prior to the creation of Yugo America, IAI received its first shipment of eight sample cars. They arrived at JFK aboard the Yugoslav national air carrier JAT (Jugoslovenski Aerotransport), which then had direct flights from Belgrade to New York. The cars were divided up and sent to various locations for testing. One group underwent baseline emissions tests, another safety and crash tests, while Ciminera studied the car's quality, drivability, and appearance at his home in New Jersey. The quality, he remembers, was atrocious . . . truly atrocious. "We put New Jersey plates on them," remembers Ciminera, "and I drove one of the cars to and from work. Twice I was almost killed by its poor quality! On one occasion I was turning into my driveway and was making a right turn. Something snapped and I couldn't steer all of a sudden. Instead of turning into the driveway it went in at a forty-five-degree angle and jumped the curb and stopped inches away from a gigantic tree! It turns out a bolt fell out of the front suspension."[3]

On another occasion Ciminera was driving the car over a wooden bridge, a historic one-lane bridge that crossed over a very busy set of railroad tracks. Passing below Ciminera was a long freight train, and just as he came to the bridge the back to his driver's seat gave way. "The weld snapped and I'm suddenly laying flat. My head was on the backseat. I was totally prone. I couldn't reach the steering wheel anymore. But the car's still moving and I'm trying to steer it with my knees, trying to reach the pedals in a panic before I crash through the bridge and land on top of the train. Twice I nearly killed myself with that car. So I really gave 'em a list."[4]

Ciminera's list, in fact, was hundreds of items long, covering everything from safety and emissions standards to body paint, windshield glass, dashboard knobs, windshield wipers, door handles, ashtrays, and screws. He was unbelievably meticulous. When Ciminera faxed the list to Zastava in August 1984, it was the longest fax that the managers there had ever seen. They called it "the four-meter fax." "We used to joke about Tony sometimes," says Pete Mulhern. "We said that Tony was an interior decorator sent to do a technical job. And it's true. He wouldn't leave things alone. We were trying to get a carburetor that worked and he was worried about a screw in the ventilator. I'm sure it drove the Yugoslavs crazy."[5]

However, Ciminera's list of Yugo design changes was a necessary step. Before that point, neither Yugo America nor Zastava had any idea how much the car would cost. So in August 1984, Ciminera returned to Kragujevac for a final cram session in which he and other Yugo America technicians met with Zastava's research and development department to explain what was needed. At the end of the session, they had a long list, but Zastava's finance department decided that since a production-ready prototype was months into the future, it was better to negotiate a preliminary price based on the Yugo 55, which was a standard Yugo model with an 1,116cc, 55-horsepower engine. By doing so, the two parties came to a base price, which in September 1984 was about $2,000. The parties also decided that once the car had passed its U.S. safety and emissions tests and included every new part needed for production, they would reconvene in Kragujevac for a second round of negotiations that spring.

The September 1984 agreement was simply a memorandum of understanding, but it stated that Bricklin's International Automobile Importers, the parent company of Yugo America Inc., was to import a minimum of 20,000 Yugo automobiles in 1985, with subsequent annual deliveries of at least 35,000 cars. The total value of the deal was an astonishing $100 million.[6] Neither Bricklin nor IAI nor Yugo America Inc. had $100 million. As of September 1984, not one of these parties had even $40 million, which was the price of 20,000 Yugo 55 automobiles at $2,000 per car.

Clearly, Bricklin's new Yugo America venture was undercapitalized. But Bricklin did have panache. In the fall of 1984, he began working the press and spreading word that a new Yugoslav automobile, priced at a stunningly low $3,990, was on the horizon.[7] "It looks a little like everything out there," he told *The Dallas Morning News* that October. "It looks like a Rabbit, it looks like a Colt, it looks like a Tercel. It looks like all the cars in the $5,000 to $7,000 price range, except it's under $4,000."[8] Bricklin also pitched the Yugo to his own IAI dealer network, which had failed with its two sports cars; to dealers of well-known automobiles such as Ford, GM, and Chrysler; and to anyone who'd listen.

Apparently he struck a nerve. It had been years since dealers had seen an automobile priced at $4,000, and as they all knew, one of their customers' key complaints was that new cars were too expensive. Piquing interest were Bricklin's own sales estimates, which, to put it mildly, were enormous. Although his company's first contract with Zastava called for at most 20,000 imports for 1985, Bricklin told the Associated Press that he was planning to import a full 70,000 cars. He also told the AP that he would import 100,000 cars in 1986 and 250,000 cars in 1987. The latter figure of 250,000 cars was 2 percent of the U.S. market, figured the Associated Press, which would put Yugo America Inc. ahead of Volkswagen of America, Inc., and American Motors. Both of these companies, stated auto analyst Arvid Jouppi, "have very very strong dealer bodies in place. The age of miracles in the auto industry has passed," he declared, and meeting Bricklin's estimates "would be a miracle."[9] But if anyone could sell cars to car dealers, it was Malcolm Bricklin, whose Yugo America Inc. began offering exclusive franchise rights in November 1984. The price was $35,850.

In addition to this first franchise fee, dealers were required to give Yugo America a $400,000 letter of credit.[10] Yugo America would then use these letters of credit to secure loans from various banks, which it then used to buy cars from Yugoslavia. The $35,850 franchise fee was supposed to remain in escrow until all signs, brochures, and sales and service materials as well as the cars had been delivered. However, as Ira Edelson states, sometime in late 1984, Yugo America Inc. ran out of money, which prompted Bricklin to begin using his franchise fees for operations. Afraid that both he and Bricklin would end up in the hoosegow, on December 8, 1984, Edelson resigned.

"Although dealer agreements are still not complete," Edelson wrote to Bricklin, "Yugo America has been signing dealers for the past three weeks and accepting deposits of $17,925 per dealer. This amount represents half of the initial dealer package consisting of an initial inventory of parts, tools, manuals, signs, etc. *Some of these monies are now being used for operations* . . . In general, [our lawyer] has stated that deposits being received from dealers should be escrowed and not used . . . [He has also stated] that use of the deposits with no apparent way to repay could lead to civil suits and possible jury awards for damages . . . Since I fully expect capital to be forthcoming before the end of the month, the decision I have made to resign is, I suppose, an extremely conservative one . . . [But] I had to weigh the relatively slight chance of being wiped out financially at age 60 versus the exciting future Yugo would offer me . . . If you believe we can work together again after the financing is in place," Edelson concluded, "you know my feelings."[11]

Edelson knew Bricklin was a risk. But he also knew that this idea, this opportunity, could be the one. In any case, the issue was soon moot. In late December 1984, Nordic American Bank and Per Arneberg came through with a $2 million investment in Yugo America. That investment was followed by an additional $3 million infusion by a series of smaller parties in the spring of 1985. Yugo America was in business. The company now had funds to cover its escrow commitments and to continue the car's safety and emissions tests as well as Ciminera's design changes in Kragujevac. As a result, Edelson stayed. He was instrumental in keeping Yugo America financially viable and at one point negotiated a company-saving $79 million loan. But that was in 1986, when *Yugo* was a household name.

In the fall of 1984, however, when Ciminera and other Yugo America engineers and consultants traveled to Kragujevac to begin prepping the car, the Yugo was still a dream. "The people at Zastava," remembers Pete Mulhern, "were elated and terrified. They were like the dog who caught the fire engine: 'What do I do now that I've caught it? Now [that] we have this opportunity, how the heck are we gonna bring ourselves up to these standards?' They were very serious about doing things right. I mean, once they caught this dream they said, 'Man, we've got to do this thing from the top down.' And they did."[12] The standards in question were those set forth by the Society of Automotive Engineers (SAE), an international professional association for members of the automotive, aerospace, and commercial vehicle industries. Since its founding in 1905, SAE's main goal was to promote minimum acceptable standards in all things automotive, a word SAE itself coined in 1916.[12] SAE standards have since become world standards, and are followed by every single manufacturer who makes cars in, or exports to, the United States.

Apart from safety, the Yugo's most important standard to meet was emissions. An armrest could squeak and be of poor quality or a dashboard could be installed incorrectly, but emission standards were set and monitored by the Environmental Protection Agency (EPA), whose Office of Transportation and Air Quality could ban noncompliant automobiles from the road. So in late 1984, job one at Yugo America was emissions. That job was overseen by an outside consultant named Roger Berry, a former emissions specialist at Ford who had founded his own company in 1982.[13] "We laid out a plan for [the Yugoslavs]," explains Berry, "which showed us taking this vehicle, which in all fairness, was probably a 1960s sort of vehicle," and bringing it forward "from the 1960s to the 1980s."[14] The Yugo, he informed them, needed a much better carburetion system than the one it had.

Now obsolete in automobiles, the carburetor was the part of the car's engine that blended air with gasoline and controlled the engine's output. If the carburetor mixed too much air with gasoline, the car would run weakly. In that case it was "running lean." But if the carburetor mixed too much gasoline with air, its engine "ran rich," which meant it produced thick clouds of very smoky exhaust. In 1984 the carburetor the Yugo used ran rich. Unless Berry could change the carburetor and replace it with a cleaner one, the Yugo had no hope of passing its EPA emissions tests. Therefore, Berry began negotiating with Weber North America, a leading producer of carburetor conversion kits with offices in Detroit. Weber agreed to provide Yugo America with ten thousand new carburetors and to work with Berry on fitting the carburetor into a Yugo prototype and testing the car's emissions.

The carburetor work was done in Detroit. When the prototype was ready in December 1984, Berry boxed up the parts and shipped them to Kragujevac, where he, too, traveled to oversee their introduction. Berry was accompanied by Tony Ciminera and Mark Bricklin, one of Malcolm Bricklin's sons. "When we got there for the first time," laughs Berry, "we walked into the airport bathroom . . . We're standing there at the urinals, talking about our upcoming plans, and Tony says something like 'Man, oh man, it's warmer here than I thought!' And Mark and I look over and the whole front of Tony's pants is getting soaked with pee because someone had stolen the little 'U' pipe on the bottom of the urinal and out it's coming all over him. And we about died. Tony couldn't believe it, but it set the tone. It's just something you would find in an Eastern bloc country."[15]

Although Yugoslavia wasn't in the Soviet bloc, it was still a communist country whose way of life and managerial institutions were foreign to American observers. Berry and his partners were floored, for instance, by the sheer number of workers that Zastava had. Unlike American companies, where worker productivity was key, Zastava was a state-owned enterprise that favored high employment. "When most Americans went there," Pete Mulhern recalled, "they expected to see something like a printing press rushing by. And the Americans would say, 'Hey, why's it stopped?' But it wasn't stopped. It was just moving really slowly. Zastava had six guys doing one job by hand that one guy could do with the right tool. But why be efficient when efficiency meant you had thousands of people hanging out on street corners without any work?"[16]

On one level Zastava's labor policies made sense, but the presence of so many workers performing so many different tasks meant mistakes. Many, many mistakes. Windows leaked, doors didn't close right, turn signals didn't work. Once, Ciminera saw workers with dirty shoes and hands fitting in the upholstery of a new Yugo car. Berry remembers a problem with the Yugo's rear windshield wiper. The wiper was connected by a thin electrical wire that ran from the dash down the length of the automobile to the rear of the car. The wire was color coded and bundled by hand with other wires into a harness, which looked like a long braid. At the end of the harness, each wire had a connector that was tested for conductivity before being installed in the car. But, as Berry noticed, when workers connected the harness to the dashboard, taped it down under the carpet, and brought it to the back of the car, the harness with the connectors attached was too big to fit through the hole.

Although Zastava had been producing the Yugo since 1980, no one had bothered to tell management that there was a design flaw: that the two holes stamped into the back of the car for its wiper, turning-light, and rear-defrost wires were too small. So instead the assembly-line workers pulled each connector off the harness, then pulled the harness through the hole before replacing the connectors. "I'm looking at this," states Berry, "and I couldn't believe it. All of this work that they did, and this guy just undid and redid it, and there's no conductivity test after that. So what would happen is that in about one out of every ten cars he got a wire in the wrong place. So a wiper wouldn't work, a defroster wouldn't work, and so on."[17] Although Berry fixed the problem, he realized early on that Zastava lacked discipline, for neither the company nor its workers had ever produced cars in a competitive environment. As a result, the Yugo's quality was low.

The Yugoslavs were eager to learn, however. "When the Americans came," remembers Zdravka Damjanic, a company English interpreter who worked with the Yugo America employees, "they came with a lot of energy. This was something our people needed at that time . . . Everyone had to get organized and respect certain quality standards. The workers were a bit surprised at first and most asked, 'Why? Why are we doing this?' But once the Americans explained it to them, they understood. They understood that just one mistake could wreck the whole car. So people started respecting these new standards."[18] Perhaps the most visible change, remembers Damjanic, was in Zastava's management team, which approached the "Yugo-A Project" with great gusto. "Everyone was enthusiastic," she states. "From a business point of view their whole mind-set changed. Zastava became more organized, more serious in its approach. Right away the management there had a well-defined agenda, and they even stuck to it. We couldn't believe it."[19]

That agenda was published in January 1985 in a fifty-six-page internal memo written by Toma Savic. Titled *Projekat Yugo-A* ("Project Yugo-A"), the memo provided a detailed description of nine separate steps, called programs, for the production, service, and sale of the Yugo car. The memo revealed, among other things, that Zastava knew exactly what it was getting into. "Apart from being truly massive," it read, "the American marketplace is a very open marketplace. It has a developed automotive industry, but is also the greatest importer of automobiles in the world. However, this does not mean that America is an 'Eldorado' for producers. On the contrary, to survive in this marketplace we must understand that apart from high standards of engine quality, American car buyers are accustomed to similar standards of quality in the car's look, interior finish, and design."[20]

Quality, in fact, became a central focus at Zastava, and although Program Two of the memo's nine separate programs specifically dealt with the issue, references to improved quality appeared throughout. At one point the memo stated, "Success will come when *all* components are produced successfully, but failure will come when *even one* component fails. With that in mind, we must constantly emphasize quality of production, because the battle for the American marketplace will be won or lost on this front."[21] The problem, however, was that in addition to improving its own quality of production, Zastava had agreed with Yugo America to make 419 different changes to the car, and to make the changes in a mere seven months. "I remember December [1984] as being pivotal," recalls Pete Mulhern, "because we had just seven months to prepare the car for the 1986 model year. I was a plodder at IAI, and I was always trained that you can only do one thing at a time, so I was really kicking and screaming at Yugo America because these guys were doing three things at once. But Malcolm wanted to import the car in June [1985], so we were crushed with work. It was really run-and-gun."[22]

At various points, there were five to ten Americans in Kragujevac (and one or two others in Belgrade at Zastava's engine supplier) who oversaw various tasks. Ciminera, for instance, handled changes to the car's fit and finish, Berry its emissions, while Pete Mulhern assembled a new parts catalog and wrote an owner's manual. Later, in June 1985, a former National Highway Transportation Safety Administration official named Bob Pavlovic, an American of Serbian descent, was hired by Yugo America to oversee quality control.[23] Although Bricklin and Yugo America president Bill Prior visited from time to time, they generally stayed in the United States. The Americans were housed in Kragujevac at the Hotel Sumarice, a one-hundred-room hunting lodge located in a forest outside of town. There they slept in very large suites, including one suite that had personally belonged to Tito.

Each day drivers from Zastava would pick up the Americans at 6:30 a.m., and after a quick breakfast the workday began with a meeting at 7:00. At first the Americans had a very bad experience with Serbian coffee. Known as "Turkish coffee" in the Balkans, the coffee in Kragujevac was sweet, concentrated, and strong. It was made from coffee beans that had been ground into a very fine powder, which was then boiled in water before being served. Thus, the coffee in Kragujevac was unfiltered and at the bottom of each cup was a thick, black sludge. Zdravka Damjanic remembers that at one of their first meetings, in December 1984, when the Americans had finished their coffee, they started to eat the sludge with their spoons. "They thought the grounds at the bottom of the cup were something you ate, like cocoa, but they weren't. They were nasty. We explained it to them and tried very hard not to laugh. But it *was* funny."[24]

Eventually the Americans in Kragujevac became coffee connoisseurs, preferring strong Turkish coffee over filtered coffee from home. But coffee was one thing. To the Americans' surprise, the workers at Zastava also drank brandy, a specific type of brandy made from plums known as *sljivovica*. Unlike in the United States, where alcohol is banned in the workplace, plum brandy was everywhere at Zastava. Employees drank it in the morning, during breaks, and sometimes even at work, and it wasn't uncommon for Zastava's management team to end meetings with a toast. "They started drinking this jet fuel at about eight in the morning," remembers Pete Mulhern, "so way before lunchtime things would get pretty sketchy. Really. They'd offer it to me and I'd say no, but not wanting to be a jerk I'd say maybe after lunch. But they'd say, 'It's really good. You should try some.' Once I asked my interpreter why he drank the stuff. And he said, 'It's wintertime. It helps to warm the body.' And I said, 'Well, I can understand that.' It's part of their culture, I guess, so I didn't pan it. But later, in the spring, the same stuff was going on. Some guy would appear out of nowhere with a tray and a bunch of little glasses. So I asked him again, 'Why are you drinking this stuff now? It's warm outside.' But this time he laughed and said, 'It cools the body down!' "[25]

Roger Berry remembers working from 7:00 a.m. to 2:00 in the afternoon, then breaking for a long, smoky lunch at a local restaurant, where everyone drank two to three shots of *sljivovica* and a glass of wine. Then they'd return to the factory and work until 8:00 p.m., before having dinner at another restaurant around 9:00. "There was just this blue, heavy, smoky haze," he remembers. "Ninety percent of the people smoke cigarettes and they're all puffing away . . . And it's a slow, European pace, so if you got there at 8:30 or 9:00 p.m., you left about 11:30 or 12:00. Then they'd get you back to your room, pretty hammered, about 12:30 or 1:00. You'd go to sleep, wake up at 5:00 or 6:00, then at 6:30 you'd do it all over again."[26]

Amazingly enough, Berry survived his workday bacchanalia, and just prior to Christmas 1984 he and engineers from Zastava's research and development department produced their first emissions-ready car. It featured a carburetor from Weber, an ignition system from Bosch, a catalytic converter from Maremont, an air filter from Fram, and a vacuum harness from McWane. Berry had negotiated a price for each of these products, had shipped samples to Zastava, and had retrofitted them to a prototype Yugo. Now he needed to send six of these Yugos back to the United States for the cars' 50,000-mile emissions test with the EPA. By law, all new cars and trucks sold in the United States had to meet federal emissions standards and be certified by the EPA. This was accomplished by having laboratory tests performed on preproduction vehicles at an EPA-approved testing facility, such as the National Vehicle and Fuel Emissions Laboratory (NVFEL) in Ann Arbor, Michigan.

The NVFEL tested the vehicles at 10,000-mile increments under various speeds and conditions and at Yugo America's expense. The purpose, in testing the vehicle for 50,000 miles, was to ensure that the car was durable enough to meet federal emissions standards over several years. Once the car passed its federal emissions test, and passed an even stricter set of tests required by the California EPA, it received an official certificate, which in effect was a license to sell cars. The Yugo received its federal certificate (and its California certificate) in April 1985. With that, the Yugo's emissions system was in place, as were most of the 419 different design changes overseen by Ciminera. One major change was that the American Yugo would have a larger engine. The Yugo 45 had a 903cc, 0.9-liter, 45-horsepower engine. However, the new Yugo, the one being exported to the United States, had an 1116cc, 1.1-liter, 55-horsepower engine.

Even so, the new engine placed the Yugo at the very slow end of the U.S. market. The car did 0 to 60 in a paltry 14 seconds and had a top speed of 86 miles per hour. The Yugo was also loud. According to a *Car and Driver* road test published in April 1986, the Yugo had an interior sound level of 81 decibels (dBA) when measured at 70 miles per hour. Of the thirty-seven cars tested by *Car and Driver* in 1986, only the Panther Kallista (at 84 dBA) and the Lamborghini Countach 5000 (at 85 dBA) were louder.[27] Although the

Yugo's new 55-horsepower engine gave the car a bit more pep, it was still, stated one analyst, "at the very, very end of acceptability on the expressway."[28]

Safety concerns were foremost in Yugo America's mind, because apart from emissions testing with the EPA, the car faced an additional series of tests with the National Highway Transportation Safety Administration (NHTSA). The NHTSA was a federal agency within the U.S. Department of Transportation whose "New Car Assessment Program" mandated that all cars sold in the United States meet certain performance standards in a head-on collision test in which two seat-belt wearing mannequins, known as "crash-test dummies," were driven into a fixed barrier at 30 miles per hour. If the mannequins received head, chest, or leg injuries above a certain set standard, then the automobile failed the test and could not be sold in the United States.

The basic NHTSA collision test was not very difficult to pass. The Yugo, for example, passed its test in the spring of 1985. However, each year the NHTSA performed a second test in which automobiles were crashed into a fixed barrier at 35 miles per hour, 5 miles per hour more than what was federally required. This second test was unofficial and had nothing to do with whether or not a car could be sold in the United States, but the NHTSA dutifully reported the results to the press. "35 mph Crash Test Shows Head Injuries Likely in Taurus, Sable Cars," stated one AP article. "Jeep Pickup Scores Poorly in US Crash Ratings," declared another.[29] In all, for 1986 ten different cars failed the NHTSA's 35-mile-per-hour crash test, including the Yugo.[30] "If a car is on the market, it's passed its tests," stated Pete Mulhern. "But dangerous? That's a relative term. When I was at IAI, people would say to me, 'What if you get hit by a Buick?' And our standard line was 'What if your Buick gets hit by a semi?'"[31]

Be that as it may, the Yugo's 35-mile-per-hour crash test was a year into the future. So was its unrelenting barrage of bad press. But in the winter of 1985, some six months before the car went into production, the Yugo was white-hot. In January of that year, Bricklin unveiled three versions of the car at the annual convention of the National Automobile Dealers Association (NADA) in San Francisco.[32] As Ciminera remembers it, Yugo America decided not to purchase a booth at the NADA convention hall, but instead rented studio space for the cars at a nearby public broadcasting station.[33] Yugo America then chartered buses to bring interested dealers from the convention hall over to the station, where Bricklin and other Yugo America execs were waiting for them.

"We brought the cars in there and lit them up," says Ciminera. "They must have had thousands of lights in the ceilings like any studio would have, so the cars were lit up magnificently like at auto shows, only better . . . It was quite spectacular. The dealers really came . . . in crowds. We had round tables of ten with a Yugo executive at each who put on a little presentation, about how much they would make, what the profits were, and so on. At the end of the presentation the dealers were asked to write a check, which they did. There were so many checks we had to get a cardboard box to put them all in."[34]

8

Destination America

Q: What do you call a Yugo with brakes?
A: Customized.

For Yugo America, the 1985 NADA convention was a stunning success. Bricklin had shaped and molded the media, and had drummed up thousands of dollars in free company PR. Dealer deposits and franchise requests were rolling in. It was decided at first that Yugo America would award just fifty franchises in anticipation of its planned August 1985 introduction date. These franchises would be located in the northeastern corridor, close to Yugo America's parts warehouse in Upper Saddle River, New Jersey, and close to the car's debarkation point, the Port of Baltimore. Through most of 1984–85, Yugo America was administered from IAI offices in Montvale, New Jersey, but as Yugo expanded, the company moved its headquarters to nearby Upper Saddle River.

Like other car importers, Yugo America had chosen New Jersey because of its proximity to New York City. Both Montvale and Upper Saddle River were approximately thirty miles due north of Manhattan, where Bricklin lived, and close to an abundant supply of car industry men with whom to staff Yugo's headquarters. Over the years, New Jersey had been home to Fiat (Montvale), Volkswagen (Englewood Cliffs), BMW (Woodcliff Lake), Rolls-Royce (Lyndhurst), Jaguar (Mahwah), Mercedes-Benz (Montvale), Ferrari (Englewood Cliffs), Subaru (Cherry Hill), Peugeot (Lyndhurst), Volvo (Rockleigh), and Maserati (Red Bank).[1] Yugo America's New Jersey headquarters was also close to the company's new PR firm, Rosenfeld, Sirowitz & Lawson, which had offices in New York City. The firm signed on with Yugo America in late March 1985.[2]

However, Yugo America's first ad campaign would not begin in earnest until the fall of 1985. Therefore, it was up to Bricklin, Prior, and Yugo America's own PR boss, Jonas Halperin, to push the automobile and field questions from the media until the true advertising blitz began. For Yugo America, the NADA San Francisco convention was a good first step. In a February 4, 1985, editorial, the highly regarded industry newspaper *Automotive News* wrote: "Perhaps the most interesting car [at the NADA convention] was the truly late starter, Yugo. Under the protection and promotion of Malcolm Bricklin, Yugo is going to take a crack at the U.S. market. It is difficult to believe anything else but that Yugo is going to be a howling success."[3] The *Automotive News* (*AN*) also criticized the *San Francisco Chronicle*, which a week earlier had chided the Yugo for being a communist-made car.

"We believe that cars do not have politics," wrote *AN*. "But we believe just as firmly that the home-country source of Yugo is going to be the biggest hurdle that Bricklin will have to overcome. We have no doubt that he can do it . . . Bricklin has struck out a couple of times, but he is still at the plate. Don't bet against a home run."[4] No doubt, Yugo America officials were thrilled by *AN*'s glowing editorial, but they were worried that if Bricklin wasn't careful, the importation of just the third communist-made automobile ever sold in the United States could backfire.[5] Whether Sino or Soviet, Yugoslavian or Vietnamese, to most Americans, communism was a ghastly mix of housing blocks, gulags, breadlines, and barbed wire.

Already in October 1984, Congressman Dennis Hertel of Michigan had claimed that the Yugo's $3,990 price tag "indicate[d] either massive subsidies or slave labor."[6] Either way, he insinuated, the car should not be sold in the United States. In early 1985, state representatives in Louisiana proposed House Bill 283, which forbade the state's purchasing department from buying any automobile made in a communist country.[7] The bill was directed at the Yugo. "I don't like the idea that a communist country such as Yugoslavia is sending its Yugo to the U.S. and selling it for $3990," wrote one letter to the editor of *Ward's AutoWorld*. "Japanese and Korean trade is bad enough."[8]

Yugo America spokesmen countered these first early attacks by stating very publicly that, yes, Yugoslavia was a communist country, but it was independent of the Soviets and its political system "was as close to Swedish socialism as possible."[9] They also formed a dealer focus group to see exactly how much the issue mattered. "The reaction was neutral to slightly negative," stated Bill Prior. "But it wasn't about communism; it was about the country's lack of association with a quality manufacturer. [In this regard,] Yugoslavia would score like Finland. Maybe Finland builds terrific cars, but I don't know of any."[10]

No doubt Congressman Hertel had criticized the Yugo because his home district included Dearborn, Michigan, the headquarters of Ford Motor Company. But Ford did not fear the Yugo, not in the slightest. What it and other American car manufacturers feared was price dumping, the "subsidies" that Hertel was referring to. Dumping is the act of exporting a product at an unreasonably low price, usually below cost. Foreign producers would do this for a variety of reasons. If, for example, a producer's home market was protected by import duties, it could sell a given product at home for high prices while "dumping" the same product at lower prices abroad. Socialist countries such as Yugoslavia, in which all companies were state owned, could in theory subsidize an industry, or even a company or product, to lower its export prices, woo consumers, and gain market share.

The first antidumping regulation in history appeared in Canada in 1904.[11] By the 1980s, antidumping regulations were a key component of the General Agreement on Tariffs and Trade (GATT), an international convention meant to lower trade barriers signed by representatives of ninety-nine different countries who met in Tokyo in 1979. GATT's antidumping regulations did not punish transgressors. Instead, they provided a framework for how a given signatory, such as Canada or the United States, could defend its domestic industries from dumping. First, the aggrieved party had to demonstrate that dumping was taking place. Then it had to calculate the value of the dumping by comparing the product's export purchase price with its purchase price at home. Then finally, GATT required aggrieved parties to show that this particular instance of price dumping was hurting their domestic industries or threatening to do so.

In the United States, companies such as Ford lodge dumping complaints with the Department of Commerce, which investigates the case to see if dumping has occurred. If it has, the case is then forwarded to the U.S. International Trade Commission (ITC), which determines the impact of foreign exports to the United States and issues penalties in cases of dumping. A usual ITC penalty involves the imposition of higher import duties, called "countervailing duties," to make up the price differential between dumped and domestically produced goods. In the 1980s, dumping complaints typically came from the beleaguered U.S. steel industry.[12] Although certainly viewed as a threat, foreign car producers were rarely accused of dumping because their sticker prices were too high. Since 1981, the Japanese had gone up-market with their automobiles: companies like Honda were producing high-quality, relatively high-priced cars specifically for the American market.

But the Yugo was different. It was the product of a state-owned socialist enterprise, which meant, at least indirectly, every square inch of the automobile had been paid for by the state—every nut, every bolt, and every belt. While Zastava itself was intended to be a profit-making enterprise, the company couldn't have been built or even have functioned without government subsidies. In and of themselves, state subsidies are not a bad thing. They involve any form of assistance given by a government to support the production and later the purchase of a good. For instance, any tax break that aids a business in any way is a subsidy. With that in mind, however, it is up to individual governments to (1) assess the value of an importing government's subsidies, (2) compare the cost of the good in foreign and domestic marketplaces, and (3) impose duties accordingly. This prevents dumping.

However, in terms of subsidies, it appears that neither the U.S. Department of Commerce nor the International Trade Commission ever officially examined the Yugo. This in spite of the fact that in September 1986, the Yugoslav journal *Ekonomska Politika* reported that Zastava had been given a 14-billion-dinar subsidy for the export of 83,000 Yugo cars.[13] That amounted to a $427 per car subsidy, which according to GATT and various U.S. anti-dumping laws, could have meant tariffs. But "the Yugoslavs knew they had no cause to worry about American laws," wrote economic historian Michael Palairet, "because of the protection they enjoyed from highly-placed friends," including former undersecretary of state and onetime ambassador to Yugoslavia Lawrence Eagleburger.[14]

Since September 1984, Eagleburger had been president of Kissinger Associates, an international consulting firm founded in 1982 by former secretary of state Henry Kissinger and General Brent Scowcroft, the national security adviser to President Gerald Ford. Though the firm's specialty was "assessing for corporate clients the strategic implications of geopolitical and economic trends and developments," critics called Kissinger Associates "a high-powered dating service."[15] Said one observer, "It's like a door opening. After all, if Henry calls up someone in Washington or Europe and asks him to meet a client, who's going to say no?"[16] Nevertheless, the client list at Kissinger Associates was short and exclusive, numbering no more than twenty-five at any given time. Clients were required to retain the firm for a period of one year, and though never made public, the firm's retainer fee was somewhere between $150,000 and $250,000. Clients included Hunt Oil, Daewoo, Ericsson, Fiat, Volvo, Anheuser-Busch, and beginning in February 1985, Bricklin Industries, the parent company of Yugo America Inc.[17]

Unlike other clients, Bricklin Industries had hired Kissinger Associates not for Henry Kissinger's expertise but for the political connections of Lawrence Eagleburger. Although Eagleburger was perhaps best known for his tenure as ambassador to Yugoslavia from 1977 to 1981, his personal connection with Yugoslavia spanned some twenty-five years. Eagleburger had joined the Foreign Service out of the University of Wisconsin in 1957, and in 1961 was a young embassy staffer in Belgrade. It was here that Eagleburger made his first Yugoslav contacts and learned Serbo-Croatian, and it was also here that he earned a certain degree of fame in the Yugoslav republic of Macedonia. In July 1963, the Macedonian capital of Skopje experienced a twenty-second earthquake measuring 6.9 on the Richter scale. The earthquake killed more than 1,000 people, leaving 120,000 homeless, and rendering 80 percent of the city's buildings uninhabitable.[18]

Shortly after the earthquake, Eagleburger drove down from Belgrade and was one of the first foreign aid workers on the scene. He was responsible for coordinating the bulk of America's relief efforts, which earned him lasting gratitude from the Yugoslavs and the very appreciative moniker "Lawrence of Macedonia."[19] Later, as ambassador to Yugoslavia during the Carter administration, Eagleburger helped to improve relations between Washington and Belgrade following a diplomatic rift in the mid-1970s. Even after leaving the embassy in 1981 and becoming undersecretary of state for political affairs, Eagleburger continued to support Yugoslavia by encouraging the approval of a $4.5 billion loan package that various banks and governments gave to the country in 1983.[20] Thus, as far as the Yugoslavs were concerned, Eagleburger was a good, good friend.

For the right price, Eagleburger was also a friend of Yugo America Inc., which not only retained Kissinger Associates as its consulting firm but named Eagleburger to the company's board of directors in February 1985.[21] "To be very candid," states Ira Edelson, "we hired Eagleburger for the credibility that we needed. He served on the board, he got reports like everyone else, [and] he made comments as any board member might. But the main reason [we hired him] was that we needed him for our original credibility."[22] It was Eagleburger, insists Edelson, who in the spring of 1985 assisted Yugo officials in setting up face-to-face meetings with Senator Tom Harkin of Iowa, Senator Frank Lautenberg of New Jersey, and Secretary of Transportation Elizabeth Dole. The purpose of the meetings was to ascertain if the U.S. Congress or the Department of Transportation had any negative and possibly deal-breaking opinions regarding the Yugo. According to Edelson, they did not. All three politicos "were very much in favor of the project," he insists, because the United States supported Yugoslavia, while Yugoslavia opposed the Soviets.[23] It probably helped that both Harkin and Lautenberg were the sons of eastern European immigrants, and that Harkin himself was of Slovenian descent.

Whatever the case, the personal opinions of Tom Harkin and Frank Lautenberg were of little consequence, for U.S. support for Yugoslavia had been a key foreign policy in Washington since 1948. The reason: Tito's break with Stalin was not simply an ideological victory for the United States, it was a geopolitical victory as well.

Prior to 1948, Yugoslavia had been the southwesternmost member of the emerging Soviet bloc. Its Adriatic coastline included sizable ports at Rijeka, Zadar, and Split, which were a stone's throw from Italy and perilously close to the Suez Canal. Control over Yugoslavia meant that Stalin had what no Russian czar had ever had: a Mediterranean port. Though the Soviet Union did have control over neighboring Bulgaria, Bulgaria's ports were on the Black Sea, which meant that Soviet ships sailing from Bulgaria to the Mediterranean sailed through the Turkish Straits, which had been demilitarized by world treaty since 1936.

Therefore, when Tito left the Soviet bloc, he took his Mediterranean ports with him, a coup of immeasurable importance to the U.S. military. From that point forward, successive American administrations treated Yugoslavia like a "pampered child," giving it billions of dollars in aid and loans, most-favored nation trading status, and tons of military equipment.[24] In the media, Tito was a "good communist," a war hero, a man who had fought Hitler, defied Stalin, and kept Yugoslavia's ethnic hostilities under wraps. However, when Tito died in 1980, there was a very real fear in Washington that the Red Army would invade Yugoslavia and force it back into the Soviet bloc. The invasion never happened, but for the rest of the 1980s Yugoslavia remained a key ally of the United States, whose unity and independence were major American concerns.

Another U.S. concern, says Lloyd George, an economic officer who served at the American embassy in Belgrade in 1985, was the promotion of Yugoslav business relations with the United States. Typically, American embassy officials assisted American firms wishing to export to or do business in Yugoslavia. In the 1970s and '80s, these businesses included Dow Chemical, Uniroyal Goodrich, General Foods, GTE, Westinghouse, Coca-Cola, and McDonald's. But in general, American embassy officials were not supposed to assist Yugoslav firms with exporting their products *to* the United States. This wasn't a law or a regulation, but a general operating procedure for American commercial attachés and economic officers in Belgrade.

"Most of us [at the embassy] thought that was a very narrow interpretation," remembers George, "because bigger issues were at stake than simply supporting American businesses. Yugoslavia was in debt, and needed to increase its exports to pay for its foreign loans. So we supported Yugoslav businesses as much as we could, including Zastava."[25] To that end, in April 1985 American embassy officials set up a series of meetings in Belgrade between Yugo America Inc., Zastava, and various high-level members of both the Yugoslav federal government and the Serbian republican government. The purpose of the meetings was to hash out any last-minute details regarding the Yugo before Bricklin traveled to Kragujevac for a final round of contract negotiations that June. In attendance were Ambassador David Anderson, Yugo America board member Lawrence Eagleburger, CFO Ira Edelson, and vice president Alex Crossan.[26]

If, in hiring Lawrence Eagleburger, the goal of Yugo America was to improve its credibility, the plan worked, because not only was Eagleburger known and respected in Yugoslavia, he was enormously influential both in the Belgrade embassy and in the Yugoslav government. The fact that Ambassador Anderson even attended these April meetings is revealing, as is a cocktail reception given in honor of Eagleburger at the ambassador's residence on April 15, 1985. The invitation list included Edelson, Crossan, and a veritable who's who in Yugoslav political affairs, including Andrija Dozet, vice president of Genex, Yugoslavia's main trading house; Budimir Kostic, the president of Investbanka, one of Yugoslavia's largest banks; Josef Snoj, Yugoslavia's federal undersecretary of foreign trade; Milos Krstic, a member of the Serbian Republican Executive Council; and, interestingly enough, Slobodan Milosevic, president of the Belgrade City Committee of the League of Communists.

It should be stated, however, that there is no evidence to suggest that Eagleburger or U.S. officials in Belgrade acted improperly vis-à-vis the Yugo America project. As a private citizen and president of Kissinger Associates, Eagleburger was free to assist Yugo America with making as many connections as possible. That was his job. Likewise, embassy officials were interested in helping any U.S. business that could earn hard currency for the Yugoslavs. But the presence of Lawrence Eagleburger on the board of Yugo America put great pressure on Zastava, because to deny Bricklin was to deny Eagleburger, who as everyone knew had the embassy's ear and Kissinger's connections and was an ally of the Yugoslav government. Thus, in June 1985, when Bricklin traveled to Kragujevac for a final round of meetings, Zastava had no leverage. It agreed almost immediately to Bricklin's price, which depending on whom you ask was either $2,500 or $2,900 per car.[27]

Bricklin's second contract with Zastava called for five hundred Yugos to be delivered to the United States by the end of August 1985, followed by an additional shipment of ten thousand cars by late December. The contract also stated that over the next four years, from 1986 to 1989, Zastava was to send Yugo America an astounding 360,000 cars, a number that in industry terms was patently absurd. In the preceding four years, for example, only seven auto manufacturers in the world—Honda, Mazda, Nissan, Subaru, Toyota, Volkswagen, and Volvo—had exported that many cars to the United States. Industry heavyweights Audi, BMW, Isuzu, Mercedes, Mitsubishi, and Saab hadn't come close to 360,000 cars, nor had Fiat in its final eight years on the American market. But Bricklin thought big: the total value of the deal, including cars and spare parts, was over $1 billion.[28]

Officials at Zastava knew Bricklin's figures were too high: 360,000 cars represented twice the company's annual output, and far more than its aging facilities could provide. "Bricklin wanted huge quantities," remembers Savic, "but we didn't have the capacity. We didn't have the money. We told him that but he said not to worry, he'd build us another plant."[29] However, to build such a plant, Bricklin needed money—lots of money—that Yugo America didn't have. Therefore, he and Bill Prior announced plans to take Yugo America public. Their goal was to raise $300 million for a paint and final assembly shop in the Kragujevac suburb of Korman, which would begin production sometime in 1987. "My attorney told me to keep my mouth shut," stated Bill Prior in an interview with *Automotive News*. "But what I can say is we are very enthusiastic about the future."[30]

Certainly Bricklin was excited. He had once taken Subaru of America public and had found himself rolling in dough. In addition to buying cars with the money, Bricklin had bought a yacht, hired a plane, and built a faux-Japanese headquarters for Subaru in Pennsauken, New Jersey. That was in 1968. Bricklin had raised $1 million by selling three hundred thousand shares on the Philadelphia Stock Exchange. But in 1985, Yugo America needed three hundred times that amount, which meant an initial public offering (IPO) that, in a word, was huge. In 1984, for example, the largest IPO on any stock exchange in the world was British Telecom, which sold three billion shares for $278,928,000. Second was Bowater Inc., a newsprint and paper firm that sold seven million shares for $131,596,434, and third was Reuters Holdings, the media conglomerate, which sold some one hundred million shares for $107,250,000.[31]

Clearly, Yugo America Inc. would not raise $300 million, nor would it import 360,000 cars through 1989. But Bricklin and Prior were unflappable. Through June 1985, they increased their dealer network to 87 and made plans for a gala send-off in Kragujevac when the first shipment of 250 Yugos was scheduled to leave Zastava for the Port of Bar. The planned production date was July 9, with the final send-off party slated just two weeks later, on Monday, July 23, 1985.

Officials at Zastava were scared but elated. They had less than a month to make final preparations for the American Yugo. Their main task was to set up a special Yugo-A assembly line, separate from other assembly lines, on which only a select group of workers worked. Tony Ciminera suggested that Zastava should handpick only its best laborers, and that it should pay them a somewhat higher wage or give them prizes or bonuses for meeting certain targets. Although Toma Savic liked the idea, the bosses at Zastava refused. "That's impossible," Ciminera remembers them saying. "In our system, we're all equal. If you give something to one worker, you have to give it to all of them." However, when Ciminera asked the executives why they themselves were chauffeured to work each day in Mercedes-Benzes while the rest of the workers arrived on bikes, they told him, in effect, "Some workers are more equal than others."[32]

In any case, as head of the Yugo-A project within Zastava, Toma Savic avoided his company's socialist bureaucracy by transferring 140 of his best workers to a special Yugo-A assembly line, one of four assembly lines within the factory in Kragujevac. The workers earned their usual wage but felt that being transferred to the Yugo-A project—and working with the Americans—was in a way prestigious. The average salary for Zastava workers was somewhere between sixty cents and one dollar per hour, a fact which Yugo America execs frequently cited to the media in explaining how they could sell a car for just $3,990.[33] They also cited a strong U.S. dollar and the additional fact that 92 percent of the car's components and raw materials were produced by Zastava.[34]

But critics continued to grumble, including Congressman Hertel of Michigan, who still claimed that Zastava was building the Yugo through the use of slave labor, and Louis Ross, the vice president of domestic auto operations at Ford, who told the AP "you'd have to be in a communist country to get prices like that."[35] However, as Yugo America's PR head Jonas Halperin retorted, "Yugoslavia is a communist country, but it's not the kind where the government runs the factory. The people who run the factory are elected by the workers, and if they don't do a good job they go back to the assembly line."[36]

This wasn't true. The people who ran Zastava were actually appointed by the communist party, but it showed that Yugo America was keenly aware that once the Yugo arrived in the United States its communist origin would be an issue. Therefore, Bricklin repeated over and over: "Yugoslavia was our ally in World War II. [It] didn't drop bombs on us like Germany and Japan."[37] Yugo America president Bill Prior repeated the same theme, adding that Yugoslavia wasn't just a nonaligned nation, it was also not a member of the Warsaw Pact. And to Congressmen Hertel's criticism that the Yugo was built using slave labor, Prior responded that it wasn't slave labor that Zastava was using, it was Slav labor.[38]

In truth, the workers at Zastava were *not* slaves, no more than average workers were in, say, Mexico or Greece. But during the 1980s there was a widespread belief in America that goods from Eastern Europe were made by prisoners. The belief was bolstered by such well-known works as *One Day in the Life of Ivan Denisovich* and *The Gulag Archipelago* by Soviet dissident Aleksandr Solzhenitsyn, and by a February 1983 report from the U.S. Department of State claiming that Soviet authorities were using thousands of prisoner-laborers to build a 2,700-mile pipeline from Siberia to Europe. But the Soviet Union was a special case. According to the International Trade Commission, the Soviets had a prison population of 4 million, of which 1.5 million were producing goods for export.[39] However, the importation of foreign goods using slave or convict labor had been banned in the United States since the Smoot-Hawley Tariff Act of 1930. Therefore, protectionist politicians who opposed U.S.-Soviet trade on ideological grounds often used the slave labor issue to bolster their case.

But Yugoslavia wasn't the Soviet Union and Zastava was no gulag. Certainly, the government of Yugoslavia maintained a prison system like those of other countries, and it also had a special concentration camp for political prisoners known as Goli Otok, the "Barren Isle." Goli Otok is perhaps one of the most infamous places in Yugoslav history and there are rumors that furniture produced there was sold in the United States. But Goli Otok was an isolated example, and neither it nor any other Yugoslav prison provided parts or labor to Zastava. If anything, Zastava had too much labor. In 1984 the company had some 22,000 employees in its passenger-car wing who produced a grand total 164,993 cars, a ratio of one worker for every 7.5 cars produced. By contrast, Ford Motor Company had approximately 114,000 employees who in 1984 produced 1,979,315 cars, a ratio of one worker to every 17.4 cars.[40]

"If it's one thing [the Yugoslavs] weren't lacking," remembers Roger Berry, "it was labor. You know that productivity thing with the number of man-hours it takes to make a car? What our worst guy was in the United States, just add a zero to it and that would be roughly the number of hours it took the Yugoslavs to build a car. I mean, they had people standing around. It was an employment effort to get as many people in there as they could."[41] However, as Tony Ciminera remembers it, the 140 workers on the new Yugo-A assembly line weren't standing around. Between the opening of production on July 9, 1985, and the send-off celebration fourteen days later, on July 23, they worked themselves into a frenzy.

Their task was to assemble a pristine automobile, one which incorporated Ciminera's 419 different design changes as well as parts from over two hundred foreign and domestic suppliers. "I'd say they did a Herculean job," insists Ciminera.[42] The Yugo was cheap, the workers knew, but it couldn't *look* cheap, otherwise U.S. consumers wouldn't buy it. Zastava's English interpreter Zdravka Damjanic remembers working until 1:00 a.m. each night assisting Yugo America technicians in giving directions at each stage of the Yugo-A assembly line. "The Yugoslav workers were all working very hard," she states, "not asking for overtime or anything. They really wanted the car to make it. We all did. So we worked like mad."[43] Even Zastava's managing director, Radoljub Micic, made frequent visits to the car's final inspection area, which he'd never done before.

However, as Zastava's big send-off celebration approached, it was clear that in spite of their efforts the workers on the Yugo-A assembly line would fall just short of 250 cars. By July 23 they'd produced 220 cars and still were working full tilt on the project just as the celebration began. By any measure, the Yugos' going-away party was over-the-top and Bricklinesque. Workers stood in the parking lot, on rooftops, and in windows, waving thousands of American and Yugoslav flags while clapping and cheering furiously as if at a rally. In attendance were Bricklin, Prior, Ciminera, and Edelson; the new U.S. ambassador to Yugoslavia, John Scanlan; various officials from the Yugoslav federal government, the Serbian republican government, and the city of Kragujevac; the head of Zastava Group, Srboljub Vasovic; the managing director of Zastava's car-making facilities, Radoljub Micic; the director of Genex, Miodrag Savicevic; and twenty to thirty future Yugo car dealers who had accompanied Bricklin from the United States. Also in attendance were Bricklin's fiancée, his former wife, his former wife's boyfriend, and two of his sons.

"The huge, 11 million square foot factory," wrote one AP reporter, "was bedecked with Yugoslav and U.S. flags, red-bannered slogans and huge portraits of late Yugoslav president and Communist Party leader Josip Broz Tito."[44] Above the dais and in big letters were the English and Serbo-Croatian words "Pravac Amerika / Destination America," and outside stood an impressively long train decorated in bunting and loaded with 220 red, white, and blue Yugo cars. "Yugoslavia should be proud of this small car," blared Bricklin. "Everyone will be talking about it in the United States."[45] From there Srboljub Vasovic gave a speech, then one of the American car dealers presented the Yugoslavs with a small tree, a sapling that Ciminera's young son planted in front of Zastava. It was a "tree of friendship," they agreed, and everyone clapped loudly when the boy had finished.

Eventually, after a delay of two days, all 250 cars made it to the

Port of Bar. They were joined a week later by a second shipment of 250 cars and loaded onto the transport ship *Erica Bolten*, which sailed for Baltimore on August 1, 1985. Toma Savic was there that day and remembers watching the ship disappear over the horizon. It had been just fourteen and a half months since Bricklin had approached the Yugoslavs, and only nine months since Berry, Ciminera, and other Yugo America technicians and consultants had begun prepping the car. "Ambitious?" wrote *The Washington Post*. "Call it audacious."[46] As far as Savic could tell, no one had ever spent so little time readying such an important car. "Would the Americans buy it?" he wondered. A few days later Savic flew to the United States. As he touched down in New York he remembers feeling, in his words, "fearfully optimistic."[47]

9

Yugo-mania

Q: Why is a Yugo like a Bic lighter?
A: You use it until it runs out of gas, then throw it away.

"Remember this date," wrote analyst Mark Knepper of *Motor Trend* magazine, "August 26, 1985. That was the day scores of otherwise rational consumers went into a feeding frenzy at dealerships in the Northeast, attacking at first light, waving checks, fistfuls of money, and first-born children in a fury that cowed even veteran salesmen. That was the day a new class, almost a new kind of car entered the American market . . . That was the day the Yugo went on sale."[1] Knepper wasn't exaggerating: people went crazy for the Yugo. At one Florida dealership, for example, buyers put down more than 140 deposits on the car and purchased 11 Yugos sight unseen. In Kalamazoo, Michigan, another dealer took deposits on 124 Yugos, while throughout the Northeast, where the Yugo debuted in approximately 50 dealerships along the Boston–Washington corridor, customers purchased every single car. In all, Yugo America sold 1,050 automobiles in a single day.[2]

"I've been in the car business my whole life," said one dealer, "and this is the most popular car I've ever seen. People are just buying it from a picture in a brochure."[3] The media called it "Yugo-mania," and for the next six months the Yugo was everywhere. It appeared on ABC's *World News Tonight*, on *NBC Nightly News with Tom Brokaw*, on the CBS *Evening News*, and in various segments of CNN's *Headline News*. The Yugo also appeared in *USA Today*, *The New York Times*, the *Financial Times*, *The Wall Street Journal*, *News-*

week, U.S. News & World Report, Car and Driver, Road & Track, Motor Trend, Automotive News, Forbes, Fortune, BusinessWeek, and *Money* magazine. "We used to come to work in the morning," remembers Tony Ciminera, "and there'd be these huge trucks parked in the street: CNN, CBS, NBC. Huge camera trucks with antennas . . . It was like a presidential election. They'd start interviewing us as soon as we walked toward the building. I'll never forget it."[4]

What was amazing about Yugo-mania was that prior to September 1985, Rosenfeld, Sirowitz & Lawson (RS&L), Yugo America's PR firm, had run only a handful of ads. The firm had delayed its advertising because Bricklin, Prior, and Yugo America's own PR man, Jonas Halperin, had done a remarkable job in attracting free press. In less than a month, they'd garnered what in Prior's estimation was $20 million in publicity.[5] However, RS&L also delayed its campaign because Yugo America was broke. From day one the company had been inches from bankruptcy. It had prepped the car, hired consultants, and paid for salaries and parts with money left over from Bricklin's IAI project (which wasn't much), money from Yugo dealer deposits made in late 1984, and money from a $2 million investment by Nordic American Bank and shipping magnate Per Arneberg.

Although Yugo America did have other investors, in September 1985 it lacked sufficient funds for a nationwide advertising campaign. As reported in *Fortune* magazine, RS&L was to oversee a $10 million PR blitz for Yugo America featuring a full range of print and television ads.[6] But as Ira Edelson insists, "we didn't have anywhere near that kind of money."[7] Therefore, Yugo America waited as long as possible to begin advertising, and out of necessity its first ad campaign was significantly scaled back. In fact, RS&L did its first studio shoot with the car on August 16, the same day that Zastava's first shipment of Yugos arrived. The shoot featured a red Yugo GV lined up with a Volkswagen Beetle and a Ford Model T, suggesting that the $3,990 Yugo was the "latest wave in low-priced reliable transportation."[8] The ad's slogan was "Introducing the Same Old Idea," with the tagline "Yugo, $3990. The Road Back to Sanity."

RS&L had gone with the Beetle–Model T motif because the Yugo, in Len Sirowitz's words, was the epitome of "solid, dependable, back-to-basics transportation."[9] Though an ad man, Sirowitz knew cars. In the 1960s he'd been a young art director for the New York PR firm Doyle Dane Bernbach, where he helped to create an entire series of Volkswagen ads. They were slick, witty, and simple, such as a 1963 ad featuring an elderly gentleman standing between a Ford Model T and a Volkswagen Beetle. The ad read: "33 years later, he got the bug." A 1967 Sirowitz ad featured three Volkswagen automobiles, including a Beetle, a Squareback, and a twenty-one-window Bus, lined up in a row, with the tagline: "It comes in three economy sizes." In a way, RS&L's first ad campaign for Yugo America was simply a continuation of Sirowitz's earlier work with Volkswagen. As a result, the Yugo's "Same Old Idea" campaign was exceptionally good.

It also helped that Sirowitz's partner, Ron Rosenfeld, was one of the best copywriters in the business. The two had made headlines in 1969 when they'd formed their own agency and run an eye-popping campaign for Swissair under the slogan "Heidi Lied." Swissair's previous agency had featured a bucolic Heidi, in peasant garb, in various scenes of repose. "This year get above the crowds," one old ad read. "Ski the Alps. Heidi wouldn't lie."[10] But in 1970, Rosenfeld and Sirowitz jump-started the Swissair campaign by replacing the innocent Heidi with a blond bombshell Heidi in a polka dot bikini. "The unknown. Revealed," stated their ad. "Heidi lied."[11] The Swissair campaign was the first of many Rosenfeld and Sirowitz hits. By 1984 they were billing $140 million a year, with such diverse accounts as *Redbook* magazine, Harlequin romance novels, Smith-Corona typewriters, International Spike fertilizer, Oppenheimer mutual funds, and a chain of Mexican hotels. "We got the cream of the crop," stated Bill Prior.[12] "Our objective [was] to create a brand and become a basic generic economy car like Volkswagen did. That takes the right dealer, the right message, and a car of quality."[13]

Quality, in fact, had been a central theme at Yugo America for over a year now, and it was imperative that the car's "Introducing the Same Old Idea" campaign address, among other things, craftsmanship. Therefore, the first generation of Yugo America ads—including the Yugo–Beetle–Model T photograph and tagline, which began running on Sunday, September 8, 1985, in ten newspapers along the

Boston–Washington corridor—described the Yugo as well-crafted transportation.[14] The ads were accompanied by an entire run of brochures, posters, flyers, information sheets, and direct-mail materials that were sent to dealers just prior to the car's introduction on August 26, 1985.

"Handcrafted?" read one glossy brochure. "You're kidding! Yugo craftsmen. Without a doubt, they're the most important ingredient in achieving our high quality standards. They take great pride in their manufacturing ability. In processes like hand-sanding and hand-painting. What about doors, trunks, and engines? They're hand-assembled. And to make sure all Yugo body parts fit precisely, there are teams of inspectors checking and testing each and every car. If a part is flawed, it goes back on the line for correction. If it's not, it is stamped by hand with the letter 'Y.' That way we know, and now you know, it passed our quality control. You'd expect such personalized attention and craftsmanship in a car that costs at least two or three times as much as the Yugo. But we give you all this craftsmanship and deliver it all for only $3990."

According to Bill Prior, Yugo America's "Introducing the Same Old Idea" campaign was targeted toward three groups: first-time car buyers, people looking for value in a second or third car or possibly a student's car, and buyers seeking an alternative to a used car.[15] Known in industry terms as "entry-level buyers," first-time car buyers were typically under thirty. They were cash-conscious, frugal, and discriminating, but willing to experiment with newer makes and models such as the Ford Escort EXP, the Honda Civic CRX, and the Nissan Pulsar NX. In 1984, entry-level buyers purchased 2.8 million cars in the United States, a 30 percent market share that was larger than any other group.[16] However, in selling cars to young people, "sportiness" was key. The average age of an Escort EXP buyer, for example, was a segment-low 24.8 years, a Civic CRX buyer 27.7 years, and a Pulsar NX buyer 27.9 years. As a rule of thumb, the cheaper and sportier a car was, the younger its owner.

"It shouldn't be surprising that the $6,697 EXP finished number one," said a Ford official. "All small sporty cars with moderate prices attract young buyers. [They] are often single or newly married and generally pre-mortgage and pre-parenthood. They're more interested in style, image and price than passenger capacity." But in the regular subcompact market, where cars were more utilitarian than sporty, the average buyer was well into his thirties. Nissan Sentra buyers were on average 32.6 years old, buyers of the base Ford Escort model 34.8 years old, Chevrolet Chevette buyers 35.1, Toyota Corolla 35.4, and Plymouth Horizon 39.3.[17] The question for Yugo America, then, was how to sell first-time buyers a car that was almost the exact opposite of sporty, a car that Bricklin himself called "a nineteen-cent hamburger with meat."[18]

Critics described the Yugo as "bland," "boxy," "primitive," "feeble," "ugly," "agricultural," "spartan," and "a car-like curiosity" that was "slightly more aggressive than a wind-up rubber band."[19] "There still has to be sex appeal in a car," stated one editor, and "I can't think of anything that is more the antithesis of sex appeal than a Yugo. [That car is] about as attractive a product as the political system that exported it."[20] In fairness, the Yugo wasn't a sports car, nor did it pretend to be. It was, in the words of Bill Prior, "a humble, almost fundamentalist product," a "very guttural, basic car."[21] But twenty-five-year-old car buyers weren't interested in "guttural." They wanted cars that were sporty, sleek, and cheap. Offering only one of these three traits, Yugo America tried to entice young buyers by sponsoring "Stuff-a-Yugo" contests on college campuses and by being a cosponsor of the U.S. Olympic Volleyball Team. Neither of these promotions worked.

Yugo America's second target group included older buyers who were looking for a bargain on a second or third family car. In general, these were suburban Americans with one or two children of high school or college age who felt that making a large car payment was unnecessary. In the mid-1980s, the average interest rate nationally for a forty-eight-month new car loan was 13.32 percent, which meant, for instance, that if a family's primary automobile was a Ford Lincoln Town Car, purchased in 1984 for $19,047, its monthly payment was $385.51. If that same family owned a second car—say, a Chevrolet Camaro purchased in 1985 for $8,530 in a sales campaign offering a thirty-six-month loan at 8.8 percent—that family's payment was $202.84. Each month that family paid out $588.35 for its two cars.[22]

Typically, new-car buyers have median family incomes that are above the national average. In 1984 that income was close to $40,000 per year, more than the national average of $24,500, and enough in this family's case to afford an annual outlay of $7,060.20 for a 1984 Lincoln Town Car and a 1985 Camaro.[23] But still, annual car payments of $7,060.20 were roughly 17.6 percent of this family's budget. The family still needed to pay for its car insurance, health insurance, utilities, and mortgage, not to mention food, clothing, entertainment, possibly tuitions, and perhaps a vacation. A new third automobile was therefore out of the question, unless of course it was cheap—dirt cheap, which the Yugo was. The car's base price was $3,990, plus a $299 destination fee and a $90 dealer preparation fee, for a final (pretax and title) price of $4,379. With 25 percent down on a forty-eight-month bank loan at an interest rate of 11 percent, in early 1986 a new Yugo cost just $87 a month. Some dealers, in fact, offered new Yugos at $99 down and $99 a month.

The Yugo was so cheap that many dealers initially wondered if its presence in the United States would undercut the used-car market, where many Americans bought their second or third family cars. "I don't have any quantified data," stated one Chevrolet executive, "but I'm sure [the Yugo and other budget imports] did take some used-car purchasers out of buying used cars, especially when you put together a payment program of $99 down and $99 a month. It does have an effect on the late-model used-car industry."[24] As Yugo America's third targeted group, used-car buyers purchased 15.9 million cars in 1985, at an average price of $5,431 each. The typical used car was 4.6 years old. It had an odometer reading of 45,270 miles and an average monthly payment of $197.18.[25]

Thus, executives at Yugo America reasoned that used-car buyers in the $5,000 range would rather buy a cheap, new Yugo, which had a twelve-month, 12,000-mile warranty, than a pricier used car with no warranty of any kind. "What we figure is that everybody ought to have that new-car smell at least once in their lives," said Ciminera. The Yugo is "a second car, a car for a student, a station car . . . It's an alternative to a used car."[26] But whether or not the Yugo "will seriously traumatize the used-car market," wrote the trade publication *Ward's AutoWorld* in late 1985, is "a resounding maybe." After all, the Yugo was but one of fourteen models sold in 1986 for under $6,000. "If the sky is in fact falling," wrote *Ward's*, "it probably should have hit ground by now."[27]

As it turned out, the real threat to the used-car industry wasn't low-priced imports like the Yugo but discount financing by Detroit's "Big Three" automakers, who, to better compete with the Japanese, in early 1985 began offering sub–8 percent interest rates on new automobiles. The low interest rates lessened demand for used cars by making new cars easier to afford. During the first nine months of 1985, for instance, new car sales totaled 8.6 million units, an 8.5 percent increase over the same period in 1984.[28] The surge in new car sales left hundreds of thousands of unsold used automobiles on dealer lots. "This is the worst year for the business I've ever seen," said one used-car dealer in San Francisco. "It almost broke me. If it lasts through the '86 model year, I'm out of business."[29]

In late 1985, however, Yugo dealers who also sold used cars found that Yugo-mania was an unexpected boon to the used-car trade. "It's helped us sell a lot of used cars," said Dick Loeher, a Chrysler-Plymouth-Yugo dealer from Kalamazoo, Michigan. "I've got two stores, and the store I've got the Yugo at is going to have a record used-car month . . . [My dealers] are using [the Yugo] as a switch car. They're moving [customers] to '84s, to cars that are in the same price range but that are used."[30] Other dealers used Yugo-mania to sell new automobiles as well—just not Yugos. In Pittsburgh, Pennsylvania, for example, one Cadillac-Yugo dealer offered a "Buy one, get one free" promotion in which customers who purchased a $24,000 Cadillac received a complimentary Yugo. A similar promotion in Mystic, Connecticut, offered a free Yugo to anyone who purchased a $20,000 Oldsmobile Toronado. "One of the things that the Yugo does for dealers is it builds showroom traffic," said Dan Prior, the brother of Bill Prior and a sales executive at Yugo America. "The Yugo helps the dealer sell other lines of cars."[31]

In terms of direct competition, however, in 1986 the low-priced Yugo faced thirteen different competitors in the sub-$6,000 market. They included the Chevrolet Chevette, the Chevrolet Sprint, the Dodge Colt, the Honda Civic, the Hyundai Excel, the Mazda 323, the Mitsubishi Mirage, the Nissan Sentra, the Plymouth Colt, the

Pontiac 1000, the Renault Alliance, the Subaru Hatchback, and the Toyota Tercel. Of these, only the Subaru Hatchback ($4,989) and the Hyundai Excel ($4,995) were priced at under $5,000. The most popular sub-$6,000 car in America was the Chevrolet Chevette, which in 1985 counted 129,927 units sold. Built by General Motors, the Chevette was an aging two-door hatchback that cost $5,645 and had been sold in the United States without any real modification since 1976. The car dominated its class, but rising labor costs as well as dated technology had made the Chevette obsolete.

In fact, by 1983 GM claimed that in spite of the car's strong sales, it was losing money on each base Chevette it produced. "The Chevette is not profitable," said Chevrolet head Robert C. Stempel in October 1983. "We cannot continue subsidizing small cars with the sales of larger cars."[32] GM's plan, then, was to discontinue sales of the Chevette in 1987 while introducing an even cheaper automobile known as the Chevrolet Sprint. Manufactured by the Suzuki Motor Company, the Sprint was a bare-bones hatchback that sold for just $2,760 in Japan. The Sprint was cheap because Japanese labor was cheap and because Japanese workers were more productive. It helped, too, that GM owned a 5.3 percent stake in Suzuki and had assisted the firm in constructing a new Sprint plant and in modifying the car for the U.S. market.

"Thus, the unthinkable came to be," wrote *Motor Trend* magazine. "A Japanese 'Chevy.' Besides negating the well-known 'USA-1' advertising campaign, the plan [to import the Sprint] has many former Chevrolet sales executives spinning in their corporate graves . . . But this is of little concern to the General's minions, who are more interested in the long-term health of the Chevrolet division and its dealer network than noble but obsolete ideas of automotive chauvinism. The [Sprint] is coming to the United States, and when it gets here it will be a Chevrolet."[33]

The move away from American-made econo-boxes wasn't unique to GM. Of the Yugo's thirteen sub-$6,000 competitors, only the Renault Alliance, produced under license by the American Motor Company, and the Chevrolet Chevette were built in the United States. The Dodge Colt and the Plymouth Colt were Mitsubishi products imported by Chrysler, while the Pontiac 1000 was a Chevrolet Sprint manufactured by Suzuki. These and other foreign-made cars with American nameplates were known as "captive imports." Captive imports were brought to the United States to increase a company's competitiveness by filling a hole in its lineup. That hole, in GM's case, was a badly needed replacement car for the dying Chevette. However, with its labor costs estimated at $23 per hour *per worker* in 1985, GM found that a sub-$6,000 automobile was impossible to build.[34] But since "time was of the essence," wrote *Motor Trend*, GM realized that "the quickest way to get Chevy its entry-level car was to send out for one," which it did with the Sprint in 1984.[35]

The Chevrolet Sprint had an introductory price of $4,949 (which for the 1986 model year was raised to $5,380), a fuel efficiency rating of 53 miles per gallon highway (!), and a nationwide network of dealers and mechanics to support it. But the Sprint was only marginally profitable and, at $5,380, was virtually the same price in 1985 as a bigger and roomier used car. What is more, GM typically used the Sprint as its "price leader," an industry practice in which an extra-low-priced automobile was used to lure buyers into showrooms, where they were talked into buying a more expensive car. Except for the Hyundai Excel or maybe the Chevette, every Yugo competitor for 1986 was a price leader, an industry gimmick. Most came loaded with a truly mind-boggling array of souped-up accessories, which increased their list prices by $1,000, $2,000, or even $3,000. Meanwhile, the cheapest base model—the one most widely advertised—was impossible to find.

In 1984, for example, Toyota shipped only 1,100 cars per month with a base price below $6,000. That amounted to just 2 percent of its shipments, or one car per dealer per month.[36] "You won't find many of those cars," wrote automotive expert Jim Mateja, "because dealers don't sell many. Quotas or not, dealers are only allotted so many cars from the factory each year. [So] when it comes to making little or no profit on a $5,000 economy job or making a hefty $5,000 on a luxury or performance number, it's the latter that gets the call."[37] The end result was that for 1985, economy-class sales for cars priced $6,500 and lower were just 3.4 percent of the market, a mere 375,000 cars out of 11 million. (And that's just passenger cars. If you include 4.7 million trucks, sub-$6,500 car sales amounted to an even more minuscule 2.3 percent.)[38]

Clearly, the world's automobile manufacturers had vacated the very low end of the American market. Margins were too slim. Mid-size cars were popular and profitable, and gas was cheaper in 1985, in real terms, than it was in 1981. "Everyone recognizes that the market for medium-sized cars is the one to be in," stated a vice president at AMC Motors. "The midsized car [is the] car of the future."[39] Yet, somewhere in the process, knew Bricklin, a market was underserved, a "segment of the American public" that *Car and Driver* wrote "[had a] compelling desire to do its shopping in flea markets and bargain basements," your quintessential Kmart shoppers.[40] "To those who believe price and economy are everything," it concluded, and "that getting to their destinations is all that counts . . . the Yugo is about as close to automotive nirvana as they believe they're entitled to get."[41]

For why else would "otherwise rational consumers" stand in line hour after hour (after hour) to test-drive a Yugo? Why would hundreds of people buy Yugos sight unseen? Certainly, Bricklin's great PR campaign had something to do with it, and Yugo-mania was, to some extent, a consumer fad. But in late 1985 it was clear to everyone that Bricklin had touched a nerve—that the Yugo had touched a nerve. Buyers wanted bare-bones, basic transportation. They wanted good quality at an affordable price. "We knew there was a market out there looking for a small car under $5,000," said Bill Prior. There was "a market in search of a product."[42]

10

"It's Going to Be a Bloodbath"

Q: What do you call a Yugo with no wheels?
A: A no-go.

Yugo America entered 1986 with 3,895 cars sold.[1] It was a small amount, by industry standards, representing less than 974 cars per month. By comparison, in 1985 import sales leader Toyota sold over 50,000 cars per month. The Yugo's econo-box rival, the Chevrolet Sprint, had sales of nearly 2,600 per month. But for the Yugo, a sales figure of 3,895 wasn't bad. In fact, it was astounding. Yugo America had a sales network of fewer than one hundred largely northeastern dealers. As of January 1, 1986, it had no West Coast dealers whatsoever. It also had no dealers in Texas, and only a handful of dealers in Michigan, Ohio, Florida, and Illinois. In addition, the company's three TV commercials had yet to air in any market, while the company's advertising, such as it was, was a very limited affair.

Even more astounding was the fact that as of late November 1985, Zastava had sent Yugo America just 3,579 cars, which meant that every car Yugo America had, it sold. By early 1986, Yugo America had received over 8,000 orders for the automobile, but just 9,889 cars had landed in the United States. "At this moment in time," stated Bill Prior, "it is obvious that supply will not keep up with demand."[2] Although Zastava was running its Yugo-A assembly line in three separate shifts, six days a week, it couldn't produce Yugos fast enough to satisfy the American market. "I'm delivering cars now that people ordered in mid-September," stated a Brooklyn Yugo dealer in December 1985.[3] That same month a Tacoma, Washington, man purchased a Yugo in Michigan and had it shipped two thousand miles to his house. He'd been on a waiting list since July.[4]

The Yugo was big news. To some, it was the freshest news to come from the automotive industry in years. But to Detroit's Big Three, the Yugo's opening sales were simply too small to warrant a response. "We have to see what the Yugo does out there," said Roger Burger, an executive at GM. "As big as we are, every time someone brings out a vehicle we can't respond [to it] unless there's some numbers. They're talking 30,000 to 40,000 cars a year. We sell 100,000 to 150,000 Chevettes [a year]."[5] But the Yugo had given the industry something to think about. If Japanese and American manufacturers failed to provide consumers with what they wanted, Yugo's early success suggested that someone else would. That was precisely the idea behind captive imports, such as the Suzuki-made Sprint, which represented Detroit's "If you can't beat 'em, join 'em" approach to small-car manufacturing.

That approach is what brought Yugo America within a hairsbreadth of being purchased by Chrysler. Sometime in January 1985, a three-man Chrysler team visited the Zastava plant in Kragujevac to see if Bricklin's emerging Yugo prototype was a viable export. The team toured the plant, drove the car, and reported back to company chairman Lee Iacocca that the Yugo was "fundamentally OK." It also reported that Tony Ciminera had "done an excellent job of assessing the product changes that are required to make [the Yugo] a contemporary model."[6] Shortly thereafter, at the Yugo's unveiling at the National Automobile Dealers Association (NADA) convention in San Francisco, Chrysler executives Gerald Greenwald and Harold Sperlich met with Malcolm Bricklin to negotiate a deal in which Chrysler would acquire the Yugo's distribution rights for a reported $15 million.

Bricklin wanted more—supposedly ten times more—but according to Tony Ciminera he refused to make a decision before first conferring with his executives. "Malcolm said, 'You're the guys who went through all this work,'" remembers Ciminera. "'You did all this work of making the car what it is. So you decide. Do we keep it, or do we sell it?' And we thought to ourselves . . . 'If Chrysler thinks we're onto something, then we *must* be onto something! This has the potential of being . . . like Toyota or Honda or even Mazda!' So like fools we said no."[7]

The $15 million figure was reported in the automotive press. If this figure is correct, Bricklin had turned a $50,000 investment in Miroslav Kefurt's Yugo 45 distribution rights into a 30,000 percent profit—not bad for a man whose International Automobile Importers had faced bankruptcy just nine months before. Of course, there was Nordic American Bank's $2 million investment to consider, as well as a $350,000 investment by John and Rebecca Bednarik and perhaps $500,000 in investments by various Yugo America shareholders. But, even so, as of January 1985 no more than $3 million had been invested in Yugo America. Thus, as a 51 percent shareholder in the company, Bricklin could have earned some $7.5 million, enough to retire on at age forty-five. However, Bricklin said no. It was a brave move, one that revealed—yet again—that what motivated Malcolm Bricklin wasn't the money, it was the chase, "the frantic rush," wrote one observer, "to get wherever it is he has to go."[8]

Company CFO Ira Edelson has another explanation. Bricklin and his Yugo America assistants refused the deal because Chrysler "wanted to buy us up and knock us out of the market . . . We knew, even then, that at $3,990 the Yugo was potentially a very valuable car."[9] No doubt Chrysler thought so, because shortly after its $15 million Yugo offer, it slashed prices on its entry-level Omni and Horizon models to compete with the Yugoslav import. It also made plans for a stripped-down version of the Omni-Horizon known as the America, which appeared in 1986. Chrysler's goal, wrote *Ward's AutoWorld*, was to "hang tough" in the entry-level market. "There are people who are going to buy little cars in America," said Lee Iacocca. "The question is . . . who'll be making them?"[10]

One oddball answer was the Intreprinderea de Autoturisme Pitesti, a Romanian manufacturer whose most famous marque was the Dacia (which rhymes with "gotcha"). In 1985, Intreprinderea awarded exclusive distribution rights to not one but *two* U.S. companies, the Miami-based Auto Dacia of America Inc. and the North American Import-Export Company of New Paltz, New York.[11] Unbeknownst to each other, the owners of the two companies had each negotiated with Intreprinderea for the rights to the Dacia 12, a four-door sedan based on a seventeen-year-old Renault model designed in France. The Dacia had been available in Canada since 1983, where it was known as the "crudest, slowest, noisiest sedan" on the road.[12] In the words of one consumer group, the Dacia suffered from "unbelievably poor manufacturing and assembly quality," which led Canada's transportation department to order seven different Dacia recalls in a single month. One was for a leaky gas tank.[13]

What was appealing about the Dacia was its price. At $4,995 Canadian (about $3,775 U.S.), the Dacia was the lowest-priced import in Canada. Thus, its two would-be importers assumed that since nearly two thousand Dacias had been sold to Canadians since 1983, perhaps ten times that amount could be sold each year in the United States. There seems to be no rational explanation as to why Intreprinderea would award exclusive distribution rights to two companies. But sometime in late 1985, Intreprinderea offered the car's rights to even a *third* party: Malcolm Bricklin. "You see, when the Yugo went on sale," explains Tony Ciminera, "automatically that attracted the attention of other countries . . . So the Romanians marched into Malcolm's office and said, 'Please, come over to Romania, we have cars! We want you to see them.'"[14]

So in late 1985 Bricklin and Ciminera traveled to Pitești, Romania, to tour the Intreprinderea plant. Bricklin's goal, ostensibly, was to see if the Dacia 12 was an exportable product and if Intreprinderea itself could actually produce a car for the U.S. market. It wasn't, and Intreprinderea couldn't. The plant was "horrible," remembers Ciminera. "It was disgusting. I walked out."[15] But Bricklin and Ciminera did tour a sparkling new plant in nearby Craiova, where a car known as the Oltcit (pronounced "olt-sit") was built. The Oltcit was a two-door hatchback based on a 1970s French Citroën model known as the Citroën Prototype Y. Like the Jugo 45, the Oltcit was technologically out of date and known for its appallingly poor construction. But because labor was cheap in Romania, in 1985 Citroën began importing the Oltcit to Western Europe, where it sold the car as the Citroën Axel.

"The car was nice and the factory was nice," says Ciminera. "Everything was new just like in Paris. So we had a couple of cars flown to Detroit [and had] engineers examine them to see what it would take to meet U.S. emissions. Meanwhile we were waiting for a letter from Citroën stating that Oltcit had permission to export the car to the United States. The letter never arrived. So we stopped. [The people at Oltcit] were bullshitters, so we sent the cars back to Romania."[16] This was sometime in 1986.

Bricklin's attempt in 1985–86 to import a second Eastern European car was perhaps the first indication that he was looking beyond the Yugo project. While still pushing the Yugo, Bricklin planned to create a Yugo America parent company known as Global Motors. As Bricklin envisioned it, Global Motors would be an automotive import firm handling multiple car marques at the same time. Thus, instead of buying a single Yugo franchise, prospective car dealers would buy a Global Motors franchise, which included (hypothetically) the Yugo, the Dacia, the Malaysian-made Proton, the Indonesian-made Lincah Gama, and others. Bricklin was envisioning an entire lineup of second- and third-world cars, with econo-box models at one end and sedans and sport-utility vehicles at the other. The idea wasn't new. At around the same time, a New York company named Universal Motors was trying to set up its own import line with automobiles from Spain, Portugal, and India. Its lead product was the Mahindra, a "straightforward version" of a forty-year-old Jeep model, built in Mumbai.[17]

"Would you buy an Indian Mahindra?" asked *The Wall Street Journal.* "A Portuguese Indian? A Romanian Oltcit? A Malaysian Proton?"[18] The answer for most Americans was no. But the Yugo had demonstrated that a niche market did exist, that for reasons of economy U.S. consumers would buy even the obscurest of automobiles as long as they were cheap. This explains why, after IAI partnered with Zastava in 1984, so many second- and third-world automakers suddenly announced their intention to export cars to the United States. There was the Romanian Dacia, the Romanian Oltcit, the Malaysian Proton, the Indonesian Lincah Gama, the Indian Mahindra, the Portuguese Indian, the Greek Desta, the Russian Lada, the Spanish Ligero, the Spanish SEAT, the Czechoslovak Skoda, and, most important, the Korean Hyundai.

Established in 1967, Hyundai was part of the Hyundai Engineering and Construction Company, which by the mid-1980s was one of the largest industrial conglomerates in the world. With over thirty subsidiaries in such diverse fields as shipbuilding, iron and steel production, building construction, computer components, hotels, department stores, tourist agencies, and cars, the Hyundai Engineering and Construction Company had over 150,000 employees and revenues of $10 billion per year.[19] Like Zastava, Hyundai had entered the automobile business by importing foreign technology. Its first car was a British Ford model known as the Cortina, which it assembled under license from Ford in 1967. But since Hyundai wanted to build its own car, in the early 1970s it brought a former British Leyland executive to South Korea to assist the company in reverse engineering the Morris Marina.[20]

Reverse engineering is the painstaking process of working backward from a product, piece by piece, to copy its design. Now common in the computer software industry, in the automotive industry reverse engineering was a technique often used by manufacturers who wished to reproduce a part, or series of parts, of a competitor's car. Although automotive manufacturers rarely if ever used reverse engineering to produce an entire car, the practice was widespread among second- and third-world companies and among companies that specialized in aftermarket parts. During the Cold War, reverse engineering was an important mode of technology transfer between the United States and the Soviet Union. In one famous example, in 1944 the Soviet army dismantled an American B-29 Superfortress into 105,000 component parts, which it examined, reproduced, and reassembled into a Soviet bomber, known as the Tu-4, in 1946.[21]

In Hyundai's case, reverse engineering the Morris Marina was far less complicated than reverse engineering a B-29. The Marina was small, technologically unsophisticated, and cheap. In addition, Hyundai engineers wisely decided not to copy the Marina's dated engine but to purchase a newer engine from Mitsubishi. They also turned to Italdesign, an automobile design and engineering company in Turin, Italy, for help with the car's exterior. Italdesign had recently penned both the Volkswagen Rabbit and the Volkswagen Passat, and chose a very modern design for Hyundai featuring a two-door pickup, a two-door hatchback, a four-door hatchback, a four-door station wagon, and a four-door sedan. With all of its component parts in place, in 1975 the car began rolling off Hyundai's assembly lines as the Pony. The Pony was intended for domestic consumption, but since it had been reverse engineered by Hyundai, it was now a Korean product. It could be exported anywhere in the world free of restrictions.

The first Pony exports, oddly enough, were to Ecuador, where Hyundai sent five sample cars in 1976 in exchange for bananas, a typical barter arrangement for countries in need of hard currency. Although production remained small, by 1980 Hyundai had exported the Pony to more than sixty countries—in the words of one author, to "virtually every country that would allow foreign-built cars through customs."[22] It helped, of course, that Hyundai's parent company owned and operated the Hyundai Merchant Marine, and that South Korea itself had encouraged the car's production through a series of loans, special subsidies, and tax breaks. In 1984, Hyundai began selling the Pony in Canada, where due to its low price and perceived durability it captured a 10.9 percent import-car market share with 25,123 cars sold.[23] The Pony's initial sales were an import car record in Canada and a surprise to everyone, including Hyundai.

"It is a mystery to us why Canadian customers reacted so positively to our Pony," said N. M. Kim, the head of Hyundai's Canadian operations. "We really didn't expect to do so well."[24] In fact, Hyundai had hoped to sell just 5,000 cars. It had no idea that its nine-year-old Pony would finish just 3,260 cars behind Nissan, Canada's number three importer, and 2,568 cars ahead of Volkswagen, which fell to number five.[25] The Pony did so well in Canada that in January 1985 Hyundai announced that in just one year's time, it would begin selling a new car, known as the Excel, in the United States. The Excel was to come in four-door sedan and four-door hatchback models with an ultra-low price of $4,995. Its planned introduction date was February 1986.

"I think the Yugoslavs thought the sky was falling," says Pete Mulhern, who was in Kragujevac in early 1985. "I mean, Hyundai's car-making division was the same size as Zastava, but its management was hell-bent on exporting cars to the U.S. and its government was willing to back it up. Yugoslavia supported Zastava and Zastava supported the Yugo, but Hyundai had Mitsubishi's help and was willing to invest some really big bucks."[26] In fact, to produce the Excel, Hyundai spent a whopping $500 million on a new three-hundred-thousand-car production facility in Ulsan. Hyundai also sold 10 percent of its shares to Mitsubishi in exchange for cash and the right to use Mitsubishi engines, transmissions, and axles on the new Excel.[27]

Introduced at $4,995, the base Excel was a front-engine, front-wheel-drive automobile with a four-speed manual transmission. In terms of power, it had a four-cylinder, 1.5-liter engine, the same Mitsubishi-built engine found in the Dodge Omni, the Plymouth Colt, and the Mitsubishi Mirage. At 160.9 inches, the four-door Excel hatchback was almost two feet longer than the Yugo, which it out-weighed by three hundred pounds. Though often compared to the Yugo because of its low price, the Excel was a larger, better-equipped car. The Excel was also pitched differently to the press. Whereas Yugo America execs described the Yugo as a generic people's car, Hyundai marketed the Excel solely in relation to the Japanese.

"We think that what we're dealing with is value," said Max Jamiesson, CEO of Hyundai Motor America. "We hope the consumer will see us as being in the Japanese category on quality and will see that they can get comparable value for less."[28] We're also "not positioning ourselves against the Yugo," Jamiesson explained. "It's a smaller car, with a smaller engine, priced $1,000 less."[29] To Hyundai, Yugo America wasn't a competitor. If anything, Hyundai was an eight-hundred-pound gorilla wrestling other gorillas, while Yugo America was a mouse. There's "going to be a war for the US [small car] market," wrote *The Washington Post* in February 1986, and "the prospective combatants are [the] Koreans and Japanese."[30]

The Korean manufacturer planned to export 100,000 cars to the United States in 1986 alone. Its two first-year goals: the highest sales per outlet in the industry, and the record for the most units sold in an import car's first year in the United States.[31] Of course, Yugo America had similar goals—35,000 cars in year one—but Hyundai had the product, the reputation, and the financial wherewithal to back them up. One GM engineer called Hyundai "the new wave of

Oriental competition." We Americans "still haven't learned to be competitive with the Japanese," he said, "and [now] even the Japanese are nervous about the Koreans."[32]

The Yugoslavs were nervous too. So was Yugo America. "We were very concerned." states Ira Edelson. "Hyundai was an upscale car. But it was a cheap car. So we definitely saw Hyundai as a competitor. It was because of Hyundai that we started pressuring Zastava to give us a larger Yugo model to compete with the Excel. But they never did. They kept dragging their feet."[33] The bigger Yugo model was the Florida, a four-door hatchback that Zastava had been working on since 1982. The car's prototype, known as the 103, was to some extent an Excel clone: it had virtually the same engine, the same length and curb weight, and almost the same design. The two cars' exteriors, in fact, had both been drawn up by Italdesign, the same Turin, Italy, firm that had earlier designed the Hyundai Pony.

Zastava failed to develop the Florida for a variety of reasons, the main one being money. Bricklin's Yugo GV model was costing the company approximately $1,000 per car in add-on parts. These parts included the car's carburetor, ignition system, air filter, vacuum harness, and perhaps two dozen other parts that Zastava imported from the West. But because Zastava lacked hard currency, and because it spent what currency it did have on the Yugo GV, a new Florida model was simply out of the question. The Florida, writes economic historian Michael Palairet, "even on the optimistic projection of a 50,000 unit a year production run, would have lost money on a heroic scale."[34] As it stood, the Florida's prototype needed the same costly emissions and safety work that the Yugo GV had undergone, as well as a new 1400cc engine purchased from Fiat.

"We [Zastava] really wanted to produce the car," states Toma Savic. "Sure we did. But we needed a lot more time and money on our end to make [the Florida] suitable for the U.S. market. We finally got things going in 1988, but the car still wasn't America-ready. Therefore, we sold it only in Europe but not in the United States."[35] The first Yugo Florida rolled off the assembly line in October 1988.[36] The car was noticeably better than its Yugo predecessor. It had four doors, a bigger engine, more legroom, and a somewhat snappier design, but its build quality, wrote London's *Independent*, was "out to lunch."[37] In all, Zastava built 18,687 Floridas between 1988 and 1991; however, not a single Florida was sold commercially in the United States. (As of 2009, the twenty-one-year-old Florida is no longer being produced in Serbia but is still manufactured, under license, by the El Nasr Automotive Manufacturing Company of Giza, Egypt. It is called the Nasr Florida 1400.)

"Zastava probably built the Yugo Florida in response to the Hyundai," insists Barbara Wendling, a Yugo America quality control specialist who worked in Kragujevac. "I remember sometime in 1986 when the engineers at Zastava purchased an Excel and brought it to the factory. They took it apart and examined it to find design ideas for the Florida. But the funny thing was, they lost some of the car's parts and couldn't put it back together again."[38] To their credit, the Yugoslavs did succeed in building a second car—not a good car, mind you, but a viable car nonetheless. The problem for Yugo America was that Zastava was simply incapable, financially, of prepping, equipping, building, and homologating the Florida for the American market. Even if Zastava had had the money and had produced the Florida at breakneck speed—which some say it did anyway—the car wouldn't have arrived in the United States until 1987, more than a year after the Hyundai Excel.

By then U.S. and Japanese car makers would have reentered the econo-box market. They'd realized that although low-priced automobiles weren't particularly profitable, they were a key component in the development of brand loyalty. For if a young college graduate bought her first car—say, a Honda Civic—she in all likelihood would purchase bigger and better Hondas, or perhaps an Acura, as her life progressed. "Automakers, whether long-established or developing," wrote the Associated Press, "have learned they need a good, inexpensive starter model to develop brand-loyalty in first-time buyers. Satisfied entry-level buyers are likely to return in a few years for a more expensive model."[39] Although GM was one company that historically cultivated brand loyalty through its entry-level Chevys, by the mid-1980s both it and its Japanese and American competitors had vacated the low-priced market. That is until the Yugo and, more important, the Hyundai Excel arrived.

"Yugo and Hyundai have reopened the market," said one analyst in late 1986. "Once a few companies start to arrive with brand-new cars, everyone has to get in. That's why five years from now this [segment] is going to be very cluttered."[40] In January 1986 the firm J.D. Power and Associates predicted that by 1991 Americans would buy nearly 1.4 million cars in the sub-$6,500 range. If true, it represented a full 12 percent of the U.S. car market.[41] Therefore, by 1986, American, Japanese, and even German manufacturers who had left the low-priced market were now scrambling to get back in. "Everybody in the automobile business [is] rediscovering the basic car," said one Volkswagen rep.[42] But "rediscovering" was a bit soft. In reality, a whole bevy of U.S. and foreign carmakers were sharpening their knives.

"It's going to be a bloodbath," said one observer.[43] *Automotive News* proclaimed in its March 1986 "Import World Extra" that "the US automobile market appears destined to become a battleground for companies around the world seeking to satisfy the American appetite for small, low-cost, basic transportation models."[44] The war, it insisted, had been touched off by "a pair of small cars" known as the Hyundai and the Yugo. The planned competitors for 1987 included the Yugo's thirteen sub-$6,000 rivals, but Subaru announced it was replacing its aging hatchback model with a smaller car called the Justy ($5,495). Also new for 1987 was the Chrysler America ($5,499), made of course in America; the Volkswagen Fox ($5,690), made in Brazil; and two new captive imports from Korea: the Pontiac Lemans ($5,995) from Daewoo, and the Ford Festiva ($5,765) from Kia.

"I think there'll be plenty of room for everybody," said Bill Prior optimistically. But industry experts such as Leonard Sherman, a partner at Booz Allen Hamilton, a consulting firm, knew otherwise. "To the extent the low end gets chewed up by [these new imports], that means there is less room for those who were there. You either say 'sayonara, we lose' or you move somewhere else."[45] Without the Florida model, however, in 1986 Yugo America had nowhere to go. It was stuck with the same diminutive Fiat model in a market that promised to be more competitive than ever. Soon the Yugo would face seventeen sub-$6,000 rivals, plus an Escort model ($6,436) that Ford would discount a full $600 in early 1987. To make matters worse, another low-priced automobile, the $6,397 Daihatsu Charade, was to arrive in America by 1988.[46]

Bricklin, Prior, and other Yugo America execs entered 1986 on a wave of Yugo-mania, but the question was: Could they sustain it? Yugo America's PR campaign had been brilliant. Sales were brisk. And, for the first three or four months, Yugo America had sold every car in stock. But competition was coming: a hundred thousand Hyundais, perhaps more, captive imports from Korea and Japan, Volkswagens from Brazil. Even Japanese automakers who had left the low-priced market were now planning to get back in. That meant Stanzas, Civics, Mirages, 323s, Justys, and Tercels—thousands of them. However, as we shall see, the Yugo's greatest opponent in 1986 wasn't another carmaker; it was itself. The car's quality was atrocious.

The Ambassador Drives a Yugo

Q: What do you call a Yugo station wagon?
A: A we-go.

Yugo America attempted to improve production at Zastava by sending a team of executives to the factory in September 1985.[1] But Yugo America was limited in what it could do. Zastava was "at least 10–15 years behind the US in manufacturing technology," wrote *Ward's AutoWorld*, "and many tasks [there were] done by hand." Its manufacturing facilities were "the antithesis of robotics and automation" while its assembly-line workers performed dozens of operations "long since automated in US plants."[2] To make matters worse, Zastava's parts suppliers within Yugoslavia were notoriously bad. One such supplier, the Ramiz Sadiku firm of Kosovo, regularly missed its deliveries. In 1986 more than half the components it sold to Zastava "were rejected or passed on for retouching."[3]

Although Toma Savic had done a good job in putting together the new Yugo-A assembly line, changes to Zastava's managerial structure, supplier network, or production schedule were simply out of the question. "The organization there wasn't geared to making decisions," insists Roger Berry. "It was geared to avoiding blame. The guys [at the middle and lower levels] were . . . absolutely able to make decisions, but because of the way the organization was set up, only the higher-ups could make them. No decision was ever made without these guys signing off, and in their entire careers they'd never been rewarded for making a decision. They'd been rewarded for not having a problem. So all of the decision-making processes and all of the planning processes and all of the negotiations with the suppliers ground to a virtual halt and moved at a glacial pace. No matter how hard we pushed. It was as if we had led a camel into a tent, but couldn't get him back out again."[4]

The crux of the matter was that Zastava was a socialist enterprise that, for most of its history, had built cars in a protected environment. Unlike capitalist enterprises, which operated in a free-market environment that established competition and decided which products would be profitable, Zastava enjoyed a state-supported monopoly. The state gave it subsidies, absorbed its losses, and protected the company from competition by taxing foreign imports and limiting domestic rivals. The result was that Yugoslav consumers had no choice but to buy Zastava's cars. The salespeople there "were living every sales manager's dream," said one American observer. "In it, the buyers come to you and ask you to please sell them [a car] and you just sit there and say, 'Yeah . . . I guess I will.'"[5] Though good for business, Zastava's domestic monopoly made it hopelessly inefficient. It also meant low product quality and a lack of investment in new technologies (which explains why, as of 1985, Zastava had built only a handful of models in thirty years).

Thus, Yugo America wasn't simply asking Zastava for more cars. It was asking the company to change its mentality. "The question wasn't whether or not the Yugo could have made it in America," says Zoran Basaraba, a former executive at Yugo America. "The question was whether or not it was possible for Zastava to change its corporate culture and to understand that change was absolutely necessary day after day after day."[6] The Japanese understood it. Since the early 1950s, they'd followed with an almost religious reverence the teachings of W. Edwards Deming, a quality-control specialist who developed an organizational theory known as "continuous improvement." According to Deming, a company's focus should not be on how many goods it produced but on small yet continuous improvements to the production process.

But Zastava wasn't geared that way. As a socialist enterprise free from competition, it moved with the slow, lumbering gait of an elephant. Decisions were made from the top down. Quantity always trumped quality. Production was slow, changes were slight, and model runs were counted not in years but in decades. By 1985, Zastava had manufactured two different car models, the Fica and the 1300/1500, for longer than Ford had produced the Model T. The Fica, in fact, had been in production since 1955, which meant, hypothetically, a laborer at Zastava could have worked on the car his entire career. Zastava was in a stasis. It was the opposite of lean. It was bland and unresponsive and had no earthly idea that in the business world, you struck while the iron was hot. "Unlike a Western automobile manufacturer," wrote one historian, "which tries to maximize output of its new models as soon as they are offered . . . Zastava expected to take several years before it could offer its new models in volume."[7]

For his part, Malcolm Bricklin attempted to turn his early supply problems into a positive. At the Yugo's official unveiling in October 1985 at the famed Tavern on the Green restaurant in New York's Central Park, he announced: "I honestly think we could sell a half-million [Yugos] a year, if we could get them."[8] That number was absurd, but so were the balloons, the rope-twirling cowboys, and the actor Bricklin had dressed up as the Statue of Liberty. (The actor stood next to a Yugo in the restaurant's parking lot.) "From the outside, the restaurant looked like a circus," wrote *Adweek* magazine, "with hundreds of red, white, and blue balloons stretched into arches above the entrance. Inside, the invited guests listened to encouraging statistics, cited by Yugo executives, and had a hearty breakfast. [But] after the formal briefing, the already festive atmosphere turned into a free-for-all."[9] Said one attendee in a Yugo hat who'd come straight from the Palladium, "We're the downtown crowd that came uptown. We haven't been to bed yet."[10]

Also in attendance was a squad of security guards that Bricklin had hired to break up potential protests. The protesters he expected weren't Ford or GM dealers. They weren't "Buy American" maniacs or even distraught Canadians still angry at his SV-1 project. No. They were Croatians, mostly immigrants and first-generation Croatian-Americans who opposed the Yugo because its home country, Yugoslavia, had in their words "denied the Croatian nation its basic human rights of self-determination."[11] As of 1985, Croatia was one of six Yugoslav republics. It enjoyed a certain degree of political autonomy, but many émigré Croats wanted the republic to leave Yugoslavia once and for all. They despised communism and typically viewed Yugoslavia as an "expansionist hoax," a plot by Serb politicians to conquer the Croatian nation through Yugoslav communism. Therefore, Croat émigré groups such as the four-thousand-member Croatian National Congress worked tirelessly to undermine Yugoslav initiatives whenever and wherever they could.

Just a month prior to the Yugo's Tavern on the Green unveiling, a thirty-six-year-old Croatian immigrant named Petar Ivcec disrupted the annual Yugoslavian Ethnic Festival in Detroit by scaling a sixty-five-foot flagpole and attempting to rip its massive Yugoslav flag from its hinges. "He's against communism and against the Yugoslav regime," explained Ivcec's wife as firemen were attempting to rescue her husband, and dozens of Serbs and Croats, some in peasant garb, were scuffling around her.[12] It was the first time that an ethnic festival had been disrupted that year, reported Detroit's police commander, who noted, though, that someone had detonated a bomb in the festival's washroom back in 1980.

Bricklin probably didn't expect anyone to bomb his Yugo opening. But who knew what to expect? In September 1976, a group calling itself Fighters for a Free Croatia hijacked a TWA jetliner in New York with almost a hundred people on board. The hijackers claimed to have a bomb, which they didn't, but to prove it they placed a real bomb in a locker at Grand Central Station that detonated while they were in flight. The hijackers then threatened to blow up a second bomb somewhere in the United States unless *The New York Times* and four other newspapers printed their appeal. The hijacking of a major airline, they explained, "was the only possible method to employ in appealing to the American people to protest the sending of any form of aid to the imperialistic Belgrade regime."[13]

Although the Fighters for a Free Croatia was definitely a fringe group, it espoused an ideology that many American Croats believed. In their minds, Yugoslavia was bad. So was Serbia. And now, with Tito gone, nothing represented Yugoslavia more than the Yugo, a car *built* in Serbia. Therefore, even prior to the car's August 1985 introduction, the Croatian National Congress initiated a nationwide letter-writing campaign in which its president, Matthew Mestrovic, sent letters critical of the Yugo to the American press.[14] "Buyer beware!" warned Mestrovic. "Yugoslav products, including their cars, are so shoddy that even the Soviets have threatened to stop buying them . . . The main thing going for the Yugo-car is its low price tag. But even that is a Yugo-mirage. It would be easier to overlook the car's many defects if it sold for $2,990 instead of the $3,990 . . . [But Yugo America] wants American consumers to believe that the Yugoslavs, with their dismal manufacturing and efficiency record, are going to succeed where Italy's Fiat failed."[15]

In the coming years, the Croatian National Congress would organize a nationwide boycott of the Yugo as well as a series of protests at Yugo dealerships and at the Yugo America headquarters in New Jersey. "Yugo out of U.S.A.! Yugo out of U.S.A.!" they chanted. "Yugo junk, go home! Yugo junk, go home!" At one point the Croatian National Congress demanded that Yugoslavia release one imprisoned dissident for every one hundred Yugos sold. "The sale of Yugos supports the communist government of Yugoslavia," it said. "[And] we object to the absence of human rights in Yugoslavia."[16] During round two of Detroit's Yugoslavian Ethnic Festival, held under heavy police guard in 1986, hundreds of Croat protesters shouted "Death to Yugoslavia!" and "Down with the Yugo!" Although this time no one climbed the flagpole, someone did throw a gasoline-soaked rag at a Yugo display.[17] "We're only doing what we think its right," said one protester. "Our objective is to inform the public of the low quality of the car and to [show that America's] support of the Yugo only serves to perpetuate another police state [while denying] the Croatian nation the basic right of self-determination."[18]

The Croatians "were savvy PR people," remembers Zoran Basaraba, "and they quickly understood that this was the first product that came from Yugoslavia that actually had an identity as a Yugoslav product. So, for political reasons, they picketed. The picket lines were a shock to the dealers. Could you imagine a dealer somewhere in Nebraska? He didn't have a clue where Yugoslavia was, and all of a sudden he wakes up one morning and there's fifty people picketing his dealership over an issue he doesn't understand."[19] The main Croat pickets were in San Francisco, Chicago, St. Louis, and Detroit, where in one three-month period they handed out over 150,000 anti-Yugo flyers. In one instance, protesters handed out

2,000 flyers alone at a U.S.-China volleyball match in Irvine, California, because Yugo America was a sponsor of USA Volleyball.

"They have every right to be doing what they're doing," said Ira Edelson in a 1987 interview. "[But] we happen to think that their allegations are not meritorious . . . If there are any human rights violations that are of a substantial nature, I doubt that Yugoslavia would have enjoyed most-favored-nation status."[20] Edelson was right—to an extent. Yugoslavia's citizens could enter and exit the country freely, own property, subscribe to foreign newspapers, and hold foreign bank accounts. But there were limits to free speech: taboo subjects included Tito, the country's single-party system, state ownership of industry, and ethnic relations of any kind. A person may "not be realistic about today's life in Yugoslavia," said one dissident, nor describe its ethnic or economic problems too critically.[21]

In 1985, Amnesty International claimed that over five hundred people per year were jailed in Yugoslavia for "non-violent political actions."[22] These included "verbal offences," such as making jokes about government leaders, painting political graffiti, and singing nationalist songs. Though the U.S. State Department frequently criticized governments who fared poorly in Amnesty's reports, it remained curiously silent regarding Yugoslavia. The country was simply too important in geopolitical terms to risk a diplomatic spat. "There is a tendency in the West to let the Yugoslavs off easy," wrote *The Washington Post*. "After all, it is said, they are more liberal than other communists and . . . being multi-ethnic and multinational, they've got to be extra careful . . . To which, the United States government . . . adds (under its breath), it is in the American interest to settle Yugoslavia down as a stable buffer against Soviet expansion . . ."[23]

It seems it was also in the American interest to support the Yugo. In June 1986 the American embassy in Belgrade leased a yellow Yugo GV from Yugo America for one dollar. The car was fitted with a tiny American flag on each fender and personally unveiled by Ambassador John Scanlan at the 1986 Belgrade Auto Show. "Here is a Balkan country," gushed Scanlan, "not an industrial giant but, by God, they're marketing a neat, inexpensive car in America. It's a source of national pride."[24] Either that, or Scanlan had lost his mind. Over the next two years he frequently used the yellow Yugo as his personal limousine. "Sometimes, when [the] Ambassador . . . feels like a bit of a lark," wrote one journalist, "he leaves his armor-plated regulation car in the garage and has the ambassadorial stars and stripes hoisted from the bumper of a tiny Yugo . . . Then, with the chauffeur at the wheel and Scanlan sitting as ambassadorially as one can in the back seat of an economy car, he makes his official calls . . ."[25] On one occasion Scanlan took the Yugo to an annual meeting of the Yugoslav League of Communists, a kind of parliament, which he attended as an observer.

"There was a lot of cheerleading going on at the embassy," remembers Patrick J. Nichols, a former economic affairs officer in Belgrade. "Basically, no one wanted to see Yugoslavia fail."[26] But, because of its binge borrowing, by the mid-1980s Yugoslavia was failing—big-time. Its foreign debt had risen from $2.4 billion in 1970 to over $20 billion in 1985.[27] The way to reduce the debt was to earn hard currency and to use the currency to pay the debt down. This could be done by increasing exports and decreasing imports; by encouraging Yugoslav citizens to work as seasonal guest workers in, say, Germany or Sweden; by promoting foreign tourism; by cutting wages and limiting social programs; and by borrowing less.

But "paying the piper," as one group of scholars called it, was easier said than done.[28] Yugoslavia could export its goods only if other countries wanted them. It could restrict imports, but without new machinery, domestic production would suffer. Yugoslavia could encourage its people to work abroad, but they'd been working abroad, and Western Europe needed only a finite number of workers. It could also promote tourism, but tourism was a seasonal business, one which also required heavy investment. Yugoslavia could cut wages, limit social programs, or even raise prices, but as one Yugoslav official said, "We can't do that anymore! They'll be rioting in the streets!"[29] The one thing Yugoslavia could do was borrow less. However, by 1983 it owed so much money that it had to borrow an additional $600 million simply to pay the *interest* on its loans.

The $600 million package as well as a $1.9 billion loan refinancing plan had been put together by a consortium of banks, governments, and international financial institutions called the Friends of

Yugoslavia.[30] The consortium had been assembled in 1983, interestingly enough, by then deputy secretary of state and future Yugo America board member Lawrence Eagleburger. In all, some five hundred banks had loaned money to Yugoslavia, including Manufacturers Hanover Trust, Bank of America, Bankers Trust, Chase Manhattan, Citibank, Marine Midland, and Security Pacific. The bank with the most exposure in Yugoslavia was Manufacturers Hanover Trust, or "Manny Hanny," which played an important role in the Friends of Yugoslavia consortium by overseeing the new $600 million multibank loan to Yugoslavia and the refinancing of another $1.9 billion in Yugoslav debt.

Founded in 1961 when Hanover Bank and Manufacturers Trust Company merged to create Manufacturers Hanover Trust, Manny Hanny was, at its height, America's fourth-largest bank. In 1974, it was also the first Western bank to open a branch office in socialist Eastern Europe.[31] By almost any measure, Manny Hanny was an aggressive lender, especially to banks, governments, and financial institutions in the developing world. In 1985, for example, the bank had over $1.6 billion invested in Mexico, a staggering 54.8 percent of its working capital.[32] Overall, Manny Hanny loaned 8.5 percent of the bank's total assets to four financially volatile nations: Mexico, Venezuela, Argentina, and Brazil.[33] During the 1970s and '80s, it also lent at least $250 million to cash-strapped Yugoslavia. And in October 1985, it lent $75 million as well to Yugo America Inc.[34]

The loan to Yugo America and the loans to Yugoslavia were unrelated. "The loan to Yugo America was not part of what we called Yugoslav exposure," remembers Fulvio Dobrich, then a senior vice president at Manny Hanny and manager of its Yugoslav accounts. "The loan to Yugo America was handled on the domestic side, not the international side. They may have told us [they were giving Yugo America the loan] but we probably read about it in the newspapers. You can imagine, banks tend to be competitive internally, and don't necessarily talk to each other as much as they should."[35] Maggie Mudd, Dobrich's associate at Manny Hanny, agrees: "That was a big loan, but it was made with a domestic guarantee. It was not considered Yugoslav risk, but if I remember correctly, Fulvio and I thought it was kind of insane. I remember thinking 'Holy smokes!' because the product they were selling was a car from Yugoslavia that had to make it to the United States."[36]

The person who negotiated the $75 million loan for Yugo America was Ira Edelson. Back in 1984, when Yugo America first incorporated, Edelson had chosen Manufacturers Hanover as the company's bank. "There was nothing special about it," says Edelson. "We had to open up a bank account, and Manny Hanny was simply the bank we decided on. We had no idea it was so heavily invested in Yugoslavia."[37] Although Edelson learned in the coming months that Manny Hanny was Yugoslavia's largest private creditor, he applied for the $75 million loan not through Fulvio Dobrich but through a vice president named John Dowling at Manny Hanny's New York headquarters. (As chairman of the U.S.-Yugoslav Economic Council, a kind of two-country chamber of commerce, Dobrich did attend the Yugo's 1985 Tavern on the Green unveiling in Central Park, where he met Bricklin for the first time.)

Manny Hanny's $75 million loan to Yugo America was actually a line of credit, which Yugo America could draw upon whenever it needed to. Of the $75 million loan amount, Manufacturers Hanover earmarked $54 million for the purchase of new cars. It also earmarked another $2 million for parts and accessories, which left Yugo America $19 million to use at its discretion.[38] The loan was collateralized, believe it or not, by the thousands of Yugo GV automobiles that Yugo America was planning to purchase from Zastava. In international business terms, Manufacturers Hanover had provided Yugo America with a "loan against imports." A loan against imports is a specific type of loan that enables an importer to stay in business during the lengthy down period in which goods are being purchased abroad and shipped to the United States.

Technically, Manufacturers Hanover still owned the automobiles, but Yugo America could run its import business and distribute the cars in any way it saw fit. Manny Hanny's only real concern was that Yugo America repay the loan with interest. Loans against imports are common in the import-export business. What was interesting in Yugo America's case was the size of the loan, $75 million, and the fact that if Yugo America went bankrupt, Manny Hanny's collateral would be worthless. "Most of that [$75 million] line of credit," remembers Edelson, "was against the cars as collateral. However, if [Yugo America] were to go bankrupt, the collateral would be worth substantially less than to a going concern, and Manufacturers Hanover would lose a substantial amount of money."[39] So why did Manny Hanny do it? Why would anyone give a fledgling Bricklin operation $75 million to sell a Yugoslavian car?

"I think you could safely assume that there was a period of time in the 1980s that banks were doing some stupid things," says Fulvio Dobrich.[40] Certainly, giving $75 million to Yugo America was one of them. Another was a sizable loan that Manufacturers had given to Drysdale Government Securities in 1981. Drysdale was "insolvent the day it opened its doors," said one observer, which didn't stop Manny Hanny from giving the company some $21 million in loans before Drysdale went bankrupt in 1982.[41] For the executives at Manufacturers Hanover Trust, however, nonperforming loans like the Drysdale loan were part of its business. You had to risk money to make money, and Manufacturers Hanover had always turned a profit. According to the trade publication *American Banker*, between 1984 and 1985, Manny Hanny's nonperforming loans rose from $1 billion to $1.84 billion, an industry-leading increase of 84 percent.[42] But during that same period Manufacturers Hanover recorded a net income of $352.5 million, up 4.6 percent from the previous year, and its twelfth consecutive year of record earnings.[43]

To be sure, the $75 million Yugo America loan was a big loan, but Manufacturers Hanover had given bigger and riskier loans before. It is also possible that officials at Manufacturers Hanover had been sucked in by Yugo-mania. After all, in October 1985, when the $75 million line of credit was extended, Yugo America's one hundred or so East Coast dealers were selling the cars as fast as they could get them. The company's future looked bright. It helped, too, that in mid-1985, Manufacturers Hanover had already given Yugo America a smaller start-up loan that the company had used to purchase its first five-hundred-car shipment from Zastava. Since this first shipment of Yugos had been an unequivocal success, Manny Hanny decided to offer Yugo America an even larger line of credit. It was, in Bill Prior's words, "a more permanent endorsement" of Yugo America by the bank.[44]

Naturally, officials at Yugo America were ecstatic. They now had $56 million for cars and parts and $19 million for operations. They'd started the company with almost no money; now suddenly they were flush. They could expand their workforce, develop a dealer network, and afford, for the first time, a nationwide media campaign. But the question was: Did the Yugo need it? In November, *Fortune* magazine named the car one of its twelve "Outstanding Products for 1985." The Yugo joined New Coke, airplane telephones, Combat Roach Killer, Nike Air Jordan sneakers, AIDS antibody tests, and the "We Are the World" single as an outstanding product, wrote *Fortune*, whose "technological innovation, originality, or risk-taking . . . created excitement in 1985."[45] Later that month, *Motor Trend* magazine nominated the Yugo for its "Import Car of the Year" award, and in December, *USA Today* named the car one of its twelve "Hot Hits" for 1985.[46]

The Yugo was popular. It was so popular, in fact, that even after Yugo America had secured its $75 million Manufacturers Hanover loan, the company felt comfortable enough to delay its nationwide media campaign until 1986. It was a fateful move. The company's ad agency, Rosenfeld, Sirowitz, and Humphrey (formerly Rosenfeld, Sirowitz, and Lawson), had warned Yugo America that bad publicity was coming—lots of it—and that Yugo America should start its campaign as soon as possible. "[Our] recommendations," said Ron Rosenfeld, "were not followed."[47] Instead, Yugo America spent its money on developing several new Yugo GV models (including the GVL, the GVS, and the GVX) and on expanding its workforce to 190 employees. It also paid its executives huge salaries and drew up plans for a massive new corporate headquarters somewhere in New Jersey.[48]

But what Yugo America didn't do was advertise, at least not nationally. "Yugo preferred to rely on the rush of favorable launch publicity," wrote *Automotive News* in July 1986, and "has yet to [unveil] a national ad campaign." That was a mistake, it implied, as now "the negative publicity [surrounding the car] has been national [in scope]."[49] Officials at Yugo America had had plenty of time to react. The first real criticism of the car had come from syndicated columnist Mike Royko only days after its August 26 introduction.[50] In October 1985, automotive writer John R. White of *The Boston Globe* called his review of the Yugo "2 Hours in Purgatory."[51] "If you are desperate for a new car and you're strapped for dough to make payments," wrote White, "go ahead and buy one . . . But right now I couldn't be interested in a Yugo purchase if the decimal point were moved two places left on the price tag." The car, in White's description, was cheap. As in bad cheap. Poor-quality cheap. Cheap cheap.

Of course, the execs at Yugo America knew early on that quality was an issue, which is why their "Introducing the Same Old Idea" ads referred to craftsmanship—"Yugo craftsmanship." "People don't want anything cheap," said Bricklin. "[So the Yugo] has to be perceived as a smart buy, like getting something really good on sale" or, for that matter, something of quality.[52] Bricklin had named his car the Yugo "GV" for a reason. He wanted people to know that the Yugo was a "good value," an intelligent purchase. But without a nationwide PR campaign, consumers didn't know that. They knew only what they had heard, and what they had heard, increasingly, was bad.

In December 1985, for example, Warren Brown of *The Washington Post* titled his Yugo review: "If Yugo for It, You Could Be Sorry."[53] "I am a sucker for the underdog," wrote Brown, "a patsy for the Davids of the world. My inclination is to cheer anyone or anything going against the odds . . . But if this automotive David gets clobbered in the market, I'm going to give Goliath a standing ovation. I do not like this little car."

He continued: "The Yugo GV [I tested] had less than 50 miles on the odometer at delivery and could be expected to be a bit sluggish. But vibrations at speeds of 40 to 50 mph? . . . You've gotta be kidding." According to Brown, even the Yugo's fuel-gauge needle was bad. He did say, however, that the Yugo started reliably, that its heater and rear-window defroster worked, and that its paint job was "competent." But "make no mistake about it," he concluded, "this is not a rebirth of the trusty Volkswagen Beetle. If the Yugo is what it means nowadays to be the lowest-priced new car in the United States, used-car salespeople have nothing to fear."[54]

Although Brown thoroughly trashed the Yugo, he stopped short of saying that it was better to buy a good used car than a new Yugo.

But was it really? So far no one had said so for sure. However, it was a valid question. Should Joe Car Buyer buy a used Honda Civic or a new Yugo? Should he buy a reliable used car or a new car that might fall apart only a year or two after he'd bought it? Decisions, decisions. But because Joe Car Buyer was an American, a true-blue car-buying American, he liked to research his purchases. He looked up used-car prices in a publication called the *Kelley Blue Book* and read new-car reviews in *Consumer Reports* magazine. *Consumer Reports* published a review of the Yugo in February 1986. From that point forward, Yugo-mania was over.

12

The Car-Buying Bible

Q: What do you call a Yugo that breaks down after 100 miles?
A: An overachiever.

In 1986, *Consumer Reports* had more than 3.3 million subscribers. It was, according to one poll, the most trusted consumer information source in America, ahead of even the Better Business Bureau and the Environmental Protection Agency.[1] The magazine had been published since 1936 by a nonprofit organization known as the Consumers Union (CU). For some fifty years Consumers Union had tested almost every product imaginable: toys, tires, food, luggage, stockings, washing machines, lawn mowers, cameras, and, of course, cars. The organization's goal, said its director, was "to make consumers skeptical of advertising and demanding of quality, and to let manufacturers know that they will be judged."[2]

Consumers Union zealously protected its objectivity, avoiding any hint of bias: it refused, for example, to accept any form of advertising in its publications, and to this day *Consumer Reports* features no outside ads. Zero. By the same token, advertisers were not allowed to use *Consumer Reports'* ratings or reviews in their own advertisements, and the magazine refused to accept gifts, wholesale goods, or samples of any kind. The testers at *Consumer Reports* purchased their products in secret. They had a team of professional shoppers who paid in cash or with personal credit cards and who bought goods in retail stores just like normal consumers would. The only difference was that once they bought the goods, they shipped them back to a facility in Mount Vernon, New York, where testers there put them through the ringer.

They tested the durability of luggage by tumbling bags two thousand times in a machine that looked like "a Ferris wheel."[3] They tested the strength of plastic trash bags by filling them with garbage and dropping them on the ground over and over again. They dirtied up dishes, stored them overnight, then stuck them in a dozen different washing machines to see how clean they would get. They tested stereo speakers in an echo-free chamber. They tested facial tissue in a homemade "sneeze machine." They tested condoms by blowing them up to the size of watermelons. They even tested the safety of baby carriages by whipping them around to see if their tiny test dummies would fall out. Perhaps the magazine's most famous test involved mattresses. These were pummeled at least one hundred thousand times in the center (to simulate sleeping) and twenty-five thousand times at the edges (to simulate sitting) by a buttocks-shaped battering ram made from two halves of a bowling ball.[4]

The Consumers Union tested everything, it seemed, and each month recorded its results in *Consumer Reports*. The public valued its judgments. Manufacturers feared them, for "passing Consumers Union tests," wrote *The Wall Street Journal*, was often "crucial to a company's success."[5] In 1983, for example, a Connecticut heater company named Kero-Sun declared bankruptcy after *Consumer Reports* wrote that kerosene heaters were generally fire hazards that could emit noxious fumes.[6] That same year, shares in Coleco Industries dropped nearly 20 percent following a blistering review of Coleco's new Adam computer, in which *Consumer Reports* wrote that of the four Adam computers it had purchased, none of them worked.[7] In April 1969, *Consumer Reports* wrote that the Subaru 360 had "displayed shockingly deficient structural integrity" in federal crash tests and that the tiny automobile was, in its estimation, "unacceptably hazardous."[8] Both Subaru and its CEO at the time, Malcolm Bricklin, nearly went bankrupt.

As of 1986, Consumers Union spent some $500,000 per year on thirty-five new cars. These were purchased from dealer lots and shipped to the organization's Auto Test Center in Orange, Connecticut, where they were scrutinized by a team of experts. At the center, the team checked fifty items in all: fenders, doors, seats, head restraints, safety belts, gas cap, windshield wipers, and so on, and there it also tested the car's bumper with a machine known as the "basher." Then, when these tests were complete, the team drove the car three or four times over a thirty-mile loop consisting of interstate highways and winding roads. It also measured the car's fuel efficiency over a separate 195-mile trip, and conducted a final braking and handling test at a closed drag strip in Lime Rock, Connecticut.[9] Though certainly not perfect, the Consumers Union "system of evaluating vehicles," wrote *The Boston Globe*, "is probably about as good as you are going to get."[10]

It definitely was good enough for the American consumer, who typically viewed *Consumer Reports* as a car-buying bible. "I don't even look at a car if *Consumer Reports* says it's not a reliable car," said one Seattle woman.[11] Her view was typical. By the early 1990s one in five Americans used *Consumer Reports* to choose a car.[12] As a result, even a lukewarm rating could affect a company's sales. A bad rating could kill them. That's what happened to the popular Suzuki Samurai in 1988, which *Consumer Reports* claimed was "not acceptable" because in its tests the tiny jeep tended to roll over in severe turns at 40 miles per hour. Although Suzuki called the results "inaccurate and defamatory" and actually sued Consumers Union for product disparagement, the public was still unconvinced.[13]

"People were frightened," said Bob Knoll, former director of car testing for Consumers Union. "They did not want to see themselves or their children in that vehicle. When a car is really bad we don't hesitate to say so."[14] Knoll wasn't lying. His team blasted the Samurai and gave it the magazine's first "not acceptable" rating in more than a decade. It even demanded that the National Highway Transportation Safety Administration issue a recall of the car, and that Suzuki itself refund the car's purchase price to over 150,000 Samurai owners. This was no joke. Consumers Union was serious. In its July 1988 issue of *Consumer Reports* (which came out in June), and in another report a month later, it so badly panned the car that Samurai sales fell 70.6 percent from the previous year, a difference of 5,280 cars. Said one Consumers Union spokesman, "If [Suzuki's losses are] a reflection in any way of the public giving credence to our findings, then I think that is a good sign."[15]

Interestingly enough, the Suzuki Samurai had been introduced to the United States in November 1985, just two months after the Yugo. "I'm sure Suzuki was terrified of *Consumer Reports*," said Pete Mulhern, a technical service manager at Yugo America, "because everybody saw how the magazine panned us back in 1986, and how sales of the Yugo just crashed."[16] The *Consumer Reports* review of the Yugo appeared in January 1986, in the magazine's February issue, which meant that Bob Knoll and his CU testing team had inspected the car in November or December 1985. The review itself was just three pages long, but *Consumer Reports* gave the Yugo top billing by placing it on the cover. "How Much Car for $3990?" asked the headline. Below it was the caption: "First Look at the Yugo." The cover photo was of a Peterbilt tractor-trailer bearing down on a gold Yugo, whose driver sat cringing in fear. It was obvious what *Consumer Reports* thought of the Yugo: it wasn't safe.

The review began with the same headline as the cover ("How Much Car for $3990?"), but this time the caption was brutal. "The price is the come-on for the Yugo," it declared. "But you can't buy it for $3990, and it's hard to recommend at any price."[17] Wow. One can only imagine the sick feeling in the stomachs of Yugo America execs who first read the review just days before the 1986 National Automobile Dealers Association convention in New Orleans, where they planned to introduce a second Yugo GV model called the GVS to over a hundred Yugo dealers and their wives.[18] "Is low price significant justification for buying the Yugo?" asked *Consumer Reports*. "We don't think so. Overall the Yugo scored below every other small car we've tested in recent years . . . Handling was competent and braking was very effective, but comfort, ride, shifting, heating, and the design of the controls were below par . . . [Then] there's a serious question of safety. Buyers of any model as small as the Yugo have good reason to worry."[19] The 1985 NADA had been a Yugo lovefest; 1986 was panning out quite differently.

According to *Consumer Reports*, the Yugo it tested "was a sorry sample indeed." It had twenty-one defects "attributable to sloppy assembly or incomplete dealer preparation," including a leak that dripped oil onto the car's exhaust system and filled the compartment with smoke. "The clutch chattered. The brakes squealed . . . The speedometer clicked. The hood became loose. The reception of the Yugo radio was so poor," it wrote, "that we played tapes most of the time. (They didn't sound great either.) The rear window washer quit. The ignition switch had to be replaced. And two bolts holding the transmission were loose." In its 5-mile-per-hour bumper test with the "basher," the Yugo sustained $620 in front-end damage and $461 to the rear. The bumpers "were badly bent and twisted," and "the grille was broken." The Yugo was a mess. The only things *Consumer Reports* found good with the car were its emergency handling and braking, and the visibility of its dashboard displays.

Although *Consumer Reports* rarely if ever editorialized about a car's importer, it did mention Malcolm Bricklin: "The importer, Yugo America Inc., is a subsidiary of Bricklin Industries, the company run by entrepreneur Malcolm Bricklin. Bricklin unsuccessfully marketed the Subaru 360, a minicar that CU tested in 1969 and rated Not Acceptable . . . Bricklin later started a factory in Nova Scotia to build a sports car that bore his name. That venture also failed. More recently he took over the import and sale of the foundering Fiat X1/9 and Spider sports cars. But even after he replaced the cars' Fiat nameplate with Bertone and Pininfarina nameplates, the cars didn't sell . . . [N]ow it's the Yugo."[20]

The implication, of course, was that Bricklin's new Yugo GV project would fail like all the others. "Will Yugo America go the way of some of Malcolm Bricklin's other ventures?" it asked. "Will Yugo owners be stranded without service or parts? How much would an 'orphaned' Yugo be worth in the used-car market?" These no doubt were valid questions, and *Consumer Reports* had every right to point out Bricklin's track record. His Subaru 360 was a dangerous car. No question about it. Likewise, his Bricklin SV-1 had had major quality issues and, after the bankruptcy of General Vehicle Inc., no company to support it. Its buyers had been "orphaned." The same could be said for purchasers of the Pininfarina Spider and the Bertone X1/9, who from 1984 onward had no one to support them. By then Bricklin's International Automotive Importers, which imported the cars, had ceased operating, and Bricklin had turned his attention to Yugo America Inc. That didn't mean anyone at Yugo America was happy about it.

"We were really annoyed that *Consumer Reports* brought up

Malcolm Bricklin," says Pete Mulhern, "because it turned people's attention away from what we were offering: decent, cheap transportation."[21] However, according to Bob Knoll, the now retired CU official who oversaw the Yugo's tests, *Consumer Reports* "had an obligation" to mention Bricklin. In fact, "we couldn't say all we wanted to say about Bricklin in our review because it wasn't very nice." Although Bricklin was, in Knoll's opinion, "one of the great American entrepreneurs," whenever Knoll heard that Bricklin had started a new business, he was skeptical. As for the car, remembers Knoll, the Yugo "was actually pretty agile. It just didn't happen to be put together very well . . . It was basically a poorly built Fiat."[22]

The *Consumer Reports* review of the Yugo was a disaster for Yugo America, but not because Knoll mentioned Bricklin. It was a disaster because in the review's very last line, CU concluded: "If $4400 is the most you can spend on a car, we think you'd get better value from a good used car than a new Yugo."[23] That line was picked up and repeated over and over again in the press. By February 1986 the Yugo was an industry laughingstock and was about to become a national joke. "You know how journalists are," said Tony Ciminera. "They copy one another. When they saw that story appear, they picked it up and duplicated it on all the wire services. And it just grew in intensity."[24] Suddenly, insists Pete Mulhern, "Yugo bashing was cool. Everybody did it."[25] Soon the Yugo jokes began, such as "How do you double the value of your Yugo? Fill the gas tank." Or "What comes in every Yugo owner's manual? A bus schedule." Or "Why does a Yugo come with a rear-window defroster? It keeps your hands warm when you push it."

Officials at Yugo America tried to downplay the *Consumer Reports* article by saying that CU had been overly critical. "The real judge is the public," said Tony Ciminera to a *Chicago Sun-Times* reporter, and "people who buy Yugos don't read *Consumer Reports*. I'm talking about people ranging from retirees to young first-time drivers without lots of money. Journalists drive Hondas and exotic cars, get jaded and can't relate to an auto such as the Yugo. They don't drive clapped-out Chevys and other old cars that Yugo buyers had been driving."[26] Ciminera had a point of sorts. Odds are the people who bought Yugos didn't read *Consumer Reports*, because if they had, they wouldn't have bought Yugos in the first place. But for everyone else, the message was clear: "You'd get better value from a good used car than a new Yugo."

Sales plummeted. In January 1986, Yugo America sold 2,823 cars. However, with the publication of the *Consumer Reports* article, in February it sold just 1,736 cars, a difference of 38.5 percent. To make matters worse, in mid-February 1986 the National Highway Transportation Safety Administration (NHTSA) ordered a mandatory recall of all 9,800 Yugos that had been sold in, or shipped to, the United States.[27] The NHTSA ordered the recall after an agency subcontractor had tested the car and found a potentially dangerous problem with its seat-belt anchorages. The fix was minuscule—the anchorages needed a washer and a screw tightening—but the subsequent PR was devastating.

In March, Yugo America received more bad news when the NHTSA released the preliminary results of its annual 35-mile-per-hour crash test. The test was part of the NHTSA's "New Car Assessment Program," in which the agency purchased twenty-six cars for 1986 and crashed them headfirst into a fixed barrier at 35 miles per hour. The 35-mile-per-hour test was not mandatory, but a 30-mile-per-hour test was. Federal regulations required that all new cars sold in the United States receive a passing score of 1,000 points or below on an NHTSA-conducted 30-mile-per-hour crash test. (The Yugo had passed its test in spring 1985.) However, to the chagrin of automakers industry-wide, each year the NHTSA performed a second test at 35 miles per hour. The test was for information purposes only and was designed to compare the crashworthiness of new vehicles.

Critics complained bitterly that the NHTSA's fixed-barrier crash tests were seriously flawed. The NHTSA, for example, insisted that any head injury of 1,000 points or more to either the driver's-side or passenger's-side test dummy would probably be fatal. But the agency couldn't prove at what score death was certain, or if occupants would survive crashes in cars with substantially lower scores. "All we can do is measure how hard the dummy is hit," said one safety expert, but "the missing link is how do you know he got hurt?"[28] Complicating matters was the fact that NHTSA researchers frequently recorded different test scores *for the same model cars*. In 1982 the agency tested fourteen Chevrolet Citations. The cars were identical and had been produced in succession at the same GM plant, but their head-injury results varied from less than 500 in one test to more than 900 in another.[29]

Although one official admitted that the NHTSA suffered from "scattered results," in 1986 the agency's 35-mile-per-hour crash test consisted of just a single test of each new car.[30] That meant that instead of testing ten new Yugos, for instance, and averaging the results, the NHTSA tested just one. The Yugo's score: a dismal 1,415 for the driver and 1,318 for the front-seat passenger.[31] The NHTSA tested the Yugo in March 1986 alongside a Buick Century two-door coupe, a Buick Century four-door sedan, and a Mazda 323 LX, which was a two-door hatchback. The other three cars fared better than the Yugo. The Buick coupe scored 647 for the driver and 928 for the front-seat passenger; the Buick sedan 699/672; the Mazda 323 LX 802/894.[32]

The NHTSA still had twenty-two more cars to test. But instead of waiting until all the results were in, the agency released its findings to the press. "Yugo Scores Poorly in Safety Agency's 35-MPH Crash Test," blared *The Wall Street Journal*. "No Go for Yugo in Crash Testing," said the *Orlando Sun-Sentinel*. "Yugo Worst in Crash Safety Test, Study Finds," trumpeted the *Chicago Tribune*.[33] The only problem was the Yugo wasn't the worst. It was simply fourth out of four cars tested. However, when all twenty-six cars were tested, the Yugo scored better in driver's-side safety than the Isuzu I-Mark, which received a frightening 2,172 points, and the Subaru GL, which received 1,728 points. In passenger's-side safety, the Yugo scored better than AMC Jeep Comanche (1,636), the Plymouth Colt Vista (1,356), the Saab 900 (1,443), and the Hyundai Excel (2,662).[34]

Overall, ten of the twenty-six cars tested had scores indicating that either one or both of their front-seat occupants would be killed in a car wreck. One failure of note was the supposedly übersafe Ford Taurus, whose driver's-side rating was 1,209. (Its sister model, the Mercury Sable, scored even higher: 1,237.) The best-performing cars in the 1986 NHTSA crash tests were the Chevy Nova (552/562), the Toyota Celica (627/430), the Oldsmobile Delta 88 (688/681), and the Buick Century Sedan (699/672).[35]

To be sure, the Yugo's scores of 1,415 and 1,318 placed it in the bottom five of the twenty-six cars tested. But in one key respect this was natural. In crash tests the world over, smaller cars tend to absorb more damage in front-end collisions than larger cars. They simply have less mass to soak up a blow before passing it on to their occupants, which is why the 1,832-pound Yugo scored so poorly on its tests. It was basic physics. The same could be said for the Isuzu I-Mark, the Subaru GL, and the Hyundai Excel, each of which weighed less than 2,200 pounds.

In addition, the NHTSA inadvertently skewed the results by removing 600 pounds of material from each car it tested, including the car's gas, radio, spare tire, door handles, and sometimes the backseats. The agency did this because the equipment it used to record the dummies' impact data weighed approximately 600 pounds.[36] Therefore, in order to test each car at its original curb weight, the NHTSA took out a comparable amount of stuff. Removing the spare tire from American-made cars was no big deal: usually the tire was located below the floor of the trunk. But the Yugo's spare tire was located in the front, where it lay flat in the engine compartment, between the engine and the firewall. Fiat's designers had put it there on purpose to assist in impact protection. "A spare tire is a big rubber doughnut," insists Pete Mulhern, who remembers the NHTSA test. "It's like a shock absorber. But [the engineers at NHTSA] took it out. So when they crashed the car the steering column got displaced, the firewall got displaced, and the dummy ate the steering wheel. It was a miserable failure and everyone was just downtrodden, but the test wasn't fair."

Mulhern wasn't the only one who complained. Robert Munson, the director of auto safety at Ford Motor Company, insisted that in Ford's own company tests, the Taurus and the Sable had earned significantly lower scores. "We were getting a lot less than what they got," he said. And "we don't understand what 1,200 means."[37] Hyundai maintained that its score was better, too, because the Excel models it'd been importing since April had had safer seat-belt systems installed. The NHTSA, said Hyundai, had tested an old model. In any case, the companies that had failed the NHTSA test all argued the same thing: the test was flawed, the test was unnecessary, the test had nothing to do with real driving conditions. And they were right. The 35-mile-per-hour standard is "a subjective number that [the NHTSA] picked out of its hat," said Tony Ciminera in a 1986 interview. It "isn't really a test" but a "guide for consumers" and "you're not required to pass it."[38]

But the NHTSA's 35-mile-per-hour crash test was a useful yardstick. In the words of one expert, "The crash test results separate the safer cars from the less safe cars."[39] Indeed, in the coming years the Yugo's occupant-death statistics would bear that out. According to a 1991 report issued by the Insurance Institute for Highway Safety, the Yugo had the eighth highest death rate of the 134 most popular 1984–88 model cars on U.S. roads between 1985 and 1989, with 3.6 occupant deaths per ten thousand cars.[40] The statistics didn't lie. Of the 134 cars listed, bigger cars had fewer deaths than smaller cars, while sports cars and subcompacts were the most dangerous. The Chevrolet Corvette Coupe was first with 4.7 deaths per ten thousand, followed closely by the Chevrolet Sprint four-door (4.5) and the Chevrolet Sprint two-door (4.3). Other small cars with high death rates were the Pontiac Fiero, which tied for ninth at 3.5; the Hyundai Excel two-door, which was eleventh at 3.3; and the Ford Escort two-door, which was twelfth at 3.1.[41]

The Yugo's high death rates weren't surprising. The car was small, by any measure; it had poor acceleration, which left it vulnerable at on-ramps; it suffered from poor visibility, low-quality build-construction; and its seat belts were bad. The Yugo was also an old car. Therefore, it lacked such newer safety amenities as antilock brakes, automatic seat belts, computer-designed crumple zones, reinforced doorsills and cross members, and air bags. But the Yugo wasn't a death trap. It simply was what it was: a European minicar from the 1970s. "It's not so much that the car is bad," said one industry analyst. "It's just that automotive technology has improved so much in the last four or five years that people have come to expect so much more than the Yugo delivers," especially in terms of safety.[42]

For whatever reason, though, it was the Yugo, and not the Chevrolet Sprint or the Ford Escort or the Hyundai Excel, that entered the public's discourse as inherently unsafe. One telling example came in the summer of 1986, when *NBC Nightly News* accidentally ran a thirty-second Yugo commercial following a grim report on the NHTSA crash tests and the apparent safety issues of small imported cars. When the commercial ended and the *Nightly News* came back on air, anchorwoman Susan Schwartz said wryly: "Buy one as your second car and let the wife and kids get killed in it."[43] At the time, *NBC Nightly News* was tops in market share and watched each night in 8.5 million homes.[44]

Schwartz, like many Americans, was probably averse to small cars, Yugo or no Yugo. In the mid-1980s, nearly 70 percent of new car purchases in the United States were for mid- or large-size models, which did not include truck, van, minivan, or even SUV purchases. "The minicar interest is a passing fad," one letter to the editor of *Ward's AutoWorld* pointed out. "When consumers learn crash test results of minicars vs. even compact cars, their interest will die quickly."[45] (To emphasize the point, *Ward's* had positioned an editorial cartoon of a subcompact car shaped like a sardine can next to the letter.) "Believing in a car is not up there with believing in God or country," wrote one columnist in the *The San Diego Union-Tribune*. "But there's something about a big Detroit car that I believe in."[46] Indeed, when gasoline prices dropped to below ninety cents per gallon in 1986, consumers began buying mid- and large-size vehicles, including trucks and minivans, in droves. In May, for example, sales of the Cadillac Fleetwood Brougham, an eighteen-foot-five-inch behemoth weighing in at 4,029 pounds, shot up 35 percent.[47]

"The Yugo wasn't any more or less dangerous than other small cars," insists one Yugo America official, "but because the Yugo was a small car, and many people despised small cars, it became a lightning rod. The more the Yugo appeared in the press, the more people said: 'You're gonna die in it! You're gonna die in it!' or 'That car's a death trap.' Mike Royko said it and he'd never seen a Yugo, let alone driven one."[48] Mike Royko was a Pulitzer prize–winning columnist for the *Chicago Tribune*. In August 1985, Royko had written an editorial entitled "This Car Is Just a Little Creep," in which he blasted the Yugo for what he claimed was its dangerously poor acceleration.

"I'm waiting with dread for the arrival on the highways of something called [the] Yugo," wrote Royko, a car "that's not much bigger than a kitchen appliance. But it isn't the size that makes me nervous.

It's the engine . . . The car will accelerate . . . from zero to 50 miles an hour in 19 seconds . . . That means that if you are moving along an expressway at about 60 miles an hour . . . and some little Yugo is creeping onto the highway . . . before he gets to 55 or 60 you will probably be upon him . . . So I'm serving warning," wrote Royko, "on all future Yugo drivers now. Stay out of the way of me and my current gas guzzler. If you don't, I'll just pull off at the next exit, go to the nearest car wash and have them brush you off my grille."[49]

Royko was wrong. The Yugo was slow, but not *that* slow. It did 0 to 50 in 9.3 seconds, not 19 seconds, and 0 to 60 in 14 seconds flat. However, Royko's point was that small cars were dangerous, and since the Yugo was a small car, it was dangerous too. At least in his opinion. The Yugo received similar criticism from Ralph Nader, the famed social activist, and from well-known *Miami Herald* columnist Bill Braucher.[50] "All the Yugo does for me," wrote Braucher, "is create more anxiety. My experience with small cars, foreign and domestic, has been harrowing. We need more of these mechanized boxes on the streets as desperately as we need more potholes . . . I admired the late Marshall Tito, but wrapping myself into a Yugo is the last thing on my mind at any price."[51]

Price, however, is what drew people to the Yugo. Interest had slowed somewhat since the first frantic days of Yugo-mania, but in April 1986, Yugo America sold its ten thousandth car.[52] The company was behind schedule. It had planned to sell at least forty thousand cars in its first calendar year—Bricklin's hundred-thousand-car projection notwithstanding—but had sold just ten thousand cars in seven and half months. But help was on the way. First, Yugo America assisted Zastava in fixing its supply problems, which meant buyers could get Yugos as soon as they wanted them, with no more lines and no more lists. Second, officials at Yugo America had scrounged up an additional $3 million from Manufacturers Hanover to finance a series of commercials on network television, which meant, at long last, the company could counter its bad PR. And third, in the spring of 1986, the California Air Resources Board announced that Yugo America could sell cars in California. The Yugo had passed its emissions tests.[53]

With over 1.1 million new car registrations in 1985 totaling

$29 billion in sales, California was one of the largest automobile markets in the world. It was just what the Yugo needed: a shot of adrenaline. To that end, the company carefully selected some twenty-nine dealers from San Diego to San Francisco and hosted not one but two formal introductions: the first, at the ultra-expensive L'Ermitage Hotel and Resort in Beverly Hills, the second at the equally expensive Mark Hopkins Hotel in San Francisco.[54] "California is very, very important to us," said Dan Prior, the brother of Bill Prior and an executive at Yugo America. "There is no car company that can do well in the U.S. and not do well in California."[55] Although Yugo America first began selling cars in the state on July 15, it hoped to sell ten thousand cars there by the end of 1986. Therefore, it increased its ad budget for California and began shipping cars to the Atlantic terminal closest to the state, in Barbours Cut, Texas.[56]

But was it a case of too little too late? Could Yugo America actually salvage its reputation and sell cars that Americans wanted? To do so, it would need to overcome a mountain of issues: bad press, poor quality, company finance, even Malcolm Bricklin. Apart from Manufacturers Hanover and a few private investors, no one would loan money to Yugo America with Bricklin at the helm. "In all honesty," said company CFO Ira Edelson, "we had trouble raising money with Malcolm in there."[57] As CEO, Bricklin drew a huge salary but left the company's day-to-day operations to Bill Prior while spending most of his time in Manhattan. In late 1986, Bricklin purchased a 4,500-acre ranch near Meeker, Colorado, where he took up residence in 1987.

As for Yugo America, the company began selling cars in California amid even more bad news. In May the Insurance Institute for Highway Safety (IIHS) found that of twenty-three cars tested, the Yugo sustained the most damage in a series of 5-mile-per-hour crash tests. According to the IIHS, the Yugo sustained $2,197 in damage, including $686 in damage in a front-angle crash into a fixed barrier, and $856 in damage in a rear-angle crash into a pole. The Ford Escort showed the least damage at $361, while the average for all twenty-three cars tested was $1,088, over $1,100 less than the Yugo.[58] The Yugo "is a relatively inexpensive car," said a leading insurance expert, "but if one hits anything [with it] it costs almost the price of the car to put it back together [again]."[59] In fact, both State Farm and Allstate insurance companies soon charged "higher-than-standard" collision rates to policyholders who drove Yugos.[60]

Clearly, 1986 had been a bad year for the Yugo. The worst thing was, it wasn't over yet. The car had been crushed by *Consumer Reports*, blasted by the NHTSA, and singled out by the IIHS. It had been ridiculed in newspapers, mocked in magazines, and criticized on TV. It had even been physically attacked by Croat nationalists. Thus, by mid-1986 public opinion had coalesced. The Yugo wasn't a bad car. It was a bad car *for the ages*. A new Edsel. A new Pacer. A new Gremlin. It was a car no teenager would be caught dead in. A car losers drove. Although sales picked up and Yugo America would have a relatively good year in 1987, the damage was done. If Yugo America was to make it in America, it wouldn't be with the Yugo. It would be with a new car, a larger car, one with four doors, automatic transmission, and electronic fuel injection. And that car was from Malaysia.

The Yugo first went on sale in America in August 1985.

Unlike American car buyers, who bought their cars and then drove them off the lot, in the 1980s Yugoslavian car buyers often waited months for delivery.

A popular Zastava model was the Fica ("Fee-cha"), a generic version of the Fiat 600.

Malcolm Bricklin was cofounder of Subaru of America. His company's first imported car was the atrociously built 360.

In 1973, Bricklin talked the government of New Brunswick, Canada, into investing millions in a "revolutionary" sports car called the Bricklin SV-1.

Bricklin's next venture, International Automotive Importers, brought the Pininfarina Spider to America in 1983.

ABOVE: As a vice president at Yugo America, Tony Ciminera was given the Herculean task of prepping the Yugo for the U.S. market. (Courtesy of Barbara Wendling)

LEFT: Malcolm Bricklin, the man who brought the Yugo to the United States

Tony Ciminera, Malcolm Bricklin, and Yugo America president Bill Prior at the Yugo's big send-off party in Kragujevac, Serbia, in July 1985 (Courtesy of Toma Savic)

A press conference at the Yugo's July 1985 send-off. Note the giant photo of the late Yugoslav dictator Tito in the background. (Courtesy of Toma Savic)

Two eighties icons: big hair and the Yugo

Yugo America spent millions on print and TV ads. These two appeared in newspapers and magazines throughout the United States.

In February 1986, *Consumer Reports* published a scathing review of the Yugo. The magazine wrote, "You'd get better value from a good used car than a new Yugo." (Copyright 1986 by Consumers Union of U.S., Inc., Yonkers, NY 10703-1057, a nonprofit organization. Reprinted with permission from the February 1986 issue of CONSUMER REPORTS® for educational purposes only. No commercial use or reproduction permitted. www.ConsumerReports.org)

In 1989, an ill-fated woman drove her tiny Yugo GV off of Michigan's Mackinac Bridge.

An American soldier stops a Yugo at a checkpoint in Kosovo on June 29, 1999. (Department o Defense photograph)

A Yugo accordian sculpture at the Yugo Next art exhibit in New York in 1995 (Courtesy of Tom Magliery)

The very last Yugo rolled off the assembly line at Zastava in November 2008. (REUTERS/Ivan Milutinovic)

13

The Proton Saga Saga

Q: What do you call a Yugo with twin tailpipes?
A: A wheelbarrow.

Malaysia is a country of some twenty-seven million inhabitants in the region of Southeast Asia. It consists of two distinct parts, Peninsular Malaysia, which is south of Cambodia at the southernmost tip of continental Asia, and East Malaysia, which occupies the northern third of the nearby island of Borneo. Dividing the two parts is the South China Sea. In 1986, Malaysia had just sixteen million people.[1] But what it lacked in population, it made up for in natural resources. The country was one of the world's leading exporters of natural rubber and palm oil, but also produced petroleum, coal, natural gas, cocoa, pepper, pineapple, tin, tobacco, and timber. Nevertheless, Malaysia yearned to industrialize—to become a new South Korea, for example—and to transform itself from an exporter of raw materials into a world-class manufacturer.

Malaysia's chief "industrializer" was Mahathir bin Mohamad, a onetime medical doctor who from 1978 to 1981 was the country's minister of trade and industry. In 1980, Mahathir oversaw the formation of a Hyundai-like industrial conglomerate called Heavy Industries Corporation of Malaysia, or HICOM. With Mahathir's backing, HICOM quickly built a cement plant, an iron and steel plant, a petrochemical plant, three motorcycle engine plants, and a paper mill.[2] In 1981, Mahathir became prime minister and announced plans to expand HICOM's holdings to include automobiles. The only problem was that Malaysia had never really made automobiles. It had assembled them. Foreign automakers such as Toyota, Nissan, Mazda, and Mitsubishi would send it their automobiles in the form of "complete knockdown" kits, or CKDs. In the 1960s and '70s, these CKDs included every single part needed to construct a new car; only the labor was Malaysian.

In time, though, Malaysia developed its own parts industry and began substituting domestically made parts, such as tires, seat belts, and batteries, for parts made in Japan. The percentage of Malaysian-made parts was generally small: in the early 1980s, maybe 18 percent.[3] But Prime Minister Mahathir, as part of his industrialization drive, insisted that Malaysia should move beyond mere assembly and into the realm of manufacturing. Therefore, in 1983 he and his HICOM industrial conglomerate joined Mitsubishi in building a $200 million stamping and assembly facility on the outskirts of Kuala Lumpur.[4] It was the biggest, most modern facility in Southeast Asia and home to the Perusahaan Otomobil Nasional, the national carmaker of Malaysia.

Called "Proton" for short, the company was 70 percent owned by HICOM and 30 percent owned by Mitsubishi. Mitsubishi had loaned HICOM approximately 36 billion yen ($144 million), but its greatest contribution wasn't money per se, it was technology.[5] Japanese experts helped build the plant, equip the plant, and run the plant, and had trained some 250 Malaysian workers at factories in Japan. They also assisted Proton in developing its first automobile, the Saga, which was almost identical to a Mitsubishi Lancer Fiore in everything but the hood ornament. Mitsubishi assisted Proton because Prime Minister Mahathir had guaranteed the company a dominant market share. At Mahathir's direction, the Malaysian government instituted a 40 percent import duty on rival CKD kits and a 140 percent duty on imported cars. It was a risky move. Mahathir hoped that by discouraging CKDs and fostering a single manufacturer, Proton, he'd be helping his country develop a true component industry while lessening its dependence on world commodity markets.[6]

But that depended on sales. In 1983, Malaysia's eleven CKD assemblers and associated component makers produced one hundred thousand cars. They employed twenty thousand workers, built a dozen different makes, and did perhaps $500 million in sales. However, with the advent of Mahathir's 40 percent duty on CKDs, their prices rose at least $2,000 per car. In some cases $4,000 per car, which killed sales. Unless Proton could suddenly make cars and pick up the slack, layoffs were expected. When it opened, though, the new Proton plant near Kuala Lumpur could produce only, at most, 80,000 cars.[7] It also employed just 2,500 people, and 7,500 people in its supply and distribution network, a significant drop from Malaysia's once-vibrant assembly and component industry. Worse yet, the Proton's new Saga, set for production in late 1985, contained just 42 percent Malaysian-made parts. It was essentially a CKD. (Because of Mahathir's support, though, its Japanese-made parts were exempt from the 40 percent CKD duty.)

"In the private sector," said Zulkifli Isahak, secretary of Malaysia's main assemblers' association, "we recognize that the decision for the national car was made, and that it is here to stay. We have to adjust to what niches are available. If that is not tenable, we'll have to wind down and the car industry will become a public sector business."[8] Isahak had chosen his words carefully. Only the truly powerful could question Mahathir, and it was unwise, certainly, for private business representatives to blast Proton in the press. The Malaysian government had harassed critics before. In 1979, for example, twenty-three trade unionists employed by the Malaysian Airline system were imprisoned due to a pay dispute.[9] By law, strikes were illegal. The police could arrest and detain people for up to two years without trial, and in Malaysia the burden of proof was on the accused. Possession of a handgun got you the death penalty. So did drug trafficking, a charge automatically applied to anyone possessing more than 15 grams of heroin, about half an ounce.[10]

As for the Proton Saga, it was Mahathir's baby. Production started in July 1985 at the plant near Kuala Lumpur, where in a celebratory speech the prime minister declared that the Saga was "more than just a quality automobile"; it was "a symbol of Malaysians as a dignified people."[11] In truth, the car wasn't bad. With their Japanese tools, Japanese parts, and Japanese advisers, the Malaysians had made a *Japanese* car. It came with either a 1.3- or 1.5-liter engine and either as a four-door hatchback or a four-door sedan. Both models had a five-speed manual transmission, but the 1.5-liter had an optional automatic. The 1.3-liter sold for $6,708, the 1.5-liter for $7,254, which included air-conditioning, tax, tag, and registration. Priced a full $1,500 below its nearest competitors, the Saga was a hit. Within six weeks of its introduction, the Saga's full 1985 production run, totaling 8,050 cars, had been sold.[12]

But demand for the Saga was artificial at best. Malaysians bought the car because other cars were too expensive. Mahathir had seen to that. To the prime minister's great chagrin, however, in 1985 the domestic Malaysian car market shrunk 28 percent, to just 53,392 cars.[13] It had dropped nearly 50 percent since 1983. The cause was a grueling economic recession brought on by falling prices in the world commodities markets, to which Malaysia, a raw goods producer, was beholden. To make matters worse, the Japanese yen rose considerably in 1985, which meant interest payments on HICOM's 36 billion yen debt to Mitsubishi were costing the company an additional 40 percent.[14] By the end of 1986, Proton would owe Mitsubishi a cool $200 million. "The Malaysian government couldn't have done a worse job on a major industry if it had intended to destroy it," said one Western economist, who cited the country's poor automobile market and Proton's disastrous effects on Malaysia's assembly industry.[15] Indeed, throughout 1986, Proton continued to build cars below capacity, while thousands of assembly workers in hundreds of companies were simply laid off.

"It's certainly not a business for weak stomachs," said Ho Tet Kheong, the general manager of Assembly Services, Malaysia's largest private assembler before Proton was formed. "If get out we must, then get out we will."[16] Ho, like his colleague Zulkifli Isahak, was completely defeated. He could only look on in silence as Toyota, which experienced an 82 percent drop in sales to Malaysia in a single year, suspended shipments to his company in November 1986.[17] A month later Ho laid off two hundred workers. However, Prime Minister Mahathir, in implementing his country's industrialization drive, had expected the assembly industry to retract—but not that much. He'd also expected fairly strong sales from the Proton Saga, which failed to materialize. Forced into a corner, Mahathir's only option—and thus Proton's only option—was to export. Said Wan Nik Ismail, Mahathir's handpicked Proton director, "Export we must. We have to. Otherwise, there is no economic volume."[18]

By "economic volume," Wan Nik meant sales, first to Asian countries such as China, Sri Lanka, Indonesia, and Brunei, and then, if that worked, sales to Britain and the United States. But that was a big if. Proton's sales to the United States depended on two things: a wealthy importer with a good distribution network, and permission from Mitsubishi, which in spite of Mahathir's national car rhetoric still owned 30 percent of Proton and provided the company with engines, transmissions, and parts. If Mitsubishi said no, Mahathir's export plans were dead. Interestingly enough, Proton's original contract with Mitsubishi did not involve exports. The Saga had been designed and Proton's plant had been built for domestic use only. But, due to Mahathir's insistence, Mitsubishi allowed Proton to sell cars to countries where Mitsubishi and its partner Chrysler had a limited stake.[19]

As of 1986, Chrysler owned 15 percent of Mitsubishi and sold two Mitsubishi-made models, the Dodge Colt and the Plymouth Colt, as captive imports.[20] The two Colt models were identical to the Mitsubishi Mirage, which was also sold in America and which was a two-door version of the Mitsubishi Lancer Fiore, the same Lancer Fiore on which the Proton Saga was based. (A simple formula: Colt = Colt = Mirage = Lancer = Saga.) Thus, officials at Mitsubishi were less than pleased when in mid-1986 Proton began its search for an American partner. The Japanese company already had three Lancer Fiore models in America. It did not need a fourth, especially if sales of the Proton Saga undercut its own sales or that of the two Colts. (The Saga's price tag was liable to be cheap: Proton's workers earned about $150 a month and Mahathir was willing to subsidize exports.) "Mitsubishi does not want [Proton] to compete with Mitsubishi products on the world market," said one analyst. It "would be crazy to do that."[21]

But Mitsubishi also knew that even under the best circumstances it would be exceedingly difficult for Proton to recondition the Saga for the American market. Though based on the Lancer Fiore, the Saga was still a third-world car, a very basic version of the Mitsubishi Mirage model sold in the United States. It needed to pass NHTSA crash tests and EPA and California Air Resources Board emissions tests, and meet hundreds of federally mandated standards for everything from hood latches and brake hoses to rearview mirrors, head restraints, and brakes. Mitsubishi could streamline the process by providing Proton with engines and exhaust systems from its American-equipped Mirage, but why? As it stood, the Saga was 58 percent Japanese, meaning more than half its parts came from Japan. But according to the Generalized System of Preferences, an international trade agreement under the World Trade Organization, the Saga needed to have at least 60 percent Malaysian content to be considered a Malaysian car.[22] If not, it was considered a Japanese-made car and thus subject to Japan's self-imposed export quota to the United States, the famed Voluntary Export Restraint. Therefore, if Proton was to sell cars in America, it would have to decrease its Mitsubishi-made content by 18 percent; otherwise the Saga was a Japanese car that would count against Mitsubishi's quota. It was a lose-lose situation for Mitsubishi.

"Officially, the Japanese promised to 'consider' [Proton's export] proposal," wrote Fred Bartu, a Swiss journalist who covered Malaysia in the 1980s. But "in reality they resisted it from the very beginning." Mitsubishi "tried to stall the idea by suggesting that extensive market research was necessary which would take up to two years, that the technical modifications to make the [Saga] exportable would last as many years, and that this export plan would require massive new investments."[23] Mitsubishi hoped that eventually Mahathir would give up, but the irascible politician ignored Mitsubishi's advice and ordered Proton to find an American distributor. This was in mid-1986, at precisely the time that Yugo America exec Tony Ciminera was searching Europe and Asia for a second compact car. "Malcolm said go around the world," remembers Ciminera. "We need more cars. There was no Yugo Florida yet, and we couldn't keep asking dealers [to sell just the Yugo]."[24]

Ciminera had tried to bring over the Romanian Oltcit but, failing that, turned his attention to the East. He'd read in *Automotive News* and heard through his own industry contacts that a Malaysian company was badly in need of a distributor, so sometime in the summer of 1986 he traveled to Kuala Lumpur. "I went to Malaysia and found this brand-new factory in the middle of a jungle," he says. "A fabulous new facility . . . You could eat off the floors, it was so spotless." The car they were building there, the Saga, "was as good as anything built in Japan." It "was basically the same car that Mitsubishi was selling as the Mirage and Dodge was selling as a Colt . . . They'd only changed the grille . . . I told Malcolm the car was unbelievable compared to the Yugo . . . He said, 'Are you sure?' and I said, 'I'm telling you, Malcolm, it's not a diamond in the rough, it's a diamond.' Malcolm said, 'All right. I'll make a few phone calls.' And he did."[25]

Bricklin called Kissinger Associates. The firm's president, Lawrence Eagleburger, was already on Yugo America's board, but Bricklin didn't need Eagleburger, he needed Henry Kissinger, because the former secretary of state knew Mahathir bin Mohamad personally: Kissinger had taught the Malaysian leader at Harvard's International Seminar in 1967. However, Kissinger's entrée came at a price: a $200,000 consulting fee "to advise [Bricklin Industries] in connection with [its] efforts to import into the United States automobiles made in Malaysia," and royalties of $10 for each Saga that Bricklin eventually sold. It was a steep price, but Bricklin's Yugo was tanking in the United States, and Yugo America and its parent company Bricklin Industries (BI) needed a second car. They were desperate. Therefore, Bricklin agreed to Kissinger's terms in a contract dated October 15, 1986.[26]

On one level, the BI–Kissinger Associates contract was unnecessary. In 1986, production at Proton had fallen to just twenty-five thousand units. At that rate, the company was losing $15,000 per car.[27] The situation was so acute that Proton would have signed an agreement with anyone. But as James Robinson, the chairman of American Express, once said, "I may have met [the client] otherwise, but when you do it under Henry's auspices, it can be a more personal involvement . . . [It's as if Henry is saying] 'I can vouch for these guys.'"[28] By vouching for Malcolm Bricklin, Kissinger gave Bricklin Industries direct access to Mahathir, who met its executives at the prime minister's residence in Kuala Lumpur in late November 1986.

"Malcolm came over with Bill Prior and some executives and lawyers," remembers Ciminera, who was already in Malaysia, "and they took us to [see Mahathir] in a police car with flags flying on the fenders and all that. He hosted us in this big enormous room. A social protocol officer came in and gave us dos and don'ts. Then [Mahathir himself] came in. Bill Prior did a presentation and [the prime minister] was very impressed. Sitting there in the room were executives from the factory itself. And the prime minister just turned to them and said, 'Sounds great. Let's do it.' Just like that. We were stunned. The factory guys were a little miffed, because it was being rammed down their throats. I don't think they minded the car being exported to the U.S., but they wanted to explore it more and have more discussion. But [Mahathir] just said 'you will do it.'"[29]

Apparently the prime minister had been sucked in by Bricklin's "bullish" projections: sales of 80,000 to 100,000 cars per year for the next five years, and sales of 250,000 cars per year by 1993. To any sane observer, Bricklin's sales figures were stupefyingly absurd. First-year sales of 80,000 to 100,000 cars would make the Saga the second best introductory-year import of all time.[30] (In 1986, the Hyundai Excel set the record, with 168,882 cars sold.) For 1993, sales of 250,000 cars would make it the seventh most popular passenger car, and the eleventh most popular automobile of any kind in the United States.[31] Nevertheless, Mahathir liked what he heard. He especially liked Bricklin's pledge of $10 million to homologate the Saga, as well as Bricklin's planned production date of February 1988, which was a mere fifteen months away. Therefore, the prime minister said yes. The two sides signed a preliminary agreement on December 3, 1986. Shortly thereafter, Proton America Inc. was born.

The new company was a subsidiary of Bricklin Industries and was housed at Yugo America's Upper Saddle River headquarters in New Jersey. It was Bricklin's fifth automobile import company in twenty years, his third since 1983. However, in January 1987, Bricklin created a sixth import company known as Global Motors.[32] Global was a subsidiary of Bricklin Industries, and the new parent company of Yugo America Inc. and Proton America Inc. The goal, in establishing Global, was to create an automotive import company offering dealer franchises that sold multiple car marques at the same time. For example, a Global Motors dealership would sell Yugos, Sagas, Romanian Oltcits, and Indonesian Lincah Gamas. Each car would have its own showroom, or "pod," but share a single sales and service staff working under one roof.[33]

"We're going to be a driving force in the international auto industry," exulted Jonas Halperin, Global Motors' new PR head and spinmeister extraordinaire.[34] Halperin had come to Global from Yugo America, but in doing so, he hadn't left his office. That was because Global, Yugo America, and Proton America were one and the same. They shared the same buildings, the same executives, the same secretaries, and for a time the same phone numbers and fax machines. They even shared a single budget—which was Yugo America's budget—because Proton America and Global Motors had no income whatsoever. In Global's case that was fine. The company existed on paper. Its parent company, Bricklin Industries, existed on paper too. But Proton America needed $10 million dollars to update the Saga, money that Yugo America, which struggled through 1986, didn't have.

In all, the company sold 35,959 cars that year through approximately 250 dealers. Considering that few cars had ever been skewered in the press like the Yugo, the company's sales weren't bad; but because Yugo America was a wholesaler of very low-priced automobiles, its profit margins were low. The car cost perhaps $2,500 freight-on-board, meaning Yugo America bought the car from Zastava for $2,500 but was responsible for all shipping costs from Bar, Montenegro, to ports in Maryland and Texas. The company then had royalties to pay. First, it owed $60 per unit to Malcolm Bricklin, whose Bricklin Industries "awarded" the car's rights to Yugo America in 1984.[35] (Thus, Bricklin's royalties-only take for 1986 was $2.15 million. This did not include his salary as CEO or any other perks or benefits.) Second, it owed an estimated $50 per unit to Per Arneberg and Fram Shipping, and third, maybe $10 per unit to Nick and Gene Pepe, two original Yugo investors who sat on the company's board.[36]

With shipping costs, taxes, import duties, and royalties, the $2,500 Yugo probably cost Yugo America $3,000 before it got to the dealer's lot. Dealers themselves paid approximately $3,500 per car, which left Yugo America with a pretax revenue for 1986 of just under $18 million. But by this time Yugo America had more than two hundred employees, to whom it paid salaries, health insurance, and other benefits, with fat compensation packages for Malcolm Bricklin, Bill Prior, Dan Prior, Tony Ciminera, Ira Edelson, Jonas Halperin, and others. (The company had no shortage of executives. As of 1986, Bricklin had at least one son in management, as did Ira Edelson.) The company also paid for warehouse and office space (there were three very large facilities in all), furniture, computers, travel (including a limousine service for executives), accounting fees, and consulting. It paid Kissinger Associates between $150,000 and $200,000 in 1986 for Lawrence Eagleburger, plus a $50,000 installment (out of four annual installments) for Kissinger's help with Proton.

In addition, Yugo America paid for the salaries and expenses of seven or eight American employees working permanently in Kragujevac, and for the design and testing of three new Yugo GV models, the GVL, the GVS, and the GVX. In 1986 it also paid for a multimillion-dollar television ad campaign, its first ever. It paid an indeterminate amount for dealer warranty claims, and hundreds of thousands of dollars in interest to Manufacturers Hanover Trust and Nordic American Bank. The bottom line: $18 million wasn't much. Of course, Yugo America was able to augment its income through dealer franchise fees and bank loans, but its lifeblood was sales. "The company survived from day to day on cash flow that was being generated by the sale of cars at wholesale," says Marcel Kole, a Yugo America executive and assistant to Ira Edelson. "To the extent that . . . wholesale sales slowed up, then obviously there [was] a crunch on the cash flow of the company."[37]

Thus, Bricklin's $10 million Proton venture was risky indeed, for rather than spending the money on jump-starting his moribund Yugo project, he was robbing Peter to pay Paul. "The Proton was a project we really looked forward to as being successful," remembers Ira Edelson, but "it was a drain on our finances. Sales of the Yugo had to take care of our overhead, plus the expenses put into the Proton."[38] One major expense was transferring the Saga's steering column, which was mounted on the right, to the car's left-hand side, for as former British colonials, Malaysians drive in the left-hand lane with their steering wheels on the right. Though seemingly a small job, a steering column transfer involves literally hundreds of changes: the steering wheel, the steering column, and the steering box must be moved; the brake master cylinder must be moved; the pedals must be moved; and the dashboard and firewall must be replaced.

Building a left-side prototype would be difficult enough; moving the prototype into production by February 1988 was probably impossible. Even then, the Saga still needed to pass U.S. safety and emissions tests and required an increased number of Malaysian-made parts. That meant workers needed training and in some cases factories needed tools. "The vehicles are designed to Malaysian requirements only," stated one observer. "Their windshield glass isn't up to European [or American] standards, dashboards are made from plastic materials that could shatter in an accident, bumpers aren't adequate, and starters aren't suitable for temperate climates."[39] In short, the diminutive Saga required major changes. No wonder Mitsubishi was shocked when Bricklin said he'd prep the car for just $10 million and sell it stateside in fifteen months. The "Mitsubishi people were surprised," said a person close to the Proton project. Their estimate was actually "much, much more."[40]

The Japanese feared, in fact, that even if Bricklin succeeded, "exports of a second-class Mitsubishi Lancer Fiore might destroy the image of high quality and reliability that Mitsubishi had built" for itself in the United States.[41] Even under the best circumstances, Mitsubishi didn't want Proton as a competitor. But it was especially loath to compete with a slapdash Saga model that Bricklin would market as a low-priced Mitsubishi in the press. They'll "find a way to torpedo [the project] sooner or later," said one industry analyst, because the managers at Mitsubishi know that "there are too many things out of [their] control."[42] But Bricklin thought he could handle the Japanese. He'd smooth-talked them before with Subaru, and this time he had Mahathir bin Mohamad and Henry Kissinger in his corner. Mitsubishi would have to relent. If not, Proton America and its benefactor Yugo America were doomed.

14

Thirty-five Hundredths
of a Percent

Q: How many teenagers can fit into a Yugo?
A: No one knows: none of them wants to risk being seen in one.

The signing of the Bricklin Industries–Perusahaan Otomobil Nasional agreement in December 1986 put Zastava in an awkward situation. For over two years now, Zastava had trumpeted Bricklin as its savior-entrepreneur, a trusted *biznisman* and visionary who could sell its cars in the United States. With little warning, however, Bricklin declared that Yugo America's parent company Bricklin Industries would soon be importing cars from Malaysia. "Malaysia!" exclaims Toma Savic. "Here I was working like a maniac trying to make the Yugo work and suddenly Bricklin's negotiating with Proton. At that point we knew something was wrong. It was clear to us at Zastava that things weren't going well at Yugo America if Bricklin was starting another project."[1]

But, oddly enough, by early 1987 things *were* going well at Yugo. In January, sales of the Yugo GV stood at 4,174, a 9.2 percent increase over December and a 71.9 percent increase over January 1986. That same month Yugo America's top performer was Yugo of Pensacola, which sold an incredible 127 units.[2] Yugo sales continued to soar in February, to 5,059, which represented a 21.2 percent jump over January and a daily sales rate of 180 Yugos nationwide.[3] In March the company sold its fifty thousandth Yugo GV, and in June *The Wall Street Journal* reported that Yugo America's year-to-date sales (22,273) placed it third among European importers. Trailing only Mercedes-Benz (37,734) and BMW (34,780), Yugo America had sold more cars in 1987 than Saab, Audi, Porsche, Jaguar, Sterling, Renault, Rolls-Royce, Peugeot, and Alfa Romeo.[4] "Consumer demand has been heartening," stated Yugo America president Bill Prior, "and our sales projections indicate that 70,000 more Americans will be driving Yugos in 1987. More and more consumers are looking for reliable transportation at [an] affordable price."[5]

Helping Yugo sales was Prior's very shrewd decision in 1986 to keep the car's price at $3,990 through October 1987.[6] That meant that while prices of other subcompact automobiles edged upward, the Yugo's stayed the same. In 1986, for example, it faced thirteen sub-$6,000 competitors, two of which were priced at under $5,000. But in 1987 the Yugo faced just twelve sub-$6,000 competitors and not a single competitor under $5,000. The Yugo's closest rivals for 1987 were the Hyundai Excel (up 4 percent to $5,195), the Mitsubishi Precis (a new offering at $5,195), and the new Subaru Justy (priced at $5,495). Used cars were even higher: by early 1987 the average used car in America sold for $5,833, over $1,800 more than the Yugo and some $400 more than your average jalopy cost in 1985.[7] Love it or hate it, the Yugo was cheap. However, *cheap* was a word that Bricklin, Prior, and the other Yugo America execs were afraid of. They preferred *inexpensive*. They claimed, in the summer of 1986, that Rosenfeld, Sirowitz, and Humphrey (their well-known ad agency formerly known as Rosenfeld, Sirowitz, and Lawson) was no longer "meshing with [their] retail need" and that, as a result, the Yugo's image "was leaning toward cheapness."[8] Never mind that RS&H had emphasized craftsmanship in its ads, or that it had produced a nationwide print and TV campaign that Yugo America *never* implemented, or that the Yugo itself had finished dead last in 1986, thirty-three out of thirty-three, in J.D. Power and Associates' consumer satisfaction survey.[9] Forget all of that. To Yugo America execs, the reason the car's image "was leaning toward cheapness" was that RS&H "wasn't doing the job."[10]

RS&H responded with a resounding pshaw. "This agency does not intend to get into a shouting match [with Yugo]," said one spokesman, "but we can't permit reckless statements. They distorted the situation."[11] As RS&H described it, Yugo America had terminated the account because Len Sirowitz and Ron Rosenfeld, the agency's cochairmen, had refused to offer it credit. Yugo America "had no track record" as a business, said Len Sirowitz, and was "told specifically [that credit] would affect our relationship."[12] Sirowitz's fear, of course, was that Yugo America would go bankrupt, in the same way that Bricklin's SV-1 venture had gone bankrupt, and leave his agency holding the bag. Therefore, RS&H said no. Yugo America would pay up front and in cash for its advertising or it would find another firm, which it did in June 1986 when it hired Lambert, Dale, and Bernhard.

A brand-new firm, Lambert, Dale, and Bernhard had the good fortune of signing on with Yugo America just as its per-month sales and new dealer signings were on an upswing. For the months of January to June 1986, for example, Yugo America sold just 9,016 cars, an average of 1,500 cars per month. However, in July sales increased to 3,020, then rose to 3,400 cars per month from August to December 1986 before peaking at 5,059 in February 1987. Over that same period Yugo America increased its dealer network by approximately fifty dealers, each of whom paid thousands of dollars in franchise fees. With cars selling fast and fees coming in, Yugo America now had enough money to advertise.

And advertise it did. Beginning in July 1986, the company unleashed a two-year media blitz that featured 114 thirty-second commercials that aired in between segments of the ABC, NBC, and CBS nightly news.[13] The commercials were professionally done and appeared in the company of such ubiquitous TV ads as Bayer, Polident, Ex-Lax, Gas-X, Xerox, Burger King, Hanes, Stanley, Rice-A-Roni, Noodle Roni, and Thompson's Water Seal, which meant the Yugo was ubiquitous too. As of early 1987, the three network news programs reached over thirty-two million households per night.[14] Although not everyone was paying attention, no doubt millions of people heard the company's three new slogans: "Everybody Needs a Yugo Sometime," "The Toughest, Most Dependable Cars a Little Money Can Buy," and "Buy a Little Freedom. Buy a Yugo."

The ads weren't cheap. As of late 1986, Yugo America claimed it had spent some $8.2 million in advertising in just four months, more than twice what it had spent in eleven months with RS&H.[15] That number was probably an exaggeration, but later, in a bankruptcy deposition, one Yugo America exec insisted the company typically spent "around $800" on advertising *per car*, a huge amount by industry standards and the equivalent of $10.2 million.[16] "We incurred a lot of expenses in advertising," said Marcel Kole, a company accountant and assistant to Ira Edelson. "The dollars that we spent were not the most productive dollars" and our "goals [were] unrealistic . . . Certainly we created a valley we were unable to get out of."[17] Whatever the case, the Yugo's short but exorbitant ad campaign was a jolt to company sales. Between June 1986 and March 1988, for example, Yugo America sold more than 81,000 cars. But with low profit margins, high salaries and expenditures, and spiraling homologation costs for the Proton Saga, the company recouped little in terms of cash.

What it did recoup was notoriety, a very deep and very lasting notoriety that few products (and even fewer automobiles) have ever had. Consider this: in calendar year 1986 Yugo America sold just 39,853 cars, a tiny .35 percent of the U.S. market.[18] That's *thirty-five hundredths* of a percent, or 287.1 cars sold for every Yugo. But— incredibly—by mid-1987 the Yugo was a household name, a pop icon, a cultural artifact, even a unit of measure. It was a comparative, a pejorative, a synonym for *cheap* and at one and the same time a synonym for *failure*. The references were endless. "What's an economic downswing?" asked the Baton Rouge *State-Times*. It's "when Big Shots drive their stretch Yugos."[19] What could America do with $1 trillion, the 1986 federal budget? It "could buy every man, woman and child a Yugo," wrote the *Winston-Salem Journal*, "with about 15 million extra Yugos to spare."[20] How strong was NFL running back Joe Morris? According to *The Dallas Morning News*, he could "strap a Yugo to his back and bend down to pick up a penny."[21]

Even *Saturday Night Live* spoofed the Yugo in one of its infamous fake commercials. "These days, everyone's talking about the Hyundai and the Yugo," said spokesman Phil Hartman. "Both nice cars, if you've got $3,000 or $4,000 to throw around. But for those of us whose name doesn't happen to be Rockefeller, finally there's some good news: a car with a sticker price of $179. That's right, $179. The name of the car? Adobe. The sassy new Mexican import that's made out of clay. German engineering and Mexican know-how helped create the first car to break the $200 barrier." The commercial then cut from the showroom to a "real-life" fender bender, in which an "actual" Adobe driver used her hands to mold the car's bumper back into shape. Intoned Hartman: "Adobe. You can buy a cheaper car. But I wouldn't recommend it!"[22]

The Yugo also appeared, in the summer of 1987, in the movie version of the famed TV show *Dragnet.* Starring Tom Hanks as the sarcastic Pep Streebeck and Dan Aykroyd as the by-the-book sergeant Joe Friday, the film's funniest line involved an unassuming Yugo. After their first car had been stolen and their second car blown up, the Los Angeles Police Department issued them "the only car the department was willing to release to us." It was an unmarked 1987 Yugo, said Friday, "the cutting edge of Serbo-Croatian technology."[23]

Stand-up comedian Jay Leno, who was then a regular substitute host for Johnny Carson on *The Tonight Show* (he would take over from Carson in 1992), often eviscerated the Yugo in his routines. It was, in some ways, his trademark. Said the Los Angeles *Daily News*: there is "no truth to reports that Jay Leno will become the national spokesman for Yugos. He is an unabashed Yugo basher."[24] Among Leno's many Yugo jokes were: "Did you hear they're finally starting to carpool in California? It's true. Yesterday, I spotted three Yugo drivers in a tow truck."[25] "More problems for Dr. Kevorkian, the suicide doctor. It seems the makers of the Yugo are suing him for copyright infringement."[26] "Yugo has come out with a very clever antitheft device. They made their name bigger."[27] One popular joke referred to the Yugo's crash tests. Said Leno, safety experts had stopped testing the car because crash-test dummies refused to ride in them. "I'm a dummy," quipped Leno, "not an idiot."[28]

Likewise, Leno's comedic rival David Letterman panned the car in close to half a dozen "Top Ten" lists through the early 1990s.[29] The Yugo, for example, was number one in Letterman's "Top Ten Mafia Euphemisms for Death." Said Letterman to a drumroll, "Bought a Yugo." The car was number two in Letterman's "Top Ten Rejected Model Names for New Cars" (the "Yugo Screw Yourself"). Other Top Ten lists that featured the Yugo included the "Top Ten Demands of Striking French Truck Drivers" (#4: "No penalty for running Yugos off the road"), "Top Ten Surprising Revelations in the New Columbus Movie" (#3: "Fourth ship which didn't make it: the Yugo"), and "Top Ten Most Frequently Recalled Fisher-Price Toys" (#6: "The Yugo"). In a bizarre tribute to Letterman, in June 1991 Governor Pete Wilson of California issued his own top ten list, in lieu of a formal press release, explaining why his office had given up two Lincoln Town Cars during a budget crunch. The number ten reason: "The governor really had his heart set on a Yugo."[30]

In the summer of 1987, sportswriter Tony Kornheiser mentioned the car in a series of fictitious and very humorous *Washington Post* articles detailing the triumphant return to Washington of the Senators, a real-life professional baseball team that had left the city in 1971.[31] As Kornheiser told it, a group of politicians led by Senator Bob Dole had decided that a one-hour drive to Baltimore to watch a professional baseball game was simply too much. In their opinion, Washington needed a team. Therefore, they pressured Major League Baseball commissioner Peter Ueberroth into approving a new Senators franchise owned by Tang Ye-lin, a Taiwanese businessman who was the number one Yugo dealer in the United States. Tang's general manager, Eliot Suskind, was also head of his Yugo operations, and it was Suskind who used a Yugo GV as the Senators' official bullpen car. He called it the "Yugo-Get-A-Reliever."[32]

When the Senators won their fictitious home opener, an 8–6 no-hitter (!) against the Baltimore Orioles, Tang ran through the clubhouse shouting: "This is the greatest victory in the history of the franchise. Yugos for everyone!" To which Pappy Doyle, the Senators' starting pitcher whose son also played for the team, responded: "Thanks, but me and the boy here drink Scotch."[33] Over the course of Kornheiser's twenty-seven-part spoof-epic, the Senators survived any number of mishaps, including the on-field bombing of the team's Yugo-Get-A-Reliever by Senators fans angry with Tang Ye-lin for threatening to move the team out of Washington, to finish in third place. Not bad for a team whose uniforms sported a shoulder patch of an upside-down Yugo sinking into a bog.[34]

Mercifully, Kornheiser ended the series in October 1987, but just over a year later the popular show *Moonlighting* featured the car in a memorable season five episode in which detective Maddie Hayes, played by Cybill Shepherd, gave her partner and love interest David Addison (Bruce Willis) a new Yugo as a gift. "Ta-daaa!!!" exclaimed Maddie, who presented the car to David in front of seven or eight beaming employees. "It's for you!" Shocked into silence, David stammered: "F-f-for me? T-t-this car?" Yes, said Maddie. "I wanted to get you something you could use, something you needed, something you could be proud of. Do you like it?" Flummoxed, David responded that, yes, he liked it, but grimaced as Maddie drove off in her slick BMW. He then spent the rest of the show trying to have the car stolen. He even parked it in a bad part of Los Angeles with the keys in the ignition, but no one wanted it.[35]

Yugo America attempted to downplay its new reputation by issuing a carefully crafted statement to the press. Sent in May 1987 through the public relations news distributor PR Newswire to media outlets throughout United States, it read: "William Prior, president of Yugo America, Inc. is delighted, of course, to hear that Yugo is becoming a household word. And he's even more pleased with the acceptance of the Yugo among American consumers . . . 'There's just one word for affordable, dependable transportation,' says Prior. That's 'Yugo'—it's the definitive term for value.'"[36] However, Yugo America's press release was simply too little too late, as by this point Americans felt, almost viscerally, that the Yugo was crap. "One man wanted to give a Yugo to his daughter," reported *USA Today*, but when he test-drove it to his house his wife came out and said: "You're not bringing that [thing] onto my property."[37]

Around the same time, a Philadelphia dealership offered a free Yugo to customers who paid full price for an MR2 sports car or a Cressida sedan, but only one of fourteen buyers wanted it. The others got discounts. "Some of the people were a little reluctant to take the Yugo," said dealer Fred Loomis, who masterminded the "Toyugo" sale. "They'd say things like, 'Don't you have a 10-speed Schwinn bike?' or 'Do I have to take the Yugo?'"[38] *The Philadelphia Inquirer* covered the event and ran a front-page article with the headline "Dead Giveaway: Take My Yugo—Please!" Due to "this marketing marriage" of Toyota and Yugo, "the automotive Rodney Dangerfield from Yugoslavia, the two-for-one sale may never be the same." According to Loomis, the dealership's next promotion would include thirty days' free cellular phone service plus a radar detector, but no Yugo.[39]

Needless to say, the Yugo GV was a bad car, a poorly built car, some would say even a dangerous car. But in June 1987, *Popular Mechanics* magazine published a survey of one thousand Yugo owners who had driven their cars, collectively, for over one million miles. Astonishingly enough, 42.4 percent of respondents said they would buy a Yugo again, 36 percent said maybe, while only 21.6 percent said no.[40] That means over 75 percent of Yugo owners surveyed would or would have possibly bought *another* Yugo. A full 22.5 percent described the car's workmanship as "excellent," 54.6 percent found it "good," 15.9 percent "average," while just 5.9 percent found it to be "poor." Wrote *Popular Mechanics*: "A Maryland physician neatly captured the majority opinion: 'I'm very satisfied with my Yugo . . . It's not for the car buff, but it provides what it advertises: simple, reliable transportation at an unbeatable price.' "[41]

So why did the average American hate the Yugo? Why was such an unassuming automobile so universally panned on television, in movies and books, and especially in the press? By mid-1987 the Yugo had been on the market for less than two years. It had been advertised nationally and sold nationally for just one year. Sales were small by industry standards, and demand for the car was light. Yet, for some strange reason, the Yugo was famous. It was an instant classic, an anticlassic. It was a turkey, a lemon, a dud, a failure, a blunder, a boondoggle, and a bust. "I have no idea why that was," insists Pete Mulhern, who worked at Yugo America from day one. "Maybe it was Bricklin. He could sure sell. Maybe it was the communist thing, or the car's quality issues or maybe the price. I really don't know. But something about the car really set people off. You know the saying: 'loved or hated, but never ignored'? It was that kind of thing."[42]

Perhaps Americans reviled the Yugo because it was cheap—cheap in terms of quality and cheap in terms of price. After all, cars are status symbols par excellence. They show people who we are. "In the beginning, the automobile was designed as a means of transportation," wrote *Chicago Sun-Times* columnist Richard Roeper, "a mechanical horse, if you will. Today, the car still gets us from here to there, but it's become much more. It's [now] a status symbol, an extension of one's personality . . ."[43] Although Roeper penned his column in June 1987, his thoughts weren't new. Beginning with Carl Benz's 1894 model, the Velo, drivers realized almost instinctively that the automobile "was a compensatory device for enlarging [the] ego . . ."[44]

Through ninety years of motoring, nothing had changed. "They buy for many reasons," said one BMW dealer. But "there's some snob appeal involved, like wearing a Gucci belt. It's a sign that one has arrived, [that he's] a success in life."[45] Indeed, the decade of the 1980s saw a meteoric rise in luxury car sales. Between 1983 and 1988, for example, combined luxury car sales for all manufacturers, foreign and domestic, rose 28 percent.[46] Between 1981 and 1986, European manufacturers saw their luxury sales increase 87 percent.[47] Even Jaguar, the once moribund company on the verge of bankruptcy, had five record sales years in a row.[48] "The baby-boomers grew up with imports," commented a researcher with Merrill Lynch. "But they often started out with small economy imports. Now they are moving into their most productive and lucrative years. They have children and egos. Bigger and fancier cars are in. Small 'econoboxes,' regardless of quality, are out."[49]

However, 1980s materialism went way beyond cars. It was a decade when "consumerism became all-consuming," when brand-name clothes and brand-name purchases weren't just popular, they were an obsession.[50] Wrote one historian: "Millions of Americans now had enough disposable cash to buy expensive goods and services once limited to the upper-crust and to use their purchases to construct a private identity and a public persona." It was in the 1980s, he continued, that "Americans' pursuit of happiness degenerated into an obsessive pursuit of pleasure, [for] both indulgent experiences and beautiful things."[51] Even a cursory glance at the decade's most popular TV shows reveals a country enthralled with excess. "May you have caviar wishes and champagne dreams," crooned Robin Leach, the host of *Lifestyles of the Rich and Famous*. "Let us be your VIP ticket to the twenty-two-karat core of success!"

In 1984, *Lifestyles* was America's third-most-popular syndicated show.[52] The country's number one network show was *Dallas*, essentially a prime-time soap opera about an oil-rich Texas family led by the unscrupulous J.R. *Dallas* spin-offs and competitors included *Falcon Crest*, which peaked at seven in 1984; *Knots Landing*, which peaked at nine; and *Dynasty*, the number one show (ahead of *Dallas*) for 1985. America's favorite entrepreneur was "The Donald," or Donald Trump, a New York property investor whose most famous building was the ultra-luxurious Trump Tower. Built in 1983, the Trump Tower was a fifty-eight-story glass-and-marble monstrosity located on Manhattan's Fifth Avenue. It featured a mall with 40 shops and boutiques, 13 floors of office space, and 263 condominiums ranging from $600,000 single-bedroom apartments to a $12 million penthouse triplex. In less than a year, 90 percent of the apartments as well as the penthouse sold.[53]

In terms of fashion, Americans bought brand-name clothes, jewelry, and accessory items like never before. Think Calvin Klein, Ralph Lauren, Tommy Hilfiger, FILA, Gucci, Rolex, Izod, Nike, Members Only, Ray-Ban, Gloria Vanderbilt, Louis Vuitton, and Guess. "When you have on the most expensive brand everyone notices you," said one fifteen-year-old. "If you can't afford it, you're left out. You're a nerd."[54] The push for brand names was so intense that, beginning in 1985, food companies Dole, Campbell, and Kraft actually branded *produce*, as in fruits and vegetables.[55] In 1986, Americans bought 1.4 billion gallons of bottled water, which included import brands Perrier and Evian. At $1.7 billion retail, the bottled water they were consuming was at least a thousand times more expensive than tap water.[56]

In short, 1980s consumers were brand crazy. They were Yuppies, Boomers, members of the "Me Generation" who used their newfound wealth to buy status. Famed sociologist Thorstein Veblen called it "conspicuous consumption," a kind of consumer gluttony in which people purchased goods to display wealth and garner attention. In the 1950s it meant "keeping up with the Joneses." However, by the consumer-crazed, "buy or die" decade of the 1980s, it meant: "If ya got it, flaunt it." "MONEY, MONEY, MONEY is the incantation of today," read a 1987 article in *Fortune* magazine. "Bewitched by an epidemic of money enchantment, Americans in the Eighties wriggle in a St. Vitus's dance of materialism unseen since the Gilded Age or the Roaring Twenties. Under the blazing sun of money, all other values shine palely."[57]

In a particularly apt sign of the times, in 1987 one California company called Faux Systems marketed and sold 45,000 "Cellular Phoneys." At $15.95 a pop, Faux Systems provided customers with a fake car phone and a stick-on car antenna. The company's motto: "It's not what you own; it's what people think you own."[58] (The Cellular Phoney, believe it or not, faced several competitors, including Sharper Image's "Phone-E" antenna.) A nationwide youth fad in 1987 was the pilfering of Cadillac and Mercedes hood ornaments for use as jewelry. Kids simply walked through parking lots and tore off ornaments with their hands. "These are the 1980s," explained one New Jersey teenager. "You have to look appropriate. People look at you [and] it's nice to be noticed." Said another, "Cadillacs stand for money and power. When you wear one around your neck, it shows you got it."[59]

Certainly, upper-crust Americans thought so. In 1988, *USA Today* polled 1,100 executives throughout the United States who were asked: "What's the most coveted status symbol in your company?" The number one answer, ahead of profit sharing, salary, private office, or even country club membership, was company car.[60] Thus, Malcolm Bricklin's Yugo GV rose and fell and became an icon in the age of eighties excess, for as a car it was exceptionally cheap. But in the 1980s few Americans wanted cheap. They wanted bargains, to be sure, and the rise of Wal-Mart, another eighties icon, clearly attests to that. But cars were a different story. Cars meant status, and if your car was a Yugo, your status was low—low, low, low.

In a tongue-in-cheek article written in February 1988, the automotive writer Brock Yates sarcastically disagreed: "People buy cars to chase women (or men), to impress their neighbors, to intimidate their enemies and to generally elevate themselves in the eyes of others. The right car is a tool by which status slaves can accelerate up the social ladder . . . [Therefore,] I recommend a truly low-rent Yugo GV . . . Why? Because the Yugo is so bad, so slow, so outrageous, so antique, so outre, so 'Third World' that it brands you as a self-confident rake with a sense of humor."[61] Actually, no. As one high school student put it, in a list of what was hot and what was not for 1988: "Forget Yugos. No one really likes them."[62]

15

Mabon In, Bricklin Out

A man walks into a gas station and says: "How about a gas cap for my Yugo?"
The attendant says: "Sounds like a fair trade to me."

In August 1987, Yugo America celebrated its second birthday. That same month it sold its seventy-five thousandth car. "Our sales successes tell the story," proclaimed company president Bill Prior. "We're here to stay, and we will continue to offer the best possible values in transportation, with more new models coming soon for more choices at attractive low prices. We blazed the trail and we're hitting our stride."[1] Prior's optimism belied a far starker reality. Costs were up, sales were down, and Bricklin's Proton Saga project was eating up Yugo's income faster than it could make it. Monthly sales at Yugo America had been strong through August 1987 when the company had sold, on average, about 4,400 cars per month. But in August that number dropped to 4,201, then declined each month to a year low of 2,480 that December. Although Yugo America sold 8,960 more cars in 1987 than it did in 1986, its fourth-quarter sales for 1987 were down 21 percent. To raise capital, Yugo America announced in October 1987 that it would increase the Yugo's price from $3,990 to $4,199.[2] It also announced that a new Yugo model, the GVX, was on the way.

The Yugo GVX was essentially a souped-up Yugo. It had a five-speed manual transmission instead of a four-speed, and a 1300cc engine. It also had fatter tires, a more aggressive suspension, bucket seats, fog lamps, and various aero-body trim components, including a front air dam. Wrote *Car and Driver*, Yugo America has taken a "simple, innocent transpo-container . . . [and] dressed it up like a sex machine . . . It's the same basic formula for success employed by all the world's economy-car manufacturers: start with a small, lightweight sedan, pump it full of vitamins . . . and wait for enthusiasts to pound a path to your showroom door." But is the GVX, it asked, "a low-rent, high-speed alternative to cars like the VW GTI and the Mitsubishi Mirage Turbo? Not on your life, running dog bargain hunter."[3]

The problem was that although the GVX looked sexy, its performance was flat. The car did 0 to 60 in 13.56 seconds, just half a second better than the base Yugo, while its quarter-mile time was a sluggish 19.38. Thus, the GVX's performance improvement was moot, but it cost over $7,000. The one *Car and Driver* tested cost $7,472. "One could make a case for a four-grand bottom feeder being less than perfect," it wrote, but "[for that price] we can name fully a dozen cars . . . that deliver livelier performance, superior ride and handling, more room, a higher level of comfort, nicer accommodations and better assembly quality."[4] Although *Car and Driver*'s review of the GVX was, in a word, brutal, the 1988 *Motor Trend* review was even worse. The GVX made "ominous noises of a guttural variety," it wrote, then in the middle of a simple suburban road test it broke down.[5]

Needless to say, the pricey though tepid GVX did nothing for company sales. In fact, it wasted money, as most of its new parts were purchased in Detroit, then shipped to Yugoslavia before reexport to the United States—not a profitable plan. The money would have been better spent on the Proton; however, by late 1987 its own homologation costs were out of control. Said company CFO Ira Edelson, "Sometime around October 1987, I realized we had a problem. I went to Malcolm and told him: 'We need $20 million to finish the Proton project and to survive until it comes in.' He said, 'Are you crazy?' I said, 'No. These are my projections.' He said, 'Well, okay, if we need $20 million, then go get it.'"[6] With that, Edelson hit the bricks. He set up meetings with close to a dozen investment firms, including Shearson Lehman Brothers, but each in turn said no. "They received [us] very well," remembers Edelson. "They asked a lot of questions and were satisfied, we thought, with our answers. But then we never heard from them. It was obvious to me what had happened. They had checked Malcolm's financial background. He'd gone bankrupt in the past and had discontinued operations that had debts. Basically, Malcolm's reputation was that he was a great entrepreneur, a dreamer, a doer, but [was] not financially responsible."[7]

Once again Bricklin's reputation had preceded him. This was unfortunate, because Bricklin had kept an exceptionally low profile for over two years now and had given day-to-day control of the company to Bill Prior, a fact he cemented by moving to his 4,500-acre ranch in Meeker, Colorado. He had purchased the ranch in late 1986 for $2.3 million.[8] It had been owned, previously, by famed oil magnate Alphonso E. Bell, the founder of Bel-Air, California, and later Bell's daughter, Minnewa Bell, the wife of Elliott Roosevelt. The "Bricklin Ranch," as Bricklin called it, was a mountain paradise. Both the north and south forks of the White River flowed through it. It had thick stands of aspen, spruce, pine, and juniper; miles of meadows; several streams and lakes; and a herd of elk.

Bricklin loved it. To the ranch's hunting lodge he added a commercial kitchen. Then to the Bell house he added a glass-enclosed swimming pool, a bathroom with a fireplace, and a master bedroom with floor-to-ceiling windows and a panoramic view. Sculptures dotted the landscape. One in particular, a giant New Age piece called *Earth Mother*, was located so far into the forest it required its own road. To incorporate a kind of city theme, Bricklin had the ranch's propane gas tanks covered in graffiti. He even had a Yugo—or at least the outer shell of a Yugo—protruding from the roof of his barn.[9] The effect was startling.

"The people in Meeker will never forget Bricklin," says Dee Weiss, who did payroll at the ranch. "He had such flare. He sometimes wore boots and a six-shooter, and flew his helicopter a lot. He even landed in our field once on my husband's birthday. That's the way Malcolm was. The horses were scattering and dust was blowing everywhere, but Malcolm just said 'C'mon! Let's go to dinner!' So off we went."[10] The magnanimous Bricklin also hosted huge cookouts, busied himself with plans for a summer youth ranch and executive retreat, bought a local bowling alley, sponsored a rodeo and a sled-dog race, and donated $10,000 a month, at one point, to the Meeker chamber of commerce.[11]

Bricklin was in Colorado when Edelson found an investor, a New York brokerage firm by the name of Mabon, Nugent & Company. Edelson had heard of the firm through Yugo America board member and shipping magnate Per Arneberg. "It was a small investment house," remembers Edelson. It "agreed to raise $20 million [for us] by selling stock to its customers and perhaps keeping a percentage for itself. Another $20 million would come from Imperial Savings and Loan, a bank located in San Diego."[12] The only catch was that Bricklin was out. Both Mabon, Nugent and Imperial refused to invest in Yugo America with Bricklin at the helm. Said one person close to the deal: "Malcolm Bricklin is a terrific promoter. I don't think anybody would argue that point. But [he has to come] to grips with the fact that he's an ideas guy and not an operations guy." His "lifestyle and a management style . . . are inconsistent with running a company that has to pay attention to the bottom line."[13]

And the bottom line, as it were, was this: Bricklin would receive $13 million for his shares in Yugo America and for the shares of his three sons. Another million would go to Bill Prior, Ira Edelson, Tony Ciminera, and various other shareholders for a total payout of $14 million.[14] Of the $13 million that went to Bricklin, approximately $6 million was up front. Bricklin used the money to repay loans on his ranch and other business ventures, and accepted the remaining $7 million over time. He also received a five-year consulting contract worth at least $1.5 million, and the right to thirty-two Yugos he'd parked in Colorado.[15] He would also receive twenty new Yugos a year, plus insurance, through 1991. Nevertheless, says Edelson, "Malcolm was furious. Furious beyond words. I mean, Yugo America was his company and to lose it was a blow to his ego. But I spoke to Malcolm's son, Nathan, and we convinced him that if he didn't do this deal, we were all going bankrupt and he'd get nothing. So Malcolm agreed. He blamed me but eventually understood. It was the best thing that could have happened to him at the time. He got $7 million for a worthless company."[16]

Edelson was right: Yugo America was worthless. As of March 1988, the company had a net worth of $3.2 million but was losing

$1.5 million a month in operations.[17] With no outside investments, it would go bankrupt in June. However, Mabon, Nugent and Imperial Savings and Loan weren't buying Yugo America; they were buying its parent company, Global Motors, which in turn was the parent company of Proton America, Inc., the distributor of the Saga. The Malaysian car still needed engine and emissions modifications and possibly new doors but was due in America that October. It already had an ad agency, a nationwide dealer network (which was Yugo's network), and first-year sales projections of thirty thousand cars. *This* was the investment, not Yugo, and it was the promise of Proton that brought a New York investment firm and a San Diego savings and loan on board.

There were differences, however, in the two institutions' commitment. Mabon, Nugent was using its money and money from its investors to buy Global Motors, while Imperial was simply providing Global Motors with a loan. The San Diego–based S&L did not own Global Motors and had no seats on the company board. Imperial was a bank, but not just any bank: it was a community-based savings and loan association whose traditional job was to accept savings deposits from lower- and middle-class Californians and to use those deposits for home loans. It was your basic S&L and its profit was the very slim margin between what it paid its depositors and what it charged its borrowers.[18] Though seemingly a rough business, S&Ls were protected by the government, and through the fifties, sixties, and seventies, business was good. "Insiders called those days the 3-6-3 days," wrote one author, "when [S&L] executives paid 3 percent for deposits, loaned the money to homeowners at 6 percent, and were in a golf cart by 3 p.m."[19]

Unfortunately, "3-6-3 days" came to an end when, in the late 1970s, inflation went haywire and interest rates soared. In 1980, S&Ls like Imperial made, on average, 8.79 percent per year on their investments, which were made up, mostly, of thirty-year fixed home mortgages in their local communities. However, that same year the inflation rate was 12.4 percent, meaning America's S&Ls were losing money faster than they could make it.[20] In addition, S&Ls faced a huge problem with their deposits. By law, savings and loan associations were limited as to the amount of interest they could pay on customer savings. As of 1980, that number was 5.5 percent. But commercial banks faced no such restraints. They offered money market mutual funds that earned upwards of 16 percent. As a result, customers shifted their money in droves. In 1981, S&L withdrawals exceeded deposits by $25.5 billion.[21] The industry itself lost some $3 billion that year and another $3.3 billion in the first six months of 1982. It also watched its net worth decline twelve consecutive months in a row.

The S&L industry was in trouble. Congress responded with two very far-reaching acts in 1980 and 1982 designed to deregulate the industry to make it more competitive with commercial banks. Among other things, S&Ls could now offer money market mutual funds with no interest rate ceilings, issue credit cards, buy stocks and bonds and even junk bonds, and invest up to 40 percent of their assets in commercial real estate. There were also fewer regulators, and rules were loosened as to who could own an S&L and what they could do with its money. The result was an S&L free-for-all, with entrepreneurs, con men, and Wall Street insiders engaging in what one economist called "the largest and costliest venture in . . . malfeasance and larceny of all time."[22] The reason was that S&L savings deposits were federally insured up to $100,000 per account. That meant that fraudulent or stupid investments resulting in an S&L bank failure became public debt.

Imperial's investments were in junk bonds, essentially high-yield, interest-bearing IOUs issued by companies with poor credit ratings or no credit ratings at all—hence the name *junk*. They were risky, volatile, and murky, not what a "3-6-3" S&L would normally trade in. But these were the 1980s, when deregulation transformed S&Ls overnight. They became "powerful money lending/development conglomerate[s]" in their own right, wrote the authors of *Inside Job: The Looting of America's Savings and Loans*. They could now "make loans on, or even own, hotels, shopping malls, mushroom and windmill farms, tanning beds, Arabian horses, Wendy's restaurants, and hot-tub spas—or invest in junk bonds or futures markets. The sky was the limit and it could all be done with federally insured deposits."[23]

As of 1988, Imperial had $1.4 billion in junk bonds, the second-largest junk-bond portfolio of any S&L in the country.[24] It also had $136 million invested in Grand Wilshire Finance, a fraudulent car-loan enterprise in Los Angeles, and $20 million in Global Motors. (Actually, Imperial dropped $16 million on Global; the $20 million figure was for the press.) Global Motors' other investor was Mabon, Nugent and Company. In 1988 the firm had capital in excess of $70 million and had recently "developed substantial institutional equity and investment banking business."[25] Its goal, in acquiring Global, was to sell shares to investors at a significant markup. However, the linchpin was the Malaysian Proton Saga. If Global Motors succeeded in bringing the car to America, the firm would make millions. If not, Mabon's partners and investors would lose their shirts.

Said one person close to the deal, "We all got sucked in. But Mabon, Nugent was stupid. I mean really stupid. They bet the ranch. A company that'd been around since the 1890s bet its capital on this thing. On the promise of a car coming to America based only on what Mahathir said to Kissinger. He said, 'Yeah, I'll give it to you.' And Bricklin and Mabon, Nugent and everybody else built a castle out of this thing."[26] The bottom line: Mabon, Nugent was exposed. So was Imperial. Its seems that neither party, in blowing millions on Global, had asked a very simple question: What if Mitsubishi refused to provide Proton with parts? After all, Mitsubishi owned 30 percent of Proton, the maker of the Saga, and was to provide the company with American-equipped engines and exhaust systems and various American spec parts. Thus, if Mitsubishi reneged on the deal—and so far the company had put nothing in writing—the Proton was a bust.

The Mabon, Nugent–Imperial–Global Motors deal closed on April 29, 1988. Although Mabon, Nugent was in charge, the firm left Bricklin's entire management team in place. Bill Prior moved from company president to chief executive officer and chief operating officer, Ira Edelson continued as chief financial officer, while vice presidents Dan Prior and Tony Ciminera headed the Saga and Yugo projects, respectively. Meanwhile, two Mabon, Nugent representatives, Jeffrey Pollock and Peter Boneparth, acquired seats on the Global Motors board. As of 1988, Pollock was a partner at Mabon, Nugent in charge of investment banking.[27] He was also indirectly

Boneparth's boss. However, it was the twenty-nine-year-old Boneparth, a lawyer by trade and a specialist in corporate finance, who ultimately headed Global Motors. Boneparth was young, full of confidence, and brash. Most Yugo officials disliked him. He was "the epitome of what was wrong with Wall Street," said one. "He was great with numbers and probably made his first million four years before [coming to Global], but was arrogant and had no idea what was going on."[28] They called him "little Iacocca" behind his back.

Boneparth's plans for Global were simple: increase Yugo sales through a new $750 cash-back program on the Yugo GV, GVL, and GVS models and a 5 percent down, sixty-month finance program for new buyers.[29] The goal was to make it through the summer and to limit Yugo losses and thus Global expenditures until the Proton Saga came through. But Yugo America simply wasn't profitable. For May, June, and July 1988, the company sold just 7,971 cars, its lowest three-month total in two years. Over that same period it spent $4 million repaying its debts, with an expected $8 million to $9 million shortfall for 1988 on the way. That's when the news came. Because of its rising debt and simple inability to produce automobiles, Perusahaan's Malaysian management team was stepping down. It was replaced in August 1988 by a Japanese team from Mitsubishi.[30] The team was led by a former Mitsubishi boss and hatchet man named Kenji Iwabuchi, who in late 1988 canceled the Proton Saga.

Global officials were livid. At a board meeting in September, they decided to sue Mitsubishi for breach of contract. However, Global Motors and Mitsubishi didn't have a contract. Global's contract, signed in late 1987, was with Perusahaan, not Mitsubishi, and it was Global's responsibility to provide Perusahaan with a working prototype.[31] If anything, Global was at fault for expecting Mitsubishi to provide it with engines and emissions systems when Mitsubishi clearly opposed the project. That was the mistake. Nevertheless, Global's board voted to sue Mitsubishi for $100 million through a Washington, D.C., law firm recommended by Lawrence Eagleburger. Only CFO Ira Edelson voted no. "I told them we didn't have a case," says Edelson, "and that, plus, if we were going to sue such a major corporation, we needed money to do it. But we don't have any money. Everyone looked at me like I was crazy, especially Boneparth. But that was my opinion and at the end of the meeting I resigned."[32]

Edelson's last day was October 31, 1988. CEO Bill Prior resigned or was fired some ten days later, while vice presidents Dan Prior and Tony Ciminera left in January 1989. With that, the Yugo principals were gone. The men who had founded the company and who had followed Bricklin through thick and thin and to Yugoslavia and back were now out of a job. Yugo America was out of business. By late 1988, it had a 133-day backlog of unsold automobiles. There were six thousand Yugos sitting portside in Texas and Georgia and another ten thousand on dealer lots.[33] Worse yet, Manufacturers Hanover had canceled its line of credit, which forced company officials to sell several thousand Yugos to an Ohio liquidator just to make payroll.[34] "Tiny Yugo has big troubles," wrote *USA Today*. It "has lost about 20 percent of its dealers" in recent months, and Mabon, Nugent & Company, "the deep pocket [that] Global needed" to solve its problems, is "selling its stake."[35]

But selling Yugo was one thing; finding a buyer was another. No one wanted it. To recoup its investment, Mabon, Nugent could have sued Mitsubishi, but the Japanese company was rich and had more attorneys potentially than Yugo America had cars. The case was also thin legally, which is why, in the end, the lawsuit was never brought. Mabon's only option then was to eat the loss, an estimated $10.5 million for nine utterly boneheaded months of work. The firm never recovered. By early 1989, it had switched to cheaper headquarters, shaken up its directors, and laid off over a hundred employees.[36] Then, in 1991, its partners sold a controlling interest in the firm to an Italian financial services company named IMI.[37] As a result, the Wall Street names Mabon and Nugent have since disappeared.

As for Imperial, the San Diego savings and loan lost $15.8 million, its entire investment. But Yugo was the least of its worries. In mid-1988 the bank discovered that Grand Wilshire Finance, a car-loan company it had given $136 million to, had been selling the same loans to different banks.[38] The loss to Imperial was $38 million. Then, in December 1988, Imperial's junk-bond vendor, Drexel Burnham Lambert, pled guilty to six counts of stock manipulation under the Racketeer Influenced and Corrupt Organizations Act. Soon after, the Drexel representative who had sold Imperial more than half its junk-bond portfolio, Michael Milken, was indicted on ninety-eights counts of racketeering and fraud. The Milken indictment presaged a veritable junk-bond collapse. By December 1989, Imperial had lost $200 million. Its capital at the end of the year was a negative $60.1 million, and since it could no longer cover deposits, it was seized by federal regulators in February 1990.[39]

By that point Malcolm Bricklin had suffered an Imperial-like collapse of his own. Although he had received at least $6 million from his April 1988 sale of Global Motors, in December he stopped making mortgage payments on the Bricklin Ranch. In 1989 he was sued by Citibank for an unpaid balance of $98,171 on his Diners Club card, his helicopter was repossessed, and the Internal Revenue Service tried to sell off his property.[40] The IRS claimed that Bricklin owed $347,321 to the government for failing to pay federal withholding, Social Security, and unemployment taxes for seventy-three workers at his ranch. But "the problem," said one IRS officer, "is [that] whenever you're selling a piece of property this unique and this expensive and it's clouded with so many liens, the number of people [who could purchase it] is limited."[41] On two occasions the IRS attempted to sell the property but failed, then in January 1990 found a buyer.

The ranch sold for exactly $347,321, but the buyer was required to settle three claims senior to the government's claim before taking possession of the ranch. (In essence, he had bought just a piece.) Bricklin in the meantime could live on the property and was still technically its owner. He had until May 1991 to settle its debts or the banks would foreclose. In April, Bricklin sold the property to Henry Kravis, the billionaire corporate raider and junk-bond investor best known for his $31.4 billion leveraged buyout of RJR Nabisco in 1988. Kravis was a main character in the 1990 bestseller *Barbarians at the Gate* and, apart from Michael Milken, was perhaps the most talked-about Wall Street investor of the 1980s. Through his company KRH Colorado, Kravis paid $5.5 million for the property, which he scoured of Yugos and other works of art and renamed West Land Ranch.[42] Bricklin saw almost nothing from the sale. Whatever he made on the deal went to liens and other debts, but even then, said his attorney, "there's [just] not enough to go around."[43]

Bricklin had hoped that he could save the ranch through his next big scheme: a nationwide chain of automobile "megadealers" who would use high-tech video "closing booths" instead of showrooms. The 10-foot-by-10-foot booths, designed and provided by Bricklin at $50,000 a pop, were to give customers "a sound and light show . . . like no other in the automotive business."[44] The booths were to be set up in no fewer than one thousand U.S. car dealerships, who would sell a majority stake in their businesses to a national group, led by Bricklin, in return for cash. The dealers would retain 20 percent of their ownership and a piece of what essentially was a dealership holding company. The idea was that by banding together, shipping cars back and forth, and setting up closing booths, the company would "sell 100 percent of all cars sold in the U.S."[45] At least in Bricklin's estimation. He also predicted $10 billion in sales by 1990.[46] How did he plan to fund this adventure? Junk bonds.

Though intriguing to some, Bricklin's new idea failed to scare up investors. Having sold his ranch to Kravis in April 1991, in June Bricklin lost a $17 million judgment in federal court to John and Rebecca Bednarik. In 1984 the Bednariks had invested $350,000 in Bricklin's International Automobile Importers in exchange for U.S. distribution rights for the Yugo. However, the court found that Bricklin had misappropriated the Bednariks' money by setting up a company of his own, Yugo America Inc. The judge ruled in favor of the Bednariks and found Bricklin guilty of breach of contract and contractual interference.[47] Two months later Bricklin went bankrupt. "I am reluctantly taking this action to resolve my present financial problems," the fifty-two-year-old Bricklin said.[48] At that moment he had less than $50,000 in assets and owed nearly $20 million to some 150 creditors.

Yugo America went bankrupt in late January 1989. It filed for Chapter 11 protection as a subsidiary of Global Motors and was marshaled through the process by a company accountant named Marcel Kole. Kole was a vice president at Yugo who became acting CEO when Bill Prior left the company in November 1988. As Yugo America's lone company officer and the only remaining member of the Global Motors' board, Kole was assisted by officials at Zastava-Impex, the Zastava export wing, which had offices in New York. Impex paid Kole's salary and kept fifty or sixty people employed at Yugo America until the company's reorganization plan was approved.[49]

The plan was for Zastava and Genex, the Yugoslav export conglomerate, to jointly invest $24 million in Yugo America. Under its terms, the two companies would pay Manufacturers Hanover $5 million and Imperial Savings and Loan $2 million. Yugo dealers who pledged to remain Yugo dealers would receive a 100 percent refund without interest for all warranty claims. Every other creditor—as well as dealers who stopped selling the Yugo—would get 9 percent back, or just *nine cents on the dollar.*[50] It was a take-it-or-leave-it scenario, a $14 million payout on a $62 million debt.[51] In exchange, Zastava and Genex would own Yugo America free and clear. They would split its shares fifty-fifty and hold every seat on the Yugo America board. The creditors had no choice: it was either that or nothing. With a judge's approval, they accepted the reorganization plan in December 1989.[52]

16

"The Yugo Is a No-Go"

Q: What's the difference between a Yugo and a golf ball?
A: You can drive a golf ball 200 yards.

"The Yugoslavs were completely out of their minds," says Zoran Basaraba. "They didn't have a clue what distributing cars in the United States entailed . . . or that buying the [car's] distribution network was just the beginning. They saw it as an end in itself." Basaraba knew what he was talking about. He was one of the few employees to work at Yugo America both before and after its bankruptcy and he was also Serbian. Basaraba had come to the United States in the mid-1980s to study political science but in 1987 began working at Yugo America as a translator. However, Basaraba's skill wasn't in translation: it was in advising Yugo America as to how to handle Yugoslavs. "I was there to clear issues that required explanations on both sides," remembers Basaraba, and "in hindsight, there was a complete misunderstanding [by the Americans] of the Serbian psyche."[1]

The Serbs, explains Basaraba, went from "absolute disbelief" that Yugo would make it in America to being resentful and envious of Bricklin once sales took off. "Instead of supporting Bricklin [and seeing that] Yugo's success in America was because of Yugo America, they became arrogant . . . Frictions developed. All they heard was that Bricklin had made a lot of money, which was anathema . . . [to the] old Marxist philosophy that workers and manufacturers were supposed to benefit from their work, not distributors." Therefore, when Bricklin left Yugo America and Zastava pulled the company out of bankruptcy, its officials felt that because they had cut out the middlemen, their problems had been solved. Hardly. By investing $24 million in Yugo, Zastava, says Basaraba, "had only just entered the game."[2]

"The game," in fact, was far more than the Yugoslavs could handle. They had gotten a taste of it in January 1989 when Basaraba accompanied Yugo America CEO Marcel Kole and Zastava manager Toma Savic to the National Automobile Dealers Association convention in New Orleans.[3] Their job was to tell several dozen assembled Yugo dealers that Yugo America was going bankrupt and that Zastava would be running the company temporarily until a reorganization plan was approved. At the time Yugo America owed its dealers at least $5 million for warranty claims and sales rebates. If it went into bankruptcy, it would be unable to pay its debts fully or finance future claims or provide new cars. "Someone told me in advance to be careful," remembers Savic. "A friend of mine said 'Those dealers are gonna be pissed. One of them might hurt you.' I thought to myself, Hurt me? But why?"[4] Then Savic understood. The assembled Yugo dealers were private businessmen, in a sense investors, but not employees. They had put money into Yugo and they wanted their money back.

"In Yugoslavia, we didn't work this way," says Savic. "We didn't have dealers like Yugo America did. We had employees at each Zastava showroom and they got paid whether they sold cars or not. It didn't matter." But in New Orleans it did matter, for once the men told the dealers what was happening, they went berserk. Some began arguing, others became physically abusive, while still others pleaded with the company not to file. "The Yugoslavs don't understand the implications of the term *bankruptcy* in the U.S. from a marketing standpoint," said one. "We're shocked [they're doing this]."[5] One group of dealers even offered to forgive its warranty claims if by doing so it would keep Yugo America out of bankruptcy. Another group simply broke off ties with the company and sued.[6]

"That was the biggest thing," remembers Savic. "The lawyers. I spent hours and hours in the courtroom, mostly in federal bankruptcy court, but there were other cases too. I'd never seen anything like it."[7] In 1989, for example, the Association of Trial Lawyers of America formed a "Yugos" litigation group to assist lawyers who were suing Yugo America because its cars were "unsafe."[8] That same year, Imperial Savings and Loan sued Mabon, Nugent and the entire Global Motors board for providing "materially false information" about the health of the company when it secured its April 1988 loan.[9] Then a Global Motors board member sued Mabon, Nugent for withholding information prior to his investment; Bill Prior sued Global for wrongful termination; and a California stereo maker named Proton Electronics sued Proton America for trademark infringement.

"Everybody sued everybody," says Savic, and Zastava "had to sort through the mess before we could buy Yugo. It took a long time."[10] However, before Yugo could even emerge from bankruptcy it was sued yet again, this time by the family of Leslie Ann Pluhar, an ill-fated Michigan woman who drove her 1987 Yugo GV off the Mackinac Bridge. The bridge was and still is one of the longest suspension bridges in the world. Five miles long from shoreline to shoreline and 199 feet high from water to road, the Mackinac Bridge is a towering steel and concrete structure connecting the Upper and Lower Peninsulas of Michigan. "Big Mac" is awesomely scary, but by 1989 drivers had crossed the bridge over sixty-four million times with just two fatalities. It was the safest stretch of highway in the state and not a single car had ever driven off it.[11]

That is until September 1989, when the thirty-one-year-old Pluhar drove her tiny Yugo over the bridge's guardrail and into the water. According to witnesses, Pluhar was traveling north on the bridge when for some unknown reason she veered suddenly to the left and onto the bridge's median, a two-foot-wide strip of steel about four inches high. She skidded down the median a full seventy feet before swerving back to the right across both lanes. She then jumped an inner guardrail onto an outer guardrail, where she skidded another forty-five feet before falling over the side. It took her six harrowing seconds to hit the water. Officials at the bridge called it a freak accident and refused to admit that the bridge's design or road or weather conditions had anything to do with it.

But witnesses claimed wind was a factor and that as far as they could tell, Pluhar's blue Yugo was "caught by a sudden gust," and "appeared to be lifted" from the road.[12] The scenario made sense. Wind speeds on the bridge commonly exceeded 30 miles per hour and were at least 35 miles per hour when Pluhar drove across. Thus, to the average person conditioned by four years of mocking media accounts critical of the Yugo, the cause of the accident was clear: the car had been blown from the bridge. It was an instant Michigan myth, an urban legend, an enduring piece of American lore. The Pluhar tale appears in paragraph two of the "Michigan" entry of *The American Midwest: An Interpretive Encyclopedia*. It also appears in the Yugo's most recent Wikipedia entry and in hundreds of blogs and websites all over the Internet.[13] (In 2007 one viewer even suggested it as a topic for the popular TV show *MythBusters*.)[14]

The only problem is, it most likely wasn't true. "Wind had very little to do with the accident," said Max Coburn, the bridge's chief engineer. And "the height of the rail [wasn't] an issue [either]. At high speed[s], when you crash into a rail, it won't hold [you] in place ... [and] if you hit it at an oblique angle with a fairly good head of steam, you're going to go right over it."[15] Later, in testimony before a Michigan House subcommittee, independent researchers agreed. A mechanical engineering professor from Michigan State testified that a 36-mile-per-hour wind buffeting a 1,840-pound Yugo traveling between 55 and 63 miles per hour, the rate Pluhar was traveling, "would have very little effect." He concluded that "Ms. Pluhar's speed was not fast enough and the wind was not strong enough to lift up her 1987 Yugo."[16]

If anything, the bridge's low center median and low inner and outer guardrails were to blame. At just four inches high, the median failed to prevent Pluhar from driving up on it and actually launched her back across two lanes and onto the inner guardrail. The inner guardrail was an eleven-inch piece of pipe-tubing designed to redirect vehicles that hit it in a north–south fashion. But for the rare vehicle careening east to west or, in Pluhar's case, west to east, the pipe tubing served as a ramp. Her car struck it, jumped it, and landed on the outer guardrail, which was just three feet two inches high. As of 1989, the center median, the inner guardrail, and the outer guardrail were all below federal code. But the Mackinac Bridge had been built in 1957, and officials claimed that changes to its median or guardrails would be dangerous to drivers, affect its structural integrity, or require a complete redesign.

F. Joseph Cady, the Saginaw attorney who represented the Pluhar family, wasn't buying it. "The bridge is unsafe," he claimed.[17] And "the proof that could happen again is overwhelming. Why they never made changes, I don't know."[18] In November 1989, Cady filed suit against the state of Michigan, the Michigan Department of Transportation, and the Mackinac Bridge Authority, claiming that "design flaws" in the bridge had caused the death of Leslie Ann Pluhar.[19] For good measure, Cady also sued the New York architectural firm that had designed the bridge, the dealership that had sold Pluhar her Yugo, and Yugo America Inc. for importing the car. His claim was that the Yugo GV "was unsafe, unstable in windy conditions and susceptible to loss of control."[20]

The Yugo case would be difficult to prove. Cady had no way of knowing why Pluhar veered suddenly to the left—she could have been reaching for something on the floor, for instance—nor could he explain why sixty-four million other vehicles, including Yugos and cars even lighter than the Yugo, had crossed unscathed. However, Yugo officials stayed mum, reasoning that a tit-for-tat media confrontation would bring even more bad press, if that was indeed possible. And besides, the company's Chapter 11 reorganization plan had just been accepted by a Newark bankruptcy court and its creditors had until December 6 to approve it.[21] The plan included a 100 percent warranty rebate for dealers who stayed with Yugo, an estimated 150 in all, so why fight with Cady publicly and risk scaring them off? It was better to keep quiet and to answer his claims in court.

Meanwhile, Yugo America focused on cars. Through October 1989, while still in bankruptcy, it sold 9,183 Yugos, the same Yugos that had been sitting in ports in Georgia and Texas and also on dealer lots. It unloaded the cars by giving dealers a per-unit rebate of $750 and by instituting a highly unusual "Sell four, get one free" program.[22] It also shipped cars to Africa, South America, and the Caribbean.[23] The goal was to clear dealer inventories so that when Yugo America emerged from bankruptcy, it could begin selling a new Yugo called the GV Plus and a convertible called the Cabrio. The GV Plus was basically a Yugo GVX; however, its fit and finish and overall quality were better and it now had electronic fuel injection.

The Cabrio was a GV Plus with the top cut off. The cars cost $4,435 and $8,990, respectively. "We are trying to move from a 'ha-ha' car that everybody makes fun of," said John Spiech, Yugo America's new president and CEO, "to 'Hey, this isn't a bad car' . . . [It] takes time to turn around an image, but it can be done and we're going to do it."[24]

Spiech was aiming high—really high. In November 1989, *USA Today* named the Yugo its number one "Lemon 'n' Loser" of the 1980s. *Fortune* magazine called it "the Edsel of the Eighties," and Fox Television featured the car in the reality-based TV show *3,000 Miles, 21 Days, 10 Cents.*[25] In it, three teams of indigent Yugo drivers raced from Los Angeles to New York while asking for and receiving hand-outs from strangers. In July 1990, Tom and Ray Magliozzi, aka "Click and Clack, the Tappet Brothers," panned the Yugo in their nationally syndicated advice column. A reader named Nick asked if he should keep his 1986 Yugo, to which Tom responded: "At this point, Nick, you really have nothing to lose by hanging on to your Yugo. It's not worth anything on the used-car market, and if Yugo comes back, you'll have all the parts you need. If it doesn't, you can always try to buy a 'parts car' from some other poor, exasperated Yugo owner who hasn't maintained his sense of humor the way you have."[26]

In 1989–90, the Yugo also appeared in sports columns nationwide as first the Los Angeles Lakers and then the Chicago Bulls drafted basketball players from Yugoslavia. With the twenty-sixth pick in the 1989 NBA draft, the Lakers selected the Serbian center Vlade Divac in hopes that Divac would replace the great Kareem Abdul-Jabbar. "Whatever else you can say about the Los Angeles Lakers and their possible drive to another National Basketball Association title," wrote *USA Today*, "add this: They are lucky shoppers. After all, their Yugo is still running. Purring, even."[27] A year later, when the Chicago Bulls selected Croatian forward Tony Kukoc with the twenty-ninth pick of the second round of the draft, the *Chicago Sun-Times* wrote: "Since they already have the NBA's version of a Rolls-Royce [i.e., Michael Jordan], the Bulls went the economy route with their only pick of this year's draft. They selected a Yugo."[28]

For both players, the papers' Yugo comparisons were jokingly positive. But other papers weren't so nice. Angered by America's 5–1

loss to Czechoslovakia in the 1990 World Cup soccer champion-
ships, *Austin American-Statesman* columnist Kevin Lyttle titled his
headline: "Lowly Americans Prove to Be Yugo of Soccer Teams."[29]
The Baton Rouge *Advocate*, in reviewing the previous week's National Football League games, sponsored a "Least Valuable Player"
award. "The winner of that award," it wrote, "will be handed the
keys to a 1987 Yugo by last year's LVP [Least Valuable Player], Brian
Bosworth."[30] The Bloomington, Illinois, *Pantagraph*, in an editorial
critical of corporate sponsorship in sports, wrote: "For years [the
Olympics] have had a jillion official sponsors for everything from
timekeepers to toothpicks . . . [It won't be long before we see] the US
Sprint 100-meter dash. Or the 200- and 400-meter Runs, sponsored
by either Kaopectate or Yugo."[31]

John Spiech, like his predecessor Bill Prior, tried to spin the Yugo's reputation to his advantage. "We can take the jokes," he said.
"When was the last time you heard people telling jokes and talking
like that about Sterling, or Peugeot, or Suzuki, or Hyundai, or Alfa
Romeo? They don't talk about them. At least they're talking about
Yugo."[32] Talking, yes, but buying, no. The Yugo GV Plus and the
Cabrio weren't due in America until April 1990, and although both
cars were better than the first Yugo, they were still Yugos. "We've
been selling the same car for three years," said one dealer, who liked
the Yugo's concept but who desperately needed a new Yugo model,
such as the four-door Florida, for his lineup.[33] But Spiech had no
control over Zastava, and the Kragujevac company hadn't the funds
or the wherewithal to produce an American-equipped Florida. The
best it could do was the Plus and the Cabrio, with automatic transmissions in both cars by 1991.

Spiech was a capable car man. Before coming to Yugo, he had
worked for Volkswagen and Fiat/Lancia and for a time was general
manager of Ferrari North America. In 1982, he cofounded Lotus
Performance Cars, the American distributor of high-end Lotus
sports cars from Britain, which he sold to General Motors in 1986.[34]
But Yugo wasn't Lotus. Lotus had a devoted corps of wealthy Americans who paid upwards of $80,000 per car. In 1989, for example, the
Lotus Esprit Turbo SE cost $81,950 and was the world's most expen-
sive four-cylinder automobile.[35] Teenage boys had posters of it. James
Bond drove it in *The Spy Who Loved Me*, Richard Gere's character

drove it in *Pretty Woman*, and in 1989 the real-life boxing champ Hector "Macho" Camacho wrapped his Esprit Turbo around a tree.[36] Lotus's reputation was one of speed and status at a wildly exorbitant price. Then there was Yugo, Spiech's new project, the number one "Lemon 'n' Loser" of the 1980s.[37]

"Mr. Spiech seems like an odd [choice] for the Yugo post," wrote *The Atlanta Journal-Constitution*. "His automotive resume includes management jobs for such exotic sports-car brands as Italy's Ferrari and England's Lotus . . . But a year after joining Yugo, Mr. Spiech is still at his post, and Yugo is still hanging on."[38] The company "hung on" because of Zastava. It bankrolled Spiech at $250,000 a year, five or six Yugoslavs, and an American sales and service force of about seventy employees. It also covered Yugo's warranty claims, the purchase of several hundred automatic transmissions from Peugeot, and the first commercials of a new $8 million ad campaign. The campaign was run by Buckley/DeCerchio Inc., an upstart ad agency whose first Yugo commercial was a prime-time spot called "the Shaker."

"The Shaker" ran during an episode of *Twin Peaks*, the surreal murder mystery by director David Lynch, and featured a red GV Plus suspended upside down from a rig. The rig, wrote one author, resembled "the one Sigourney Weaver used to fight off the enemy in *Aliens*."[39] It shook the car violently, but by the end of the commercial only a quarter had fallen out. Said a spokesman: "The reliable new Yugo. Now for just $4,400—and some change." Spiech loved it. "That's the statement we need to make," he said. "We want people to look at this commercial and say, 'Hey, this car is reliable.'"[40] "The Shaker" was cool, very cool. *USA Today* gave it four out of five stars and rated it one of the best automotive commercials of 1990.[41] Unfortunately, it did nothing for company sales. Yugo America sold just 6,359 cars that year, fewer even than during the bankruptcy and Mackinac Bridge–plagued year of 1989.[42]

Spiech, however, was optimistic. "I have news for [the] analysts," he said. "Times are tough for everyone, not just Yugo."[43] Indeed, times *were* tough for everyone, automakers included, because in 1990 America was in a recession. Car sales for the year by domestic and foreign manufacturers were down 5.3 percent, with sales of the number one car, the Honda Accord, down 13 percent.[44] But even with the recession, 6,300 cars was a disaster, a complete and total disaster. By comparison, in 1990 Sterling and Peugeot sold just 3,317 and 4,261 cars, respectively.[45] Less than a year later they were gone. Daihatsu sold 14,984 cars in 1990 and by early 1992 it, too, was gone.[46] "I don't believe the Yugo project will last the next two years under the current situation," said economist Kazimir Zivko Pregl. And "I don't think it would be good to push this project when there is no demand in the U.S. . . ."[47]

Pregl was spot-on. But he wasn't just an economist; he was deputy prime minister of Yugoslavia's Federal Executive Council, a kind of congressional subcommittee that formulated legislation before passing it on to a federal assembly for debate. Pregl's boss was Prime Minister Ante Markovic, a reformist Croat whose objective, wrote one scholar, "was to transform Yugoslavia into a developed, Western-style democracy with a modern, market economy." To that end, Markovic liberalized trade by freeing imports, converted the dinar from a soft currency to a hard currency, lifted restrictions on small business, and called for state-run enterprises, such as Zastava, "to operate without subsidies in accordance with the laws of the market."[48] Thus, under Markovic's program, Zastava would either sink or swim; it would make money or go bankrupt. But Markovic was the federal prime minister. He had no say over the republican affairs of Serbia, Croatia, Slovenia, Bosnia, Macedonia, or Montenegro, whose presidents opposed his plan.

Chief among them was Slobodan Milosevic, the president of Serbia. Although previously a die-hard communist and supporter of multiethnic Yugoslavia, in 1987 Milosevic shifted course and became a Serb nationalist. His goal was to position himself as a protector of Serbs living not only in Serbia but in Bosnia, Croatia, and in two autonomous provinces within Serbia known as Vojvodina and Kosovo. In 1989, Milosevic stripped the two provinces of their autonomy, a move that was illegal under Yugoslavia's federal constitution and that prompted Slovenia and Croatia to resist. They resisted by legalizing all noncommunist political parties, which meant no more Marxism-Leninism in Yugoslavia, and by installing national leaders of their own, such as Milan Kucan in Slovenia and Franjo

Tudjman in Croatia. Standing on the sidelines was Ante Markovic, the federal prime minister. Markovic believed in a peaceful, unified Yugoslavia, which, with Milosevic in charge, wasn't going to happen.

The Serb president controlled the Yugoslav army and since mid-1990 had been giving weapons to Serb paramilitary groups in Croatia and Bosnia. If either republic attempted to leave Yugoslavia, the Serbs there would go to war. However, Slovenia was ethnically homogenous. It had very few Serbs and was located at the far northwest corner of Yugoslavia next to Austria and Italy, somewhat distant from Serbia. Therefore, Milosevic did (relatively) nothing when Slovenia declared its independence in June 1991. But Croatia and Bosnia were a different story. The two republics bordered Serbia. They also had over two million Serbian inhabitants, who promptly rebelled when Croatia in June 1991 and Bosnia in March 1992 declared their independence. The Serbs set up small guerrilla states, one in Bosnia, one in Croatia, and began killing or ejecting all non-Serbs from their territories. This was "ethnic cleansing." The Croats of Croatia and the Muslims and Croats of Bosnia responded in kind. The fighting was door-to-door, house-to-house, and very, very bloody.

"Can there be a Yugo without Yugoslavia?" asked *The Washington Times*.[49] The answer was no. The Yugo GV contained parts from all six Yugoslav republics, and as of 1991, it had 205 different domestic suppliers. Almost all of its plastic came from Croatia. Its alternators came from Slovenia. Its seats came from Kosovo. "That was Tito's system," says Barbara Wendling, who worked in Kragujevac. "Zastava was, like, the second biggest business in all of Yugoslavia, so [government planners] very consciously spread things out."[50] In fact, Zastava had just 124 suppliers within Serbia and Montenegro (its sister republic) and only 7 within Kragujevac itself. The other 81 were outside of its borders, some in war zones such as Knin, Osijek, Borovo Selo, Bjeljina, Brcko, Gorazde, Mostar, and even Sarajevo. "We've always been proud to be a Yugoslavian factory," said one Zastava official, but "we can't cooperate with those people [anymore]."[51]

But no parts meant no cars, and without cars Zastava ground to a halt. "The enterprise was so broke," wrote one scholar, "it could only import its sheet metal against advanced payment and for

months had been paying its increasingly mutinous workforce . . . in
its own IOUs."[52] Back in the States, Zastava tried to ignore the war
and attempted to jump-start Yugo sales by replacing John Spiech
with Bill Prior, who returned to the company in mid-April 1991.[53]
By this point Serbs and Croats were fighting intermittently in southern Croatia: in a national park called Plitvice, in a Serb enclave called
Pakrac, and in a tiny village on the Serb-Croat border known as Borovo Selo. The village was home to a Zastava supplier; it was also
home to a group of radical Serbs who in May 1991 killed and allegedly mutilated twelve Croat policemen in an ambush. Known in
Croatia as the Borovo Selo "Massacre" and in Serbia as the Borovo
Selo "Incident," the ambush was the first act of the Yugoslav Wars.

Prior ignored it; his job was to sell cars. "I [needed] to come back
and give it a try," he said. "It was unfinished business, from my
standpoint. I basically asked myself three things. The first was, 'Is
there a place for this car?' The second was, 'Is there a way to effec-
tively and efficiently communicate the benefits of this car?' And the
third was, 'Could I envision a significant improvement in sales?' I
thought so, although I cannot be very definitive at this time."[54] Prior
did say that Yugo America was "in triage" and that in May 1991 at
least 60 of its 175 dealers "sold no cars at all."[55] To increase sales,
Prior announced customer incentives of $550 per car on 1991 mod-
els and $700 per car on 1990 models. He also gave dealers $300 per
car for advertising and bought old Yugo models from dealers if they
bought new Yugo models in return. The plan didn't work. In June,
Yugo America sold just 228 cars, a 55.5 percent drop from June
1990.[56] The company, along with its country, was doomed.

By this point, the usual Yugo jokes, already popular, took on a
somewhat darker appeal. "In Eastern Europe, Slovenia and Croatia
are still fighting for their independence because they don't want to
be associated with Yugoslavia," quipped Jay Leno in July 1991. "I can
understand that. Would you want to be associated with any country
that has the name Yugo in it?"[57] Jeff Danzinger of *The Christian Science Monitor* ran a political cartoon that showed a driver staring in
disbelief as his Yugo's bumper, wheel, and various other parts began
falling off. Read the caption: "Why Yugo owners are not surprised
by recent events."[58] A few years later, in an episode of the acclaimed

show *TV Nation*, filmmaker Michael Moore drove a blue Yugo back and forth between the Serb and Croat embassies in Washington, D.C. Moore called it "shuttle diplomacy." It was his way of getting the two countries "to knock it off." Said Moore to the Croat ambassador: "I have a Yugo, and I'd like to know which one of you sovereign nations is responsible for the warranty." To which the Croat replied, "The Serbs."[59]

Bill Prior left Yugo America for a second time in November 1991. The company's ten-month sales figures were a super tiny 2,461 cars, less than two cars per dealer per month.[60] Yugo hung on until April 1992, when finally its last director, a Serb by the name of Ilija Pavlovic, filed a Chapter 7 bankruptcy petition in a Newark, New Jersey, court. The company's petition listed $600,000 in assets versus $15 million in liabilities. They "notified me by regular mail," said one dealer, "not even special delivery. And the letter was unsigned."[61] Said another, "I just got a fax of a fax . . ."[62] It stated that Zastava was withdrawing from the United States because "uncertainties in Yugoslavia" had "made it impossible to provide Yugo America with a regular and dependable supply of vehicles and necessary financial support." It said nothing of warranties, which Zastava was responsible for, but claimed it would investigate "the possibility" of supplying spare parts.[63]

"[I have] Yugo parts coming out of my you-know-what," exclaimed a Nevada dealer. What he wanted was a reimbursement. According to *Automotive News*, both Sterling and Daihatsu, "last year's . . . dropouts," had promised to honor warranty claims by retaining parts and service operations in the United States.[64] But neither company was bankrupt: Yugo America had sold its chairs. It gave one employee a Yugo GV Plus in lieu of a paycheck. "A Chapter 7 means it's done and over," said one company official.[65] The "Yugo is a no-go."[66] Said Vernon Vig, a New York attorney who assisted Daihatsu with its warranty claims: "There are a whole host of duties and obligations to various constituents—dealers, customers, and government agencies—even if they're not as clear as they might be. But I don't know what happens in a case like Yugo. I think everybody's probably out of luck."[67]

17

"ZMW, Get It?"

Q: Why are Yugo drivers like corned beef?
A: They both come in tin cans.

On May 30, 1992, the United Nations Security Council voted unan-imously to impose a series of very strict sanctions on Serbia and Montenegro for supporting Serb rebels in Bosnia. They included bans on all Serbian imports and exports except for food and medi-cine and the seizure of Serbian property, businesses, and bank ac-counts worldwide. That same day President George H. W. Bush issued Executive Order 12808, which froze Serb accounts and pro-hibited American businesses and individuals from conducting trade and other transactions with Serbia and Montenegro. "The measures that I have taken today," wrote Bush in a letter to Congress, "express our outrage at the actions of the Serbian and Montenegrin govern-ments, and will prevent those governments from drawing on monies and properties within U.S. control."[1] In all, Executive Order 12808 (and later 12810 and 12831) blocked an estimated $450 million in Serb holdings.[2]

Federal agents from the Office of Foreign Assets Control (OFAC) in the U.S. Department of Treasury quickly assembled a Serbian blacklist of over one thousand individuals and businesses whose names they printed in the *Federal Register*.[3] Among them were Zastava, Zastava-Impex, and Genex, the three companies who owned or ran Yugo America, as well as Jugobanka, the New York–based bank where they got their money. When agents seized assets they often descended on a Serb-owned business in dark cars, suits, and sunglasses à la Eliot Ness. "They took all our keys and changed the locks," recalled the president of a Philadelphia machine-tools firm. "They [even] changed the code on the burglar alarm . . . [and] told me to cut up our credit cards."[4] In several East Coast ports, Serbian and Montenegrin ships were grounded for over two years while their poor, unfortunate sailors were stranded aboard. In Baltimore the nine-man crew of the *Durmitor* survived on church donations, Nintendo video games, and daily episodes of *Days of Our Lives*. Their only link to the world: a seventeen-foot dinghy provided by a U.S. representative and Serbian-American named Helen Delich Bentley.[5]

One very famous casualty of America's Serbian sanctions was the chess player Bobby Fischer. In fall 1992 the reclusive Fischer emerged from a twenty-year-long retirement to play Boris Spassky, his old Russian rival, in a series of televised matches in Sveti Stefan, Montenegro, and Belgrade, Serbia. The winner got $3.35 million, the loser $1.65 million. But, according to the U.S. Department of Treasury, even playing in the tournament was "a violation of U.S. law" punishable by up to ten years in prison and a $250,000 fine.[6] Therefore, it told Fischer to cease and desist. Fischer played anyway, defeating Spassky ten games to five. He was indicted by a federal court and a warrant was issued for his arrest. Said Richard Newcomb, the director of OFAC, Fischer "ignored our written opinion" and his indictment is "a message to other would-be violators."[7] Known for his outlandish opinions, Fischer blamed the indictment on a worldwide Zionist conspiracy. He refused to return home and spent the rest of his life in exile, dying in Iceland in 2008.

Fortunately, Yugo America's Chapter 7 bankruptcy proceeding spared it and its dealers a similar confrontation with OFAC. They were lucky. Toma Savic claims that certain Serb officials at Yugo America began hiding assets even before the bankruptcy, and that in conjunction with Zastava they established a private shell company, unknown to OFAC, called Car Parts Accessories International (CPAI). "Instead of being Zastava-owned or government-owned," said Savic, "which meant it would be subject to UN sanctions, CPAI was registered by a private citizen and Zastava's half was hidden by a lawyer from Switzerland."[8] CPAI moved cars, parts, computers, fax machines, furniture, money, even two refrigerators and a microwave. Yugo's 57,000-square-foot headquarters was picked clean.

Nevertheless, in September 1992, the owner of the property held an auction to sell what was left: a forklift, some potted plants, office supplies, company memorabilia, and parts. "Yugo key rings!" shouted the auctioneer. "You'll never see these again!"[9]

Yugo America's Chapter 7 bankruptcy wasn't a surprise. But war, sanctions, and bankruptcy were too much for Zastava to bear. By November its parent company, Zastava Group, had laid off more than thirty thousand employees. They each received unemployment benefits of $50 to $100 a month. "I remember we cried with joy when the first Yugo left our factory for America," said one worker. "Now, many of us are crying because tomorrow we may not have bread to eat . . . How are we going to survive?"[10] Zastava survived by manufacturing machine guns, mostly AK-47s, popular in Bosnia and Croatia and in conflict zones worldwide. Its car production came to a halt. From June to October 1992, Zastava produced just three thousand cars, but its workers blamed America, not Slobodan Milosevic, and rallied behind the Serb leader when President George H. W. Bush and Secretary of State Lawrence Eagleburger began criticizing him.[11]

Eagleburger became secretary of state in August 1992 after a three-year stint as deputy secretary of state under James A. Baker. Eagleburger's appointment was highly controversial. After all, he was a partner and protégé of Henry Kissinger, whose pragmatic foreign policy and secretive business interests irked conservatives, such as North Carolina senator Jesse Helms, who grilled Eagleburger for two straight days in confirmation hearings in March 1989. Eagleburger had left the Yugo board in January. He'd also left Kissinger Associates and its partner firm Kent Associates and had "terminated . . . each and every prior business and commercial affiliation [he] ever had."[12] But Helms was skeptical. He called Kissinger a "revolving, peripatetic entity . . . a political entity," and questioned whether Eagleburger's work for Kissinger "conflicted with laws [requiring] those who lobby for foreign governments to register their activities" with the United States."[13] At issue was Kissinger's client list, which included Yugo America Inc. and a New York branch of a Yugoslavian bank named LBS.

"If Lawrence Eagleburger is confirmed as deputy secretary of state," wrote an op-ed in the San Francisco Chronicle, "he will bring with him a wealth of experience dealing with Yugoslavia—maybe too much wealth. Eagleburger has revolved in and out of the diplomatic door. While he was in, he hustled loans from American banks for Yugoslavia. While he was out, he joined the board of directors of a Yugoslavian bank that benefited from those loans. While he was in, he encouraged Yugoslavia to generate hard cash by producing exports. While he was out, he became the top American representative for one of those exports—the Yugo car."[14]

Eventually, Helms approved of Eagleburger's candidacy, which passed 19–0 in committee and was rubber-stamped by the Senate. However, Eagleburger agreed "to disqualify himself from all matters involving former clients of the firm during his government service" and to take a hands-off approach with Yugoslavia.[15] "I stayed out of [Yugoslavia]," he later told *The New York Times*, "partly because [Secretary of State] Baker was involved with it and partly because I was previously involved there."[16] Once the Yugoslav Wars began, though, critics claimed that Eagleburger was pro-Serb, and that he, national security advisor (and former Kissinger Associates partner) Brent Scowcroft, and successive ambassadors to Yugoslavia John Scanlan and Warren Zimmermann had "a longtime, sentimental attachment to Yugoslavia and the Belgrade regime, a kind of clientism, which affected their views and had an influence on American policy."[17]

America's policy, such as it was, was noncommittal. Although Croatia and Slovenia had been independent since June 1991, Washington refused to recognize the two governments until April 1992. It also withheld its support for UN sanctions against Serbia until late May, which was after Serbia's eighty-seven-day siege of Vukovar, a Croatian border town, and after Serb irregulars, supported by Milosevic, had "liberated" huge stretches of Bosnia and Croatia. "Perhaps we should have been tougher on the Serbs," said one diplomat. "But some argue that the Serbs were going to do what they did anyway. Maybe the policy didn't work, but it seemed to Eagleburger the best of a series of lousy options."[18] Whatever the case, America's standoffishness aided Milosevic, and it wasn't until after Eagleburger left office that Washington got tough with the Serbs. It did so reluctantly, but the Croatian and Bosnian Wars ended, finally and through U.S. mediation, in November 1995.[19]

Milosevic remained in power. He agreed not to meddle in the

internal affairs of either Croatia or Bosnia in exchange for the lifting of UN sanctions and the return of Serbia's property and bank accounts. But Milosevic was in trouble. He had spent or stolen Serbia's foreign currency reserves, had given whole industries to his friends, family members, and political cronies, and had run the economy into the ground. Said one businessman: "Milosevic's power is based . . . on nepotism. Those who support him get rich, really rich. [And] those who do not, starve."[20] According to one source, 20 percent of Serbs were "at or below the poverty line," and "while a family of four need[ed] $250 a month for basic necessities, the average monthly salary [was] $100."[21] In Kragujevac, workers languished. They survived by pooling their unemployment checks, living in tiny apartments with in-laws and extended family members, and generally by shverz-ing, the art of the black marketeer. "When I had job, I had dignity," said one worker. "Now I have to make do with smuggling cigarettes and chewing gum, and we still can't make ends meet."[22]

Zastava had hoped that with the end of sanctions it could attract a foreign buyer. But Milosevic was fickle, and Serbian law at the time prevented foreigners from owning more than 49 percent of any one business. "Foreign companies come in here, take one look at what is going on and pack up and leave," said a Western diplomat. "We don't even bring in trade delegations now; it's no use."[23] Nevertheless, in March 1996, the director of Zastava's automotive operations announced that Renault, Fiat, and Toyota were all interested in purchasing the company and that soon he'd be toasting the workers with "champagne, cappuccino or sake."[24] What they got was sour milk. "Who is going to invest in this country while [Milosevic is] in power?" said one critic. "You can't even begin to discuss [privatization] until you actually create the institutions of a legal state," which Serbia didn't have.[25]

In November 1996, for example, a coalition of opposition parties known as Zajedno (Together) defeated Milosevic's Socialist Party in over thirty local elections, but a court controlled by Milosevic annulled the results. To protest, thousands took to the streets. They blew whistles and horns, set off fireworks, gave speeches, sang songs, and brought traffic in Serbia to a halt. In Kragujevac, an estimated 15,000 people protested every day for two months. But the workers weren't among them. In August and September 1996, they had struck for five full weeks but had come away empty-handed. Over 250 had been fired. Thus, during the Zajedno protests, workers stayed home for fear of reprisal. "The workers are so beaten down that they just don't feel like defying the system now," said one Zastava mechanic. "We just want to survive."[26]

However, it was Milosevic who survived. In February 1997 he reinstated the election results but used a series of Machiavellian measures to break the coalition and to co-opt one of its members. He then focused Serbia's attention on Kosovo. The tiny province in the south of Serbia was the cradle of Serbian identity, a kind of Serbian Jerusalem, a region whose cultural heritage included hundreds of Serbian Orthodox churches and monasteries yet whose people were 90 percent Albanian. The Albanians were also Muslim. In 1989, Milosevic stripped Kosovo of its autonomy and began a decade-long suppression of the province through the use of apartheid-like policies and a brutal military police. The Albanians fought back. Thousands joined a shadowy guerrilla movement known as the Kosovo Liberation Army (KLA), which began attacking Serb forces in early 1998. When the Serbs counterattacked, they drove the KLA deep into the mountains, then began burning their villages one by one.

By fall 1998, there were an estimated 250,000 Albanian refugees living in makeshift camps in Albania and Macedonia.[27] With casualties mounting, and Serb forces committing one grisly atrocity after another, the international community gave Milosevic a choice: withdraw from Kosovo or face NATO bombardment. He chose bombardment. NATO began bombing Serbia on March 24, 1999. For seventy-eight straight days, it hit every military target in sight. It bombed bases, radar installations, missile silos, tank columns, troop convoys, airports, shipyards, and even "dual-use" targets such as Zastava. In two different strikes—one on April 9, the other on April 12—NATO destroyed Yugo's main assembly line, paint shop, computer center, and power station, injuring 124 workers in the process.[28]

The damage was severe. Mangled Yugos swung from conveyor belts. Pieces of metal and concrete and even steel girders covered the floor. Wires were everywhere. One witness described "a junkyard of twisted metal, blackened machines, oozing chemicals" and "oil-soaked floors."[29] The damage, claimed Zastava, came to at least $200 million. "They think that because we produce cars we can help make military vehicles," said Milan Beko, chairman of the Zastava board. "If they follow this logic through they should start poisoning our wheat because it goes into the flour that makes the bread that we give our soldiers."[30] Beko scoffed at claims that Zastava produced arms. We make "only sports weapons and hunting rifles," he said, ignoring the fact that in February 1999, just two months before the NATO bombing, Zastava had "trumpeted a new product," an M-93 multiple grenade launcher that was "ideal for combating 'terrorists.'"[31]

Beko was friends with Milosevic and had formerly served as Serbia's "minister of ownership transformation." His job was to raise money for Milosevic by selling whatever assets Serbia had. In June 1997, for example, he sold a 49 percent stake in Telekom Serbia to Italian and Greek investors for $918 million.[32] He also sold portions of a Serbian electric company and an oil refining company before coming to Zastava in June 1998. Beko tried to sell the company to Volkswagen, Fiat, Hyundai, and Daewoo, then in July 1998 announced that Zastava was entering into a "strategic partnership" with Peugeot, which apparently wasn't true.[33] The company sputtered on until April 1999, when NATO's "Operation Allied Force" intervened. Beko knew Zastava was a target. Even after the bombing began, he made frantic calls to Fiat and Peugeot "remind[ing] them of [their] past and future business relations" and "offer[ing] any sort of deal to save the factory."[34]

In June the war ended. Milosevic declared victory but agreed to pull Serb forces out of Kosovo and hand the province to the UN. Serbia was a mess. The NATO air campaign had caused at least $30 billion in damages. "We have been thrown back to the economic level of the 1950s," said one Serbian economist. "Without foreign assistance, we need forty years to reach the economic level we had ten years ago when Milosevic came to power."[35] But Milosevic wasn't defeated, at least not yet. He quickly staged one building project after another to present the illusion that Serbia was back in business. He called it "heroic reconstruction."[36] In September, for example, he "reopened" Zastava. It produced about ten cars a day for two or three days, then stopped. By Christmas, everything in Serbia had stopped.[37] The country was poorer than Albania. Pensioners received $40 a month. Power, in some regions, was three hours on, three hours off. Over half of all Serbian adults were unemployed.

Finally, mercifully, in September 2000 Milosevic stood for re-election and lost. He was replaced by a coalition government of democrats and reformers and was subsequently sent to The Hague. He died in prison in March 2006. Meanwhile, Serbia's new government promised to keep Zastava afloat but cut its production force to 4,500 and put everyone else on "paid leave." They received just $7 a month.[38] "Humiliation is in our souls at Zastava," said one worker. "Will anyone bring dignity back to us? We almost don't think about money anymore, but just the chance to live and work with some dignity."[39] The only hope, of course, was a foreign buyer. In September 1999, French automaker Renault purchased a 51 percent stake in Dacia, the formerly atrocious Romanian manufacturer known at the time for its poor-quality cars.[40] If Dacia could do it, then why not Zastava?

But Zastava had too many negatives, including a weak government, an aging and only semirepaired facility, and parts suppliers that had literally been blown up. (One supplier in Kosovo had been captured by NATO.) It had also had three or four different management teams in ten years. In October 2000, for example, in the chaos following Milosevic's fall from power, members of the Kragujevac chapter of the Christian Democratic Party of Serbia "stormed [the Zastava plant] and took control."[41] Its new vice chairman, Gvozden Jovanovic, was "owner of a pest-control firm," while its new director, Zoran Radojevic, was a former "low-level" plant manager at Zastava who became its factory boss. There was "a yawning gap between their qualifications and [their] high positions," wrote one journalist, and this "led to charges that . . . control of Zastava had passed into the hands of incompetents and opportunists."[42] These were the men tasked with soliciting a foreign buyer. They had zero luck. "We tried to find a partner in some well-known major firm that makes cars," said Radojevic, "but nobody wants us."[43] Nobody but Malcolm Bricklin.

To the astonishment of automotive hacks worldwide, in April

2002 *Forbes* magazine reported that Bricklin had signed a new deal with Zastava.[44] Under its terms, Bricklin would pay the Serbian government $150 million for 80 percent of the company, while the government would assume Zastava's debts. Those debts in 2002 were $200 million to $300 million. Zastava had approached Bricklin through Ira Edelson, the former Yugo America CFO who was living in Florida. Zastava's export director, Dragan Ranisavljevic, sent Edelson a promotional disk, which Edelson copied before sending to Bricklin. "I figured it was for my archives," says Edelson. "[But] Malcolm got the disk . . . called me and said 'Ira, I'm ready to roll!' "[45] Bricklin *was* ready to roll. Since going bankrupt in August 1991, he had founded two new businesses, the Electric Vehicle Corporation and the Electric Bicycle Company, and both had failed.

Established in 1993, the Electric Vehicle Corporation (EVC) was a three-way partnership between Bricklin, the former Hughes Aircraft chairman and undersecretary of defense Malcolm Currie, and the electric battery guru Chaz Haba. Its product, essentially, was an electric motor and battery conversion kit that EVC would retrofit to preexisting cars. The price was $7,900 to $10,000 per kit, installed.[46] The problem, however, was that EVC's business model made no sense. Why would car buyers spend ten grand to install batteries in a used car when the base Honda Accord, Toyota Camry, Ford Taurus, and Nissan Altima were all reasonably priced at fifteen grand? In addition, the cars' batteries provided just eighty miles of drive time per charge, and EVC needed tens of millions of dollars to produce them. With no money and no market, Bricklin's newest company went belly-up.

His next venture was the Electric Bicycle Company, which he cofounded with Currie in late 1993. The company's twenty main investors included author Sidney Sheldon and St. Louis Rams owner Georgia Frontiere; they put up a collective $5 million to produce the EV Warrior, an everyday mountain bike with a battery pack attached to its rear wheel.[47] Priced at $800 to $1,000, the 82-pound EV Warrior featured a 12-volt electric motor and had a top speed of 20 miles per hour. Bricklin's plan was to sell the bike through car dealers, and not through bike shops, because car dealers had "far more display space" and "might be tempted to use . . . [the] bikes to build traffic."[48] In a maneuver reminiscent of his famed Handyman, Subaru, SV-1, Pininfarina, Bertone, and Yugo ventures, Bricklin awarded "exclusive distribution" rights to approximately one hundred dealers at a cost of $18,500 apiece. He called them "launch packages."[49]

The bikes were unveiled in June 1995 at a Cadillac dealership in San Diego. "Between now and the year 2000," said Bricklin, "things electric are really going to take off."[50] To which he added, "[And] these [bikes] are not made in Yugoslavia."[51] But, indeed, there was something Yugo-esque about Bricklin's bicycle company. Dealers took deposits but didn't get bikes. The bikes' manufacturer didn't get paid. Dealer warranties weren't reimbursed. "We never paid anyone," said a company employee, "not suppliers, not vendors, nobody. Everything we used was rented, and we never paid for it until they threatened to seize."[52] In the meantime, however, Bricklin lived in a beachfront condo in Malibu, California. Needless to say, in March 1997 the Electric Bicycle Company went bankrupt. It owed its creditors $10.5 million.[53] Bricklin lost $5 million on the deal, he claimed, to which one investor scoffed: "Malcolm reminds me of a balloon you blow up and let go, then it fizzles all around the room. [He's just] an empty piece of rubber. He used us for his own aggrandizement. But I can't sue him because he has nothing."[54]

Even with nothing, beginning in 1998 Bricklin formed a fuel-cell company to develop licenses he had acquired from NASA's Jet Propulsion Laboratory near Los Angeles. Bricklin then traded the licenses to a former dialysis firm called Techsys, sued, was countersued, then defaulted on $700,000 in loans.[55]

Next up: Zastava. In April 2002, Bricklin signed the first in a series of agreements to acquire Zastava and sell its cars through a New Jersey–based distributor called Zastava Motor Works, USA, or "ZMW" for short. "ZMW, get it?" laughed Bricklin. "That'll drive people [at BMW] crazy."[56] (It did, and BMW threatened to sue.) The three new ZMW models included a Yugo, a Florida, and a Florida pickup truck, with updated engines by Peugeot and new exterior designs. Priced at $5,000 to $9,000 retail, they would be the cheapest cars in America: Yugo part deux. "I know you're thinking: 'Who needs to start that up over again?'" Bricklin told *Automotive News*. "I thought the same thing myself, at first. [But] what's different this time, is we'll be in charge of quality."[57]

All Bricklin needed was cash—cash and a promise from Serbia that it would liquidate $200 million to $300 million in debt. "Evidently [the Serbian government] didn't think we could do the deal," says Ira Edelson. "[So the Serbs] made no effort . . . They never liquidated the debt. And since they never liquidated the debt, we weren't able to raise the money [to buy Zastava]. The deal was dead at the end of 2003."[58] By 2004, Bricklin was in China. His new company, Visionary Vehicles Inc., tried to import a car known as the Chery, lost out to Chrysler, and has since switched to plug-in electric hybrid cars. Bricklin's newest pitch: a luxury car the size of a Mercedes S that costs $35,000 and gets 100 miles per gallon. "I'm not starting a revolution," says Bricklin, "[I'm] helping the evolution."[59]

As for Zastava, the Serbian manufacturer spent several years searching for a buyer; in April 2008, its prayers were answered. In what officials called "the biggest investment in the history of Fiat," the Italian carmaker agreed to invest a staggering $1.09 billion in Zastava for a 70 percent stake and to transform the Serbian plant into a state-of-the-art manufacturing center for Central and Eastern Europe.[60] The one caveat: no more Yugos. Zastava's sole product, it seems, will be the new Fiat Topolino, a tiny micro-car shorter than the Mini.

Epilogue

Yo' mama drives a Yugo.

On November 11, 2008, the last Yugo rolled off the assembly line. There was no reception to commemorate the car, no VIPs or dignitaries in attendance—only workers. Some took pictures, some laid flowers, and others left messages on the car with white sticky tape. A sign on the back of the car read, in English and in Serbian, "The End!!"[1] However, for most workers, the Yugo's final day at Zastava wasn't particularly festive. The new Fiat-Zastava operation, called Fiat Automobili Srbija, planned to employ just 2,400 workers. That meant 1,200 workers, still on the books at Zastava, were being laid off. There was even talk that the world financial crisis would push Fiat into postponing the deal or, worse yet, into canceling the deal altogether. "Nostalgia and uncertainty pervade the factory," wrote SeeNews, and "cloud the advent of a new era as [Zastava's] remaining workers, and managers, fear for their jobs."[2]

The "uncertainty" was understandable. People needed work. But "nostalgia"? Nostalgia for what? The Yugo? Did workers at Ford miss the Pinto? Did workers at AMC miss the Pacer or the Gremlin? Probably not. But workers at Zastava *miss* the Yugo. In fact, thousands of former Yugoslavs, in Croatia, Slovenia, Bosnia, Serbia, Macedonia, and Montenegro, all now independent countries, miss the Yugo too. They suffer from what's commonly known as "Yugonostalgia," a nostalgia for not just the car but the country.[3]

In 1999, just four years after the Bosnian and Croatian wars and during the NATO bombardment of Serbia, a popular rock-and-roll song throughout the region was "Jugo 45" by the Sarajevo group Zabranjeno Pusenje. "They say the African pyramids are wonders of the world," it went. "They say the long Indian rivers are wonders of the world / But no wonder was equal to the one when my old man parked a Yugo 45 in the garden . . . Those were good times—all on credit, all for the people my friend / Put some gas in the car and drive to Trieste to buy some jeans / Those were good times—we went to picnics and sometimes to the beach / In the house a lot of laughter / In the garden a Yugo 45."[4]

Meanwhile, in America, the Yugo continues to appear as a retro-eighties joke. Released in 2000, the Hollywood comedy-mystery *Drowning Mona* featured Bette Midler in the role of Mona Dearly, a woman who died, mysteriously, when her yellow Yugo GV plunged into the Hudson River. The film's setting was Verplanck, New York, a real town, but one the film fictitiously described as a former Yugo testing ground. "In 1985," intoned the film's trailer, "the Yugo Car Company [*sic*] chose Verplanck, New York, to test its new vehicles. But that's a whole other story."[5] Besides Mona herself, every person in town except for Danny DeVito, the police chief, drove a Yugo.

These two conflicting visions—Yugo as eighties nostalgia and Yugo as retro-eighties joke—are just two ways of viewing the car. There are others. For one, the Yugo was a Cold War phenomenon, the product of an independent communist country propped up by the United States but still badly in need of currency. The Yugo was a failed product, perhaps the greatest failed product of all time. (Today, it's in the same class as New Coke, 12-inch laser discs, MC Hammer's rapping career, Eddie Murphy's singing career, and the infamous Ford Edsel.) The Yugo was a botched people's car, not in Yugoslavia, where Zastava made close to 800,000 of these things, but in the United States, where importers and manufacturers have yet to re-place the Model T.

The Yugo was a 1980s consumer fad, the automotive equivalent of Cabbage Patch Kids or parachute pants, but with a $3,990 price tag. The Yugo was a product of eighties excess, the strange if not sur-real mixture of a Bricklin sales pitch, a Wall Street investment firm, and a San Diego savings and loan, and status-crazed Americans who wanted cars with . . . well, status—status the Yugo didn't have. And then, finally, there's Bricklin. Malcolm Bricklin. The Yugo was, after all, a Bricklin idea, another Bricklin idea in a long line of Bricklin ideas that went south. But remember, he made millions on the car. So was he a genius? A visionary? A shyster? A kook? Perhaps a bit of each. "There's a saying that applies to Malcolm," said Per Arneberg, an early investor in the Yugo deal. "Where there is plenty of sun, there is also some shadow."[6]

In any case, the Yugo is the worst car in history. *That* is how we view the car. But for those of us who love the Yugo, or for those of us who simply love Yugo jokes, there's still hope. As of late 2008, the Serbian government was negotiating with officials in the Congo about moving the Yugo to Africa.[7] Yes, to Africa. Will there be a Yugo-Mobutu? A Yugo-Congo? Stay tuned.

Notes

Introduction

1. Dan Bischoff, "History Go 'Round: Grand Central Carousel Horses Around with Pop Culture," *The Star-Ledger* (Newark), August 13, 1999.

2. "Yesterday's High-tech Machine Is Type Cast as Art," *Journal Sentinel* (Milwaukee), June 14, 2001.

3. To see pictures of O'Callaghan's most recent student shows, visit design .schoolofvisualarts.edu/class.html (site accessed April 29, 2009).

4. Stephen Williams, "Yugo Your Way; They'll Go Theirs—Sad Little Cars Given New Life as Sculpture," *The Dallas Morning News*, May 30, 1995; Clifford Pugh, "Way Off-the-Road Vehicles/Yugo Art Is Also Off the Wall," *Houston Chronicle*, March 23, 1996.

5. Cathleen Falsani, "Yugos Build Image of Functionality—as an Art Form," *Chicago Tribune*, October 14, 1996.

6. Laura Outerbridge, "Scrap-Heap Artistry: Used-up Yugos Renewed," *The Washington Times*, July 15, 1995.

7. Dee Ito, "Redemption of the Hapless Yugo," *Graphis* 52:301 (1996): 92.

8. Laura Outerbridge, "Scrap-Heap Artistry—Used-up Yugos Renewed."

9. Henry Mietkiewicz, "Yugo Car-toons Funny Festival Fare," *The Toronto Star*, July 23, 1996.

10. Cathleen Falsani, "Yugos Build Image of Functionality—as an Art Form"; Diane Toroian, "Lemon Aid—Deceased Yugos Achieve a Sublime Afterlife as Auto-Show Art Exhibit," *St. Louis Post-Dispatch*, January 23, 1997; Diana Lundin, "Turning Lemons into Lemonade," *Daily News* (Los Angeles), January 8, 1996; Maria Speidel, "Art Yugeaux," *People* 45:4 (January 29, 1996): 88.

11. Paul Dean, "Laughed into Oblivion as a Car, the Yugo Bounces Back—as Art," *The Buffalo News*, January 2, 1996.

12. Keith Martin, "For Worst Performance by a Car: The Envelope, Please . . ." *The New York Times*, April 2, 2000.

13. Yahoo! Answers, "What Is the Worst Car Ever Sold in the U.S.?" answers.yahoo .com (site accessed July 2, 2008).

14. Rateitall.com, "Worst Cars in History," www.rateitall.com/t-3218-worst-cars -in-history.aspx; bestandworst.com, "Worst Car Ever?" www.bestandworst .com/r/104438.htm; and automotoportal.com, "Worst Cars Ever Made," www

.automotoportal.com/article/Worst_cars_ever_made (sites accessed July 2, 2008).

15. "What Was the Worst Car of All Time?" *Via* 129:4 (July/August 2008): 59; Rob Douthit, "Poll Results: The Three Ugliest Cars of All Time," *The Atlanta Journal-Constitution*, September 15, 2007.

16. Richard Porter, *Crap Cars* (New York: Bloomsbury, 2005), 104–05. Time.com, "The 50 Worst Cars of All Time," www.time.com/time/specials/2007/article/0,28804,1658545_1658533_1658529,00.html and Dan Lienert, "The Worst Cars of All Time," www.forbes.com/2004/01/26/cx_dl_0126feat.html (sites accessed July 2, 2008).

17. Eric Peters, *Automotive Atrocities: The Cars We Love to Hate* (St. Paul, Minnesota: Motorbooks International, 2004), 56–57; Craig Cheetham, *The World's Worst Cars* (New York: Barnes and Noble, 2007), 66–67; and Giles Chapman, *The Worst Cars Ever Sold* (London: Sutton Publishing, 2007), 146–47.

18. Urbandictionary.com, "Yugo," www.urbandictionary.com/define.php?term=Yugo (site accessed July 2, 2008).

19. Tom Incantalupo, "For Yugo, It's No Go," *Newsday*, April 21, 1992.

20. There is also a song named "Jugo 45" by the ex–Yugoslav rock band Zabranjeno Pusenje.

21. See Robert F. Hartley, "The Yugo: A Socialist Fiasco in a Competitive Environment," in *Management Mistakes and Successes* (New York: John Wiley and Sons, 1994), 303–319.

22. Eric Peters, *Automotive Atrocities*, 56–57.

23. Frank Cerabino, "Search Shows Yugo Bombed Years Before Kosovo Crisis," *The Palm Beach Post*, April 14, 1999.

24. Jack Keebler, "Increasing Cost of Certification Slows Importers," *The Tampa Tribune*, August 24, 1991.

25. Ibid.

26. Tony Assenza, "Yugo GV: Revenge of the Kmart Shoppers," *Car and Driver* 31:10 (April 1986): 48.

27. John Carey, "Look Out America: Here Comes Yugoslavia," *Periscope*, July 23, 1984, p. 13.

28. Jeremy Clarkson, "Wherever You Go, Steer Clear of Yugo," *The Sun* (London), July 4, 1996.

1: Yugo Girls!

1. Miroslav Kefurt, interview with author, July 7, 2004.

2. Richard Mooney, "Fiat Autos Driving for Red Markets," *The New York Times*, August 4, 1965.

3. Miroslav Kefurt, interview with author, July 7, 2004.

4. Ibid.

5. See *Recent Developments in the Production of Passenger Automobiles in the European Communist Countries*, Intelligence Memorandum, Directorate of Intelligence, CIA, November 1967, 25. (The report was declassified in 2000 and is available through the Declassified Documents Reference System.)

6. Miroslav Kefurt, interview with author, July 7, 2004.

7. Ibid.

8. The Yugo 45 went on sale in Great Britain in mid-1983. See Peter Waymark, "Yugo 45 Eastern Europe's Best So Far," *The Times* (London), July 8, 1983.

9. During the 1980s, Yugoslavia also had honorary consuls in Kansas and Louisiana.

10. Michael Palairet, "Mismanaging Innovation: The Yugo Car Enterprise (1962–1992)," *Technovation* 13:3 (1993): 119.

11. When the new Zastava factory opened on July 6, 1962, it had an annual capacity of thirty-two thousand vehicles, with floor space for eighty thousand. See "Yugoslavs Expand Production of Cars," *The New York Times*, July 22, 1962.

12. David C. Smith, "Yugo: Zastava Emerges from the Dark Ages," *Ward's AutoWorld* 23 (November 1986): 68.

13. Fiat announced it was leaving the American market in January 1983. See Donald Woutat, "Fiat Expected to End Direct Sales in U.S.," *Los Angeles Times*, January 18, 1983.

14. John R. Lampe, Russell O. Prickett, and Ljubisa S. Adamovic, *Yugoslav-American Economic Relations Since World War II* (Durham, NC: Duke University Press, 1990), 137–38.

15. Miroslav Kefurt, interview with author, July 7, 2004.

16. Ibid.

17. Edwin Pope, "Yugoslavia: World Wars to Winter Whirl," *The Miami Herald*, February 6, 1984.

18. John Powers, "Sarajevo: Modern Marvel," *The Boston Globe*, February 4, 1984.

19. Ibid.

20. Organizing Committee of the XIVth Winter Olympic Games, *Final Report: Sarajevo '84* (Sarajevo: Oslobodenje, 1984), 3.

21. Kenneth Reich, "Ready to Play, Sam?" *Sports Illustrated* 60:10 (March 5, 1984): 77.

22. Gerald F. Seib, Earl C. Gottschalk Jr., Bill Abrams, and Frederick Kempe, "Soviet Squeeze Play: Moscow to Shun Olympics in Action Seen as Bid to Avert Talks with U.S.," *The Wall Street Journal*, May 9, 1984.

23. Andrew Rosenthal, "Boycott Called Irreversible," *Lexington (KY) Herald-Leader*, May 15, 1984.

24. Joe Gergen, "L.A. Has Come Long Way Since Games in 1932," *The Record* (New Jersey), July 23, 1984.

25. Chris Jenkins and Bill Center, "Games Less than Olympian Without Red Bloc," *The San Diego Union-Tribune*, May 10, 1984.

26. George Vecsey, "Sports of the Times: Great Red Hopes in the Olympics," *The New York Times*, June 28, 1984.

27. Gerald F. Seib, Earl C. Gottschalk Jr., Bill Abrams, and Frederick Kempe, "Soviet Squeeze Play."

28. Ibid.

29. George Vecsey, "Sports of the Times: Great Red Hopes in the Olympics."

30. Doug Cress, "Toplak, Yugoslavs Play for National Pride," *The Washington Post*, July 28, 1984.

31. Aleksandar Lebl and David Buchan, "European News: Moscow Throws Line to Struggling Yugoslavs," *Financial Times*, March 29, 1983.

32. Lloyd George, interview with author, August 25, 2004.

33. William Oscar Johnson, "History's New Imprint" *Sports Illustrated* 56:12 (February 6, 1984): 55.

34. Steve Twomey, "Olympian Change in Sarajevo," *The Philadelphia Inquirer*, January 22, 1984.

35. James Christie, "President Mixes Up Speech: Glassed-in Reagan Opens Games," *The Globe and Mail* (Toronto), July 30, 1984.

36. Miroslav Kefurt, interview with author, July 7, 2004.

37. By 1983, most major car manufacturers had adopted fuel injection or were in the process of doing so.

38. Miroslav Kefurt, interview with author, July 7, 2004.

39. Ibid.

40. Paul Dean, " 'Old-Tech' Yugo 45 Plans an End to Autos' Planned Obsolescence," *Los Angeles Times*, June 8, 1984.

41. Ibid.

42. Ibid.

43. Ibid.

44. "New-Car Costs at Record High in '84," *Automotive News*, March 11, 1985. When released, the Sprint cost $4,949, but Chevrolet raised its price to $5,151 in mid-1984. "Prices Hiked on Fiero, Sprint," *The Boston Globe*, July 31, 1984.

45. William Chapman, "Tokyo Official Bars 20% Cut in Cars to US," *The Washington Post*, March 29, 1981; "Foreign Cars," *The Washington Post*, January 23, 1980.

46. Larry Kramer, "VW and Chrysler Imports Tops in Mileage Ratings," *The Washington Post*, September 19, 1979.

47. Japanese fuel efficiency ratings taken from *Standard Catalog of Imported Cars, 1946–2002*, 2nd ed. (Iola, WI: Krause Publications, 2002).

48. "Detroit Tilts with Imports for Car Buyers' Confidence," *The Wall Street Journal*, March 20, 1980.

49. Dean Calbreath, "You Call This Tough? Think '70s: With OPEC Embargo, Rationing, Long Lines Were Order of the Day," *The San Diego Union-Tribune*, May 29, 2005.

50. "Detroit Tilts with Imports for Car Buyers' Confidence"; Agis Salpukas, "1980 Car Sales at 19-Year Low," *The New York Times*, January 8, 1981.

51. "Chrysler Makes 3-Month Profit, First Since 1978," *The New York Times*, July 23, 1981.

52. Arthur T. Denzau, "The Japanese Automobile Cartel," *Regulation* 12:1 (Winter 1988), www.cato.org/pubs/regulation (site accessed November 24, 2005).

53. Ibid.

54. The 1984 Honda Civic four-door and wagon models had a wheelbase of 96.5 inches.

55. Warren Brown, "U.S. Small-Car Market to Spark 'Blood-Bath,' " *The Washington Post*, February 9, 1986.

56. Edward Clifford, "Sales of Imported Cars Increase 5% in Month," *The Globe and Mail* (Toronto), April 17, 1984.

57. Urban C. Lehner, "Korean Auto, Priced at $4,530 and Up, Sells Well in Canada, Plans U.S. Debut," *The Wall Street Journal*, April 13, 1984.

2: The Habitual Entrepreneur

1. For the Subaru 360 review, see "The Subaru 360 (Not Acceptable)," *Consumer Reports* 34 (April 1969): 220–22.

2. Bricklin actually appears as a case study in a business management article on "habitual entrepreneurship." See Claus Rerup, "Learning from Past Experience: Footnotes on Mindfulness and Habitual Entrepreneurship," *Scandinavian Journal of Management* 21 (2005): 451–72.

3. H. A. Fredericks and Allan Chambers, *Bricklin* (Fredericton, New Brunswick: Brunswick Books, 1977), 6. The best sources on Bricklin's early career include: *Bricklin*; Barry Rosenberg, "Would You Buy a Car from This Man?" *Philadelphia* (April 1975), 96ff; and Randall Rothenberg, *Where the Suckers Moon: An Advertising Story* (New York: Knopf, 1994).

4. Rosenberg, "Would You Buy a Car from This Man?" 168. Handyman investor Lawrence I. Fish told Rosenberg that Bricklin had just sixteen stores total, "all but two in Orlando."

5. Fredericks and Chambers, *Bricklin*, 8.

6. Ibid., 10.

7. Ibid., 10–11.

8. Steve Spence, "What Do Henry Ford and Malcolm Bricklin Have in Common? They Make Cars," *Motor Trend* 26:8 (August 1974): 68.

9. Rosenberg, "Would You Buy a Car from This Man?" 167–68.

10. Fredericks and Chambers, *Bricklin*, 11.

11. Rosenberg, "Would You Buy a Car from This Man?" 101.

12. Fredericks and Chambers, *Bricklin*, 11–12.

13. "Subaru Safe? Crash Tests Raise Doubts," *Chicago Tribune*, February 14, 1969.

14. Mark Schilling, *Encyclopedia of Japanese Culture* (Boston: Shambhala Publications, 1997), 37.

15. Randall Rothenberg, *Where the Suckers Moon*, 43.

16. See "Ten Ugliest Cars," *Car and Driver* 32 (January 1987): 62.

17. "The Subaru 360 (Not Acceptable)," 220, 222. *Consumer Reports* estimated the 360's fuel efficiency at 25–35 miles per gallon, but most other publications estimated 66 miles per gallon. See John McDonnell, "Great Future Seen for Japanese Car," *Chicago Tribune*, February 14, 1969.

18. Contract provisions summarized by Rothenberg, *Where the Suckers Moon*, 46.

19. Ibid.

20. Rosenberg, "Would You Buy a Car from This Man?" 103

21. Ibid., 102.

22. Rothenberg, *Where the Suckers Moon*, 48.

23. Rosenberg, "Would You Buy a Car from This Man?" 103.

24. Rothenberg, *Where the Suckers Moon*, 49.

25. "The Subaru 360 (Not Acceptable)," 220.

26. Ibid., 222.

27. "Lightweight Subaru Called Japan's Safest Automobile," *The New York Times*, February 19, 1969.

28. Rosenberg, "Would You Buy a Car from This Man?" 158, 160.

29. Ibid., 160.

30. Ibid., 161.

31. Ibid., 162–63. According to Ira Edelson, Bricklin's friend and later Yugo collaborator, Bricklin raised approximately $400,000 dollars by increasing the mortgage on Stern's Vacation Valley property. Ira Edelson, interview with author, May 27, 2004.
32. "Over $2 Million Settlement in Pact Breach," *Daily Courier* (Connellsville, PA), December 26, 1974.
33. Rosenberg, "Would You Buy a Car from This Man?" 163–64.
34. Ira Edelson, interview with author, May 27, 2004.
35. Rosenberg, "Would You Buy a Car from This Man?" 164.
36. Figures cited in Rothenberg, *Where the Suckers Moon*, 52–53.
37. Max Showalter, "Subaru Hits Sales Milestone," *Journal and Courier* (Lafayette, IN), January 4, 2007.

3: A Canadian Sports Car?

1. H. A. Fredericks and Allan Chambers, *Bricklin* (Fredericton, New Brunswick: Brunswick Books, 1977), 14–20.
2. Estimate cited in David Halberstam, *The Reckoning* (New York: William Morrow and Company, 1986), 333. By comparison, in 1946 industrialist Henry J. Kaiser raised over $50 million for the Kaiser-Fraser Corporation. Although Kaiser-Fraser produced over 150,000 cars, it was out of business by 1953.
3. Bricklin's problems with building workable production molds are well documented. For an interesting account, see Bill Snow, "The Composite Car That Should Have Been," *Composite Technology* (August 2005), www.compositesworld.com/columns/the-composite-car-that-should-have-been.aspx (site accessed March 20, 2006).
4. Fredericks and Chambers, *Bricklin*, 26. For a fascinating study of the politician Richard Hatfield's role in the Bricklin SV-1 project, see Richard Starr, *Richard Hatfield: The Seventeen Year Saga* (Halifax, Nova Scotia: Formac Publishing, 1988), 85–104.
5. Steve Spence, "Adventures on the 'Yellow Bricklin Road,'" *Motor Trend* (November 1974): 64.
6. Philip H. Dougherty, "Lois's New-Car Account Is a Hush-Hush Matter," *The New York Times*, September 13, 1973.
7. Fredericks and Chambers, *Bricklin*, 37.
8. Steve Spence, "What Do Henry Ford and Malcolm Bricklin Have in Common? They Make Cars," *Motor Trend* 26:8 (August 1974): 70.
9. Barry Rosenberg, "Would You Buy a Car from This Man?" *Philadelphia* (April 1975): 98.
10. Fredericks and Chambers, *Bricklin*, 38.
11. Ibid., 1–2.
12. Ernest Hulsendolph, "Acrylic 2-Seater Sells for $6,500," *The New York Times*, June 26, 1974.
13. "Safety Fast," *Playboy* 21:9 (September 1974): 158.
14. Production expenses cited in Fredericks and Chambers, *Bricklin*, 50–51, 58.
15. "Bricklin Sports Car Output Halted; Receiver Named," *The New York Times*, September 27, 1975.
16. Cited in Karl Ludvigsen, "The Bricklin: Is It Trying to Tell Us Something?" *Motor Trend* 28:1 (January 1976): 14.

17. Randy Richmond and Tom Villemaire, *Colossal Canadian Failures* (Toronto: Dundurn Press, 2002), 93.
18. Fredericks and Chambers, *Bricklin*, 60–61.
19. Mark Miller, "The Bricklin: So Many Want to Own Them, but So Few Do," *Chicago Tribune*, January 26, 1975.
20. Fredericks and Chambers, *Bricklin*, 101.
21. Ibid., 115.
22. "Bricklin Canada to File Chapter XI," *The New York Times*, September 30, 1975.
23. "Bricklin Gets New Lease on Life," *Chicago Tribune*, October 8, 1975.
24. Fredericks and Chambers, *Bricklin*, 105.
25. Lyrics published in *How to Brickle: The New Brunswick Funny Book* (Fredericton, New Brunswick: Omega Publishing, 1977), 34.
26. Fredericks and Chambers, *Bricklin*, 106.
27. Ibid., 120.
28. Ibid., 121.
29. "$10 Million Needed to Save Car: Bricklin," *Chicago Tribune*, September 27, 1975.
30. Fredericks and Chambers, *Bricklin*, 131–32, quote on 132.

4: Walkin' Down a London Street

1. James Mateja, "Bricklin Gearing Up for Another Try," *Chicago Tribune*, January 13, 1976; Bob Levey, "Owning a Brainstorm," *The Washington Post*, November 30, 1978.
2. Ira Edelson, interview with author, May 27, 2004.
3. Tony Ciminera, interview with author, June 14, 2004.
4. Ibid.
5. Rodney A. Brooks, "Subaru Posts Record 1982 Sales, Profit," *The Philadelphia Inquirer*, January 15, 1983.
6. Tony Assenza, "Bertone X1/9 vs. Pontiac Fiero SE," *Motor Trend* (May 1984): 62.
7. Tony Ciminera, interview with author, June 14, 2004.
8. Ira Edelson, interview with author, May 27, 2004.
9. Ibid.
10. The seven distributors were G.W. Imports Co. (Thousand Oaks, CA), Mid-States International Automobile Distributors (Lenexa, KS), Gulf States Imports (Houston, TX), Intercontinental Imports (Little Rock, AK), Southeastern Import Car Distributors (Boca Raton, FL), R.V.D. International Distributor (Ramsey, NJ), and Mid-Atlantic International Imports (Accokeek, MD).
11. Marshall Schoun, "Spider and X1/9 Are Reborn with Changes for the Better," *The New York Times*, January 29, 1984.
12. Tony Ciminera, interview with author, June 14, 2004.
13. Kevin Smith, "Pininfarina Azzurra," *Motor Trend* (June 1984): 119.
14. Merrill Brown, "The Return of Malcolm Bricklin," *The Washington Post*, December 27, 1983.
15. Ira Edelson, interview with author, May 27, 2004.
16. "Mr. Malcolm Bricklin, Founder of International Automobile Importers, Believes That the Success of BL's Jaguar in the US Market Has Paved the Way for More UK Cars to Be Sold in the US," *Financial Times*, April 16, 1984.
17. Tony Ciminera, interview with author, June 14, 2004.

18. Ibid.
19. Stephen J. Sansweet, "Occidental Signs Accord in Trade with Yugoslavia— Company Again Makes Use of Chairman's Old Links to Communist Regimes," *The Wall Street Journal*, February 6, 1984.
20. Thomas M. Chesser, "Barter Becomes Big Business in World Trade," *The New York Times*, July 26, 1981.
21. Ibid.
22. Carl Blumay, *The Dark Side of Power: The Real Armand Hammer* (New York: Simon & Schuster, 1992), 243.
23. Scot J. Paltrow, "Unrealized Dreams: Occidental Petroleum Hasn't Always Thrived from East Bloc Deals," *The Wall Street Journal*, August 30, 1984.
24. Ibid.
25. Steve Weinberg, *Armand Hammer: The Untold Story* (Boston: Little, Brown and Company, 1989), 225.
26. Stephen J. Sansweet, "Occidental Signs Accord on Trade with Yugoslavia."
27. *World Motor Vehicle Data, 1984–85* (Detroit: American Automobile Manufacturers Association, 1985), 280.
28. Ibid., 282.
29. Ira Edelson, interview with author, May 27, 2004.
30. Miroslav Kefurt, interview with author, July 7, 2004.
31. Ibid.
32. Ibid.
33. The purchase price of $50,000 was also reported in the *Los Angeles Times*. See Paul Dean, "Wild and Crazy Car," *Los Angeles Times*, January 1, 1985.
34. Miroslav Kefurt, interview with author, July 7, 2004.
35. John A. Russell, "Pininfarina Spider Leaving U.S. Market," *Automotive News*, August 26, 1985.
36. "Judge Orders Bricklin to Pay $17 Million for Contract Breach," *The Wall Street Journal*, June 11, 1991.
37. The number of shareholders and the breakdown of who owned what stock were provided by Ira Edelson, interview with author, May 27, 2004.
38. Pete Mulhern, interview with author, June 16, 2004.
39. Figures cited in Michael Palairet, "The Rise and Fall of Yugoslav Socialism: A Case Study of the Yugo Automobile Enterprise, 1954–92," in David F. Good, ed., *Economic Transformations in East and Central Europe* (New York: Routledge, 1994), 101.
40. Philip H. Dougherty, "Rosenfeld to Handle Yugoslav Car Import," *The New York Times*, April 1, 1985.

5: The Serbian Detroit

1. Peter Englehard, "A Summary of the Yugoslav Auto Industry's Historic Evolution and Its Economic Drivers Until the Crisis of the 1990s," *Automotive History Review* 48 (Fall 2007): 29.
2. Figures from the Zastava Oruzje website. See www.zastava-arms.co.yu/english/zastava.htm (site accessed April 24, 2009).
3. James Foreman-Peck, "The American Challenge of the Twenties: Multinationals

and European Motor Industry," *Journal of Economic History* 42:4 (December 1982): 870–71.

4. Ivan T. Berend and Gyorgy Ranki, *Economic Development in East-Central Europe in the 19th and 20th Centuries* (New York: Columbia University Press, 1974), 309.

5. James J. Flink, *Automobile Age* (Cambridge, MA: MIT Press, 1990), 265.

6. S. H. Beaver, "Railways in the Balkan Peninsula," *The Geographical Journal* 97:5 (May 1941): 275.

7. Stevan K. Pavlowitch, *Hitler's New Disorder: The Second World War in Yugoslavia* (New York: Columbia University Press, 2008), 17–18.

8. John R. Lampe, *Yugoslavia as History: Twice There Was a Country* (Cambridge: Cambridge University Press, 1996), 211.

9. Denison Rusinow, *The Yugoslav Experiment, 1948–1974* (Los Angeles: University of California Press, 1977), 19.

10. Hannah Fischer, *American War and Military Operations Casualties: Lists and Statistics* (Washington, DC: Congressional Research Service, 2005), 2.

11. Mihailo Crnobrnja, *The Yugoslav Drama* (Buffalo: McGill–Queen's University Press, 1996), 67.

12. Figures from the Zastava Oruzje website.

13. Aleksandar Vlajic and Milovan Zekovic, *Dvadeset godina proizvodnje automobila, 1954–1974* (Kragujevac: Zavodi "Crvena Zastava," 1975), 29.

14. *Od topa do automobila, 1853–1973* (Kragujevac: Zavodi "Crvena zastava," 1973), 57.

15. Aleksandar Vlajic and Milovan Zekovic, *Dvadeset godina proizvodnje automobila, 1954–1974*, 30.

16. Ibid., 30–31.

17. Michael Palairet, "Mismanaging Innovation: The Yugo Car Enterprise (1962–1992)," *Technovation* 13:3 (1993): 126.

18. Ibid.

19. Information on the 1955 and 1957 deals between Zastava and Fiat provided by Toma Savic, e-mail communication with author, October 12, 2006.

20. Raymond H. Anderson, "An Increasingly Motorized Yugoslavia Has a New Headache: Wild Turkish Drivers Dashing Home," *The New York Times*, July 24, 1972.

21. "Europe's Motor Makers Look to Soviet Bloc," *The Times* (London), April 13, 1966.

22. George Maxcy, *The Multinational Motor Industry* (London: Croom Helm, 1981), 166.

23. "Yugoslavs Expand Production of Cars," *The New York Times*, July 22, 1962.

24. An Argentinean version of the Fiat 600 was known as the Fitito.

6: Bricklin's Next Big Thing

1. Unless otherwise noted, Zastava's production and export figures taken from untitled internal documents produced by the Zastava marketing department.

2. "Zestful Performance of the Fiat 1500," *The Times* (London), January 16, 1962.

3. "Camry: Best-seller for Toyota," *Republican-American* (Waterbury, CT), February 20, 2005.

4. David E. Nye, *Consuming Power: A Social History of American Energies* (Cambridge, MA: MIT Press, 1999), 178.

5. Pamela Walker Laird, " 'A Car Without a Single Weakness': Early Automobile Advertising," *Technology and Culture* 37:4 (October 1996): 803.

6. Daniel M. G. Raff, "Making Cars and Making Money in the Interwar Automobile Industry: Economies of Scale and Scope and the Manufacturing behind the Marketing," *Business History Review* 65:4 (Winter 1991): 724–25.

7. For an outstanding article on GM's advertising campaigns of the 1920s and the advent of the GM "family," see Roland Marchand, "The Corporation Nobody Knew: Bruce Barton, Alfred Sloan, and the Founding of the General Motors 'Family,' " *Business History Review* 65:4 (Winter 1991): 825–75.

8. Ford's lineup and prices taken from the Ford website, www.ford.com/vehicles (site accessed April 25, 2009).

9. Ford of Britain's 1969 car lineup included the Escort I, the Cortina II, the Taurus P6, the Taurus P7, the Corsair, the Zephyr 4/6, the Zodiac 3, and the Capri I.

10. John R. Lampe, Russell O. Prickett, and Ljubisa Adamovic, *Yugoslav-American Economic Relations Since World War II* (Durham, NC: Duke University Press, 1990), 76.

11. For an outstanding discussion of regional misinvestment in Kosovo, see Michael Palairet, "Ramiz Sadiku: A Case Study in Industrialization in Kosovo," *Soviet Studies* 44:5 (1992): 897–912.

12. GMP stands for "gross material product." The Yugoslav GMP percentages are for 1971 and come from Dijana Plestina, *Regional Development in Communist Yugoslavia: Success, Failure, and Consequences* (Boulder: Westview Press, 1992), 180–81. Cited in John R. Lampe, *Yugoslavia as History: Twice There Was a Country* (Cambridge: Cambridge University Press, 1996), 328.

13. GMP and personal income figures from Harold Lydall, *Yugoslavia in Crisis* (Oxford: Clarendon Press, 1989), 41. Cited in Lampe, *Yugoslavia as History*, 317. Trade deficit figures cited in Lampe, Prickett, and Adamovic, *Yugoslav-American Economic Relations*, 98.

14. Yugoslav debt figures cited in Lampe, Prickett, and Adamovic, *Yugoslav-American Economic Relations*, 221.

15. William Zimmerman, *Open Borders, Non-Alignment, and the Political Evolution of Yugoslavia* (Princeton: Princeton University Press, 1987), 80.

16. Fred Singleton, *A Short History of the Yugoslav Peoples* (New York: Cambridge University Press, 1985), 244.

17. "Giant Test," *Car* (March 1970): 43.

18. George Maxcy, *The Multinational Motor Industry* (London: Croom Helm, 1981), 166–67.

19. Srboljub Vasovic was general manager of Zastava from 1984 to 2000. As of 1984, Vasovic's three deputy managers were Toma Savic (deputy manager for marketing, sales, and export), Zivorad Prokic (deputy manager for production and technique), and Radovan Petrovic (deputy manager for finance).

20. "New Fiat Models for Yugoslavia," *The Globe and Mail* (Toronto), December 30, 1978.

21. It is possible that Tito gave the two cars to other foreign dignitaries as presents. In 1976 he gave Soviet premier Leonid Brezhnev a Zastava 101 as a gift.

22. Zastava began selling cars in Great Britain in the spring of 1981, when it first ex-

ported the 101. See "In April Yugoslav Motor Cars Made by Zastava Will Be Imported into Britain for the First Time," *Financial Times*, January 14, 1981.

23. According to the Croatian Hydrographic Institute, a *jugo* is "a warm, humid wind of the direction ESE through SSE." See www.hhi.hr/peljar/vjetrovi.htm (site accessed April 29, 2009).

24. Peugeot has used three-digit model names with zeros in the middle since 1929, when it first introduced the Peugeot 201.

25. Peter Waymark, "Yugo 45 Eastern Europe's Best So Far," *The Times* (London), July 8, 1983.

26. Tony Ciminera, interview with author, June 14, 2004.

27. Toma Savic, interview with author, July 28, 2006.

28. Tony Ciminera, interview with author, June 14, 2004.

29. Ibid.

30. Ibid.

31. Ira Edelson, interview with author, May 27, 2004.

7: The "Four-Meter Fax"

1. Ira Edelson, interview with author, May 27, 2004.

2. Ibid.

3. Tony Ciminera, interview with author, June 14, 2004.

4. Ibid.

5. Pete Mulhern, interview with author, June 16, 2004.

6. "Contract for Export of Yugo Cars in 1985," BBC Monitoring Service, September 20, 1984.

7. Interestingly enough, Bricklin publicly announced the final U.S. sales price for the car as $3,990 some two months *before* he had negotiated with Zastava. The $3,990 price tag first appeared in an article in *The Wall Street Journal* in July 1984. See "Looking for a New Car? See If Yugo for This One," *The Wall Street Journal*, July 18, 1984.

8. "Entrepreneur Imports Unique Cars: Yugoslavian Model Costing Less than $4,000 to Make US Debut," *The Dallas Morning News*, October 7, 1984.

9. Edward Miller, "Would You Go for a Yugo Costing $3,990?" Associated Press, February 15, 1985.

10. The $400,000 letter of credit was cited in a February 1984 article by the *Financial Times*. See "The Financial Times Looks at Plans to Launch Yugoslavian Cars on the US Market," *Financial Times*, February 27, 1985.

11. Edelson read his resignation letter to the author during a taped interview in 2004. Ira Edelson, interview with author, May 27, 2004.

12. Pete Mulhern, interview with author, June 16, 2004.

13. From the Society of Automotive Engineers website, www.sae.org/about/general/history (site accessed April 25, 2009).

14. Berry's company was Intelligent Controls.

15. Roger Berry, interview with author, June 23, 2004.

16. Ibid.

17. Pete Mulhern, interview with author, June 16, 2004.

18. Roger Berry, interview with author, June 23, 2004.

19. Zdravka Damjanic, interview with author, July 29, 2006.

20. Ibid.

21. From page 10 of the Zastava internal publication *Projekat Yugo-A*, published in January 1985. This publication is in the possession of the author.
22. Ibid., 28.
23. Pete Mulhern, interview with author, June 16, 2004.
24. See "Ex-NHTSA Aide to Head Yugo's Quality Control," *Automotive News*, June 24, 1985.
25. Zdravka Damjanic, interview with author, July 29, 2006.
26. Pete Mulhern, interview with author, June 16, 2004.
27. Roger Berry, interview with author, June 23, 2004.
28. "Roast Test Review," *Car and Driver* 32:10 (April 1987): 175.
29. Edward Miller, "Would You Go for a Yugo Costing $3,990?" Associated Press, February 15, 1985.
30. "35 mph Crash Test Shows Head Injuries Likely in Taurus, Sable Cars," Associated Press, June 30, 1986; and "Jeep Pickup Scores Poorly in US Crash Ratings," *The Toronto Star*, May 20, 2006.
31. "Ten of 26 Cars Flunk Crash Test—Hyundai, Yugo Fare Worst," *The Seattle Times*, August 16, 1986.
32. Pete Mulhern, interview with author, June 16, 2004.
33. "$3,990 Pricetag—U.S. to Get Communist Car," *The San Francisco Chronicle*, January 28, 1985.
34. The cars were shown at Studio A of Golden Gate Productions at 500 Eighth Street in San Francisco. See John A. Russell, "Yugo to Be Displayed at NADA," *Automotive News*, January 28, 1985.
35. Tony Ciminera, interview with author, June 14, 2004.

8: Destination America

1. Joseph R. Perone, "Did You Know?" *The Star-Ledger* (Newark), December 9, 2001.
2. Philip H. Dougherty, "Rosenfeld to Handle Yugoslav Car Import," *The New York Times*, April 1, 1985.
3. "New Kids on the Block," *Automotive News*, February 4, 1985.
4. Ibid.
5. According to the *Standard Catalog of Imported Cars, 1946–2002*, the other two communist-made cars sold in America were the Skoda from Czechoslovakia and the Moskvitch from the Soviet Union.
6. Quoted in Michael Palairet, "The Rise and Fall of Yugoslav Socialism: A Case Study of the Yugo Automobile Enterprise, 1954–92," in David F. Good, ed., *Economic Transformations in East and Central Europe* (New York: Routledge, 1994), 104.
7. "Hold the Red Cars," *Motor Trend* 37:10 (October 1985): 21.
8. "Letters to the Editor," *Ward's AutoWorld* 21:10 (October 1985): 21.
9. Ron Stepneski, "Make Way for $3990—Car Dealers Welcome Yugoslav Import," *The Record* (New Jersey), July 23, 1985.
10. Rebecca Fannin, "Yugo: The Little Engine That Could," *Marketing and Media Decisions* 20:11 (November 1985): 40.
11. For a history of antidumping regulations, see J. Michael Finger, *The Origins and Evolution of Antidumping Regulations*, PRE Working Papers Series (Washington, DC: World Bank, 1991).

12. Jane Seaberry, "Made in U.S.A.: The Import Flood," *The Washington Post*, November 22, 1981.

13. *Ekonomska Politika*, September 29, 1986. Cited in Michael Palairet, "The Rise and Fall of Yugoslav Socialism: A Case Study of the Yugo Automobile Enterprise, 1954–92," 104.

14. Ibid.

15. Lenny Glynn, "The Sovereign State of Kissinger Inc.," *The Globe and Mail* (Toronto), July 26, 1985.

16. Ibid.

17. The exact client list of Kissinger Associates has never been revealed. The clients listed above were some that Eagleburger had worked with, which he attested to publicly during Senate confirmation hearings in 1989. Eagleburger underwent the hearings prior to being named deputy secretary of state by President George H. W. Bush.

18. Raymond H. Anderson, "Nine Years Later, Fear in Skopje: '63 Quake Stirs Anxieties," *The New York Times*, September 24, 1972.

19. David Binder, "Eagleburger Anguishes over Yugoslav Upheaval," *The New York Times*, June 19, 1992.

20. Clyde H. Farnsworth, "Washington Watch: Infighting on Europe Loans," *The New York Times*, May 10, 1982.

21. "Eagleburger Joins Board of Directors of Yugo America," *Automotive News*, February 18, 1985.

22. Ira Edelson, interview with author, May 27, 2004.

23. Ibid.

24. Warren Zimmermann, *Origins of a Catastrophe* (New York: Times Books, 1996), 7.

25. Lloyd George, interview with author, August 25, 2004.

26. Crossan was a former executive vice president at Occidental Petroleum who had taken part in the original IAI-Zastava-Occidental negotiations in May 1984. Apparently, Crossan was so thrilled by the Yugo project that he quit his job at Occidental to become vice president at Yugo America Inc. See "Former Executive of Occidental Takes Yugo Post," *Automotive News*, March 4, 1985.

27. Yugo America CFO Ira Edelson states that the negotiated price was "about $2,500 per car," while Toma Savic insists the price was $2,900.

28. "Medium-Term Contract for Export of Yugo Cars," BBC Monitoring Service, June 27, 1985.

29. Toma Savic, interview with author, July 28, 2006.

30. Richard Feast, "Yugo Investors to Help Build Plant," *Automotive News*, November 11, 1985.

31. "*Going Public* Magazine Reports on the '84 Initial Public Offering Market," PR Newswire, January 21, 1985.

32. Tony Ciminera, interview with author, June 14, 2004.

33. In late 1986, Ron Glantz, an analyst at Montgomery Securities in San Francisco, estimated that Yugoslavia was the world's lowest-cost producer of automobiles. See "Cash Flow," *Car and Driver* 32:7 (January 1987): 27.

34. Warren Brown, "Yugo Minicar to Debut in D.C., Baltimore," *The Washington Post*, July 22, 1985. The 92 percent figure seems exceptionally high, as the Yugo's entire engine was built by a separate company in Belgrade called DMB.

35. "Tiny Price for a Tiny Car Making Yugo a Big Deal," *Houston Chronicle*, August 28, 1985.

36. Ron Stepneski, "Make Way for $3990—Car Dealers Welcome Yugoslav Import."

37. Doron P. Levin, "Communist Cars to Try US Market," *The Wall Street Journal*, October 22, 1984.

38. Kathleen Hamilton, "Yugo Captures American Fancy," *Automotive News*, September 2, 1985.

39. "U.S. Trade Unit Reports on Prison-Good Imports," *The New York Times*, December 20, 1984.

40. "The US Motor Industry Sold 7.95m New Cars in 1984, a Rise of 17% on 1983," Textline Multiple Source Collection, January 7, 1985.

41. Roger Berry, interview with author, June 23, 2004.

42. Tony Ciminera, interview with author, June 14, 2004.

43. Zdravka Damjanic, interview with author, July 29, 2006.

44. "Big Send-off: First Yugoslav Car Shipment to the U.S. Departs," *Lexington Herald-Leader* (Kentucky), July 25, 1985.

45. Ibid.

46. Warren Brown, "Yugo Minicar to Debut in D.C., Baltimore."

47. Toma Savic, interview with author, July 28, 2006.

9: Yugo-mania

1. Mike Knepper, "The Yugo Phenomenon," *Motor Trend* 37:12 (December 1985): 11. Of all the articles written about the introduction of the Yugo, Knepper's article is far and away the best.

2. Figure cited in Philip H. Dougherty, "Affordable Legends Evoked," *The New York Times*, September 6, 1985.

3. "A Case of Yugo Mania," *San Francisco Chronicle*, August 28, 1985.

4. Tony Ciminera, interview with author, June 14, 2004.

5. John A. Russell, "Yugo Adjusts to Publicity Barrage," *Automotive News*, November 4, 1985.

6. Jaclyn Fierman, "Can a Beetle Brain Stir a Yearning for Yugos?" *Fortune* 111:10 (May 13, 1985): 73.

7. Ira Edelson, interview with author, May 27, 2004.

8. Al Fleming, "First Yugos Arrive at U.S. Docks," *Automotive News*, August 19, 1918.

9. William Meyers, "A Communist Car for the Capitalist Masses," *Adweek*, November 4, 1985.

10. Philip H. Dougherty, "Advertising: How to Get Nation Airborne," *The New York Times*, March 16, 1970.

11. Ibid.

12. Philip H. Dougherty, "Rosenfeld to Handle Yugoslav Car Import," *The New York Times*, April 1, 1985.

13. Philip H. Dougherty, "Affordable Legends Evoked."

14. Ibid.

15. Jon Lowell, "Minicars in the U.S.: Fad or Real Thing?" *Ward's AutoWorld* 21:12 (December 1985): 91.

16. Dan Jedlicka, "Ford's EXP Leads Appeal to Youngest Car Buyers," *Chicago Sun-Times*, December 19, 1985.

17. Ibid.

18. John Carey, "Look Out America: Here Comes Yugoslavia," *Periscope*, July 23, 1984, 13.

19. Mike Royko, "This Car Is Just a Little Creep," *Chicago Tribune*, August 29, 1985.

20. John R. White, "The Rise and Fall of the Yugo," *The Boston Globe*, February 5, 1989.

21. Warren Brown, "Minicar Market Gearing Up: Detractors Question Quality of 'Import Cheapies,'" *The Washington Post*, March 29, 1987.

22. The monthly payments based on an initial down payment of 25 percent of the cars' purchase prices. John Holusha, "Buying a Car on Credit? Shop for the Best Deal," *The New York Times*, May 20, 1984.

23. Average new-car-buyer income figures provided by J.D. Power and Associates. See Robert L. Simison, "Driven Down: Despite Strong Sales, Auto Makers Believe Real Booms Are Over," *The Wall Street Journal*, May 3, 1984.

24. Jon Lowell, "Minicars in the U.S.: Fad or Real Thing?" 90.

25. Used-car figures were from the Hertz Corporation. See Kenneth Eskey, "Used Car Sales Fall; Prices Stay Steady," *Houston Chronicle*, June 9, 1986. The average used-car payment figure of $197.18 was tabulated by the Motor Vehicle Manufacturers Association and reported in the *Chicago Sun-Times*. See Richard C. Noble, "American Car Debt $193 Billion," *Chicago Sun-Times*, March 9, 1986.

26. Marshall Schuon, "About Cars: Yugoslavia Unveils a Bargain Beauty," *The New York Times*, October 13, 1985.

27. Jon Lowell, "Minicars in the U.S.: Fad or Real Thing?"

28. Carole Gould, "On the Lots: A Bumper Crop of Used Cars," *The New York Times*, November 17, 1985.

29. Thomas G. Keane, "Used Car Dealers Say 1985 Was a Clunker—New Wheels Almost as Cheap," *San Francisco Chronicle*, December 30, 1985.

30. Jon Lowell, "Minicars in the U.S.: Fad or Real Thing?"

31. John R. McCarty, "Caddy Dealer: Buy One, Get One," *Houston Chronicle*, March 23, 1986.

32. John Holusha, "Chevy Turns to the Japanese," *The New York Times*, October 6, 1983.

33. Jim Hall, "Baseball, Hot Dogs, Apple Pie, and . . . Suzuki?" *Motor Trend* 36:1 (January 1984): 31.

34. Maralyn Edid, "The Auto Workers' Strategy: Straddle the Fence," *BusinessWeek*, April 22, 1985, 80.

35. Jim Hall, "Baseball, Hot Dogs, Apple Pie, and . . . Suzuki?" 31.

36. Thomas Moore, "Maxi Hopes Ride on New Mini Cars," *Fortune*, January 20, 1986, 58.

37. Jim Mateja, "Inexpensive Japanese Imports Scarce," *Chicago Tribune*, November 10, 1985.

38. Passenger car sales for 1985 were 11,042,797, truck sales 4,669,700. "Car, Truck Sales in U.S. Break Seven-Year-Old Record," *The Charlotte Observer*, January 7, 1986.

39. Stephen Taub, "The Auto Wars," *Financial World*, September 18, 1985.

40. Tony Assenza, "Yugo GV: Revenge of the Kmart Shoppers," *Car and Driver* 31:10 (April 1986): 47.

41. Ibid., 51.

42. Suzanna Wetflaufer, "Demand High for Yugoslavian Import: Customers Putting Down Cash Even Without a Test Drive," Associated Press, August 28, 1985, and Tom Incantalupo, "A Shift to New Automakers Beyond the Big Three: Sales Are Speeding Up for Low-End Cars from Overseas," *Newsday*, July 20, 1986.

10: "It's Going to Be a Bloodbath"

1. Unless otherwise noted, Yugo America sales figures provided by company CFO Ira Edelson. Document is in possession of the author.

2. "A Second Shipment of 1,580 Vehicles of the 1985 Model Yugo Has Arrived at the Port of Baltimore," PR Newswire, October 3, 1985.

3. "Yugo Extols Price and Reliability: Auto Firm Will Use the Old 'Beetle' Philosophy to Push Sales," *Akron Beacon Journal*, December 8, 1985.

4. "Believer Goes to Great Lengths to Buy a Yugo," *Automotive News*, January 13, 1986.

5. "GM Unfazed by Mad Rush for Yugos," *Chicago Tribune*, September 30, 1985.

6. "Yugo Says Chrysler Likes Its Minicar," *Ward's AutoWorld* 22:5 (May 1986): special unnumbered insert.

7. Tony Ciminera, interview with author, June 14, 2004.

8. Barry Rosenberg, "Would You Buy a Car from This Man?" *Philadelphia* (April 1975): 174.

9. Ira Edelson, interview with author, May 27, 2004.

10. "Chrysler Says 'No' to Yugo, 'Yes' to America," *Ward's AutoWorld* 22:3 (March 1986): 23.

11. John A. Russell, "U.S. Rights to Romanian Car Subject to Three-Way Squabble," *Automotive News*, March 3, 1986.

12. Alan Freeman, "When Is a Renault Not a Renault? When It's a Dacia," *The Wall Street Journal*, March 14, 1986.

13. Ibid.

14. Tony Ciminera, interview with author, June 14, 2004.

15. Ibid.

16. Ibid.

17. Dale D. Buss, "Mahindra, Oltcit and More: New Wave of Car Imports Set to Hit U.S. Market," *The Wall Street Journal*, February 6, 1987.

18. Ibid.

19. Paul Lienert, "Powerhouse Firm to Go Head-to-Head with Japan in U.S." *Detroit Free Press*, September 9, 1985.

20. Andrew E. Green, "South Korea's Automobile Industry: Development and Prospects," *Asian Survey* 32:5 (May 1992): 416. See also Jonathan Mantle, *Car Wars: Fifty Years of Backstabbing, Infighting, and Industrial Espionage in the Global Market* (New York: Arcade Publishing, 1997), 84.

21. David Ensor, "How the Soviets Copied America's Best Bomber during WWII," CNN.com, archives.cnn.com/2001/US/01/25/smithsonian.cold.war (site accessed June 25, 2008).

22. John Burgess, "South Korea Eyes U.S. Auto Market Quality, Protectionism Among Obstacles," *The Washington Post*, October 7, 1984.

23. Christopher Waddell, "Pony, Luxury Cars Make Gains in Canadian Import Car Market," *The Globe and Mail* (Toronto), January 10, 1985.

24. Bryan Johnson, "Unheralded Pony Gallops into Canadian Hearts," *The Globe and Mail* (Toronto), March 18, 1985.

25. Christopher Waddell, "Pony, Luxury Cars Make Gains in Canadian Import Car Market."

26. Pete Mulhern, interview with author, August 5, 2004.

27. "Mitsubishi Corp and Mitsubishi Motors of Japan Are to Acquire Jointly a 10% Stake in Hyundai Motor of South Korea," *Financial Times*, April 2, 1982.

28. John Holusha, "Q&A: The South Korean Script for Success," *The New York Times*, September 26, 1986.

29. Matt DeLorenzo, "Hyundai Sets Two First-Year Goals," *Automotive News*, February 10, 1986.

30. Warren Brown, "Car Wars: Koreans, Japanese Maneuvering for Position in U.S. Auto Battle," *The Washington Post*, February 23, 1986.

31. Matt DeLorenzo, "Hyundai Sets Two First-Year Goals."

32. Colleen Belli, "The New Price Leaders," *Automotive News*, March 11, 1985.

33. Ira Edelson, interview with author, May 27, 2004.

34. Michael Palairet, "The Rise and Fall of Yugoslav Socialism: A Case Study of the Yugo Automobile Enterprise, 1954–92," in David F. Good, ed., *Economic Transformations in East and Central Europe* (New York: Routledge, 1994), 105.

35. Toma Savic, interview with author, July 28, 2006.

36. "Yugo-Florida Car in Production at Crvena Zastava," BBC Monitoring Service—Central Europe and the Balkans, October 20, 1988.

37. "Motoring: Marques of the 20th Century—Yugo/Zastava," *The Independent* (London), August 12, 2000. The Yugo Florida was sold in Great Britain as the Sana.

38. Barbara Wendling, interview with author, June 12, 2007.

39. Janet Braunstein, "Inexpensive Car Market Offerings Increase," *The Record* (New Jersey), October 15, 1987.

40. Janet Braunstein, "Inexpensive Automobiles Making Comeback: Firms Struggle for Market Share," *The Record* (New Jersey), December 16, 1986.

41. Thomas Moore, "Maxi Hopes Ride on New Mini Cars," *Fortune* 113:2 (January 20, 1986): 57.

42. "Think Small—Minicars, Import and Domestic, Vie for Hearts and Checkbooks," *The Seattle Times*, March 29, 2006.

43. Warren Brown, "Car Wars: Koreans, Japanese Maneuvering for Position in U.S. Auto Battle."

44. Richard Johnson, "Cheapies by the Dozen," *Automotive News*, March 10, 1986.

45. Tom Incantalupo, "A Shift to New Automakers Beyond the 'Big Three': Sales Are Speeding Up for Low-End Cars from Overseas," *Newsday*, July 20, 1986.

46. "Another Mini-car Rival," *Chicago Tribune*, November 11, 1987.

11: The Ambassador Drives a Yugo

1. John A. Russell, "Yugo Seeking Production Increase," *Automotive News*, September 16, 1985.

2. David C. Smith, "Yugo: Zastava Emerges from the Dark Ages," *Ward's AutoWorld* 23:11 (November 1986): 67.

3. Michael Palairet, "Ramiz Sadiku: A Case Study of Industrialization in Kosovo," *Soviet Studies* 44:5 (1992): 905.

4. Roger Berry, interview with author, June 23, 2004.

5. Al Urbanski, "American Abroad: Iveco's Man in Yugoslavia," *Sales and Marketing Management* 138 (June 1987): 76.

6. Zoran Basaraba, interview with author, June 23, 2004.

7. Michael Palairet, "The Rise and Fall of Yugoslav Socialism: A Case Study of the Yugo Automobile Enterprise, 1954–92," in David F. Good, ed., *Economic Transformations in East and Central Europe* (New York: Routledge, 1994), 100.

8. Ron Stepneski, "Yugos Rev Up for Sales Race: $3,990 Car Introduced in New York," *The Record* (New Jersey), October 10, 1985.

9. "Yugo and Yoko Unveiling in Central Park," *Adweek*, October 14, 1985.

10. Ibid.

11. Sam Enriquez, "Small but Persistent Group Protests Yugoslavian-made Car," *Los Angeles Times*, February 23, 1987.

12. Bill McGraw, "Flagpole Climber Is Arrested in Yugoslavian Fest Protest," *Detroit Free Press*, September 9, 1985.

13. "Text of 'Croatian Fighters,'" *The New York Times*, September 11, 1976.

14. Kathleen Hamilton, "Croats Wage War of Words against Yugo," *Automotive News*, September 23, 1985.

15. "Letters: Unsafe at Any Speed? Of Belts, Bags, Bombs, and 'Bargains,'" *The Record* (New Jersey), August 18, 1985.

16. Elizabeth Lu, "Rights Activists Picket Yugo Office," *The Record* (New Jersey), August 25, 1987.

17. "Yugoslav Fest Marred by Protests," *Detroit Free Press*, September 8, 1986.

18. Mary Connelly, "Croatian Group Calls Yugo Boycott," *Automotive News*, August 25, 1986.

19. Zoran Basaraba, interview with author, June 23, 2004.

20. Elizabeth Lu, "Rights Activists Picket Yugo Office."

21. Wolfgang Saxon, "Yugoslavs Allow Mihajlov to Leave," *The New York Times*, June 11, 1978.

22. "Amnesty Criticizes Yugoslavia," *The Washington Post*, May 29, 1985.

23. "Belgrade Six," *The Washington Post*, January 30, 1985.

24. Henry Kamm, "Yugoslavs Take Pride in Yugo's Success in America," *St. Petersburg Times*, July 1, 1987.

25. Ibid.

26. Patrick J. Nichols, interview with author, July 11, 2004.

27. Yugoslav debt figures cited in John R. Lampe, Russell O. Prickett, and Ljubisa S. Adamovic, *Yugoslav-American Economic Relations Since World War II* (Durham, NC: Duke University Press, 1990), 221.

28. Ibid., 148.

29. Russell O. Prickett, interview with author, June 28, 2004.

30. "Yugoslavia Said to Complete 1983 Bank Debt Rescheduling," *The Wall Street Journal*, October 7, 1983.

31. "Sole U.S. Bank Branch in East Bloc Does Business as Usual," *The Wall Street Journal*, March 6, 1980.

32. Jack Anderson, "Horrendous Mexican Debt," *San Francisco Chronicle*, June 20, 1986.

33. Eric N. Berg, "At Manufacturers, Banking Is Sluggish," *The New York Times*, August 2, 1986.

34. "Yugo America Gets $75 Million Line of Credit," *Automotive News*, January 6, 1986.

35. Fulvio Dobrich, interview with author, June 7, 2007.

36. Maggie Mudd, interview with author, June 7, 2007.

37. Ira Edelson, interview with author, May 21, 2007.

38. Yugo America's $75 million line of credit and its various sub-lines were approved by Manufacturers Hanover in a letter from bank vice president Robert P. Hannan to Ira Edelson dated October 25, 1985. The letter is in the possession of the author.

39. Ira Edelson, interview with author, May 27, 2004.

40. Fulvio Dobrich, interview with author, June 7, 2007.

41. E. R. Shipp, "Three Indicted in Drysdale Collapse," *The New York Times*, July 28, 1983.

42. John P. Forde, "Bad Loans Make Minor Dent in Earnings," *American Banker*, April 24, 1985, 3.

43. "Manufacturers Hanover Corp. Records Fourth Quarter Financial Results," PR Newswire, January 15, 1985.

44. "Yugo America Gets $75 Million Line of Credit."

45. "*Fortune* Picks Outstanding Products for '85," Associated Press, November 20, 1985.

46. See "*Motor Trend* Magazine Nominates the Yugo GV for Its Import Car of the Year Award," PR Newswire, November 22, 1985; and "*USA Today* Selects the Yugo as One of Its 12 Hot Hits for 1985," PR Newswire, December 26, 1985.

47. John A. Russell, "Ouster of Yugo's Ad Agency Sparks War of Words," *Automotive News*, July 7, 1986.

48. Ron Stepneski, "Yugo to Diversify Its Line: First-Year Sales Were a Letdown," *The Record* (New Jersey), October 5, 1986.

49. John A. Russell, "Ouster of Yugo's Ad Agency Sparks War of Words."

50. Mike Royko, "This Car Is Just a Little Creep," *Chicago Tribune*, August 29, 1985.

51. John R. White, "A Heavenly Week in a Porsche; 2 Hours in Purgatory with Yugo," *The Boston Globe*, October 20, 1985.

52. Jaclyn Fierman, "Can a Beetle Brain Stir a Yearning for Yugos?" *Fortune* 111:10 (May 13, 1985): 73.

53. Warren Brown, "Weekend Wheels: If Yugo for It, You Could Be Sorry," *The Washington Post*, December 20, 1985.

54. Ibid.

12: The Car-Buying Bible

1. "Low Grades for Consumerism," *The New York Times*, March 27, 1983.

2. Betsy Brown, "Analysis Shows Consumers Union Is 50," *The New York Times*, February 2, 1986.

3. Mark Lacter, "Scrappy Consumers Union Turns 50," *San Francisco Chronicle*, January 31, 1986.

4. Christiane Bird, "Consumers Union: Testing, Testing," *Newsday*, August 14, 1988.

5. Mary Williams Walsh, "Consumers Union Tests Products in Ways Manufacturers Won't," *The Wall Street Journal*, January 14, 1985.

6. Henry Gilgoff and Braden Phillips, "First 50 Years: How Does *Consumer Reports* Rate?" *Newsday*, June 2, 1986.

7. "Coleco Stock Down on Article in *Consumer Reports* Magazine," Dow Jones News Service, December 21, 1983.

8. "The Subaru 360 (Not Acceptable)," *Consumer Reports* 34 (April 1969): 220–21.

9. Fern Shen, "A Consuming Interest in Cars," *The Record* (New Jersey), April 21, 1986.

10. John R. White, "Who Are Those Guys at Consumer Reports?" *The Boston Globe*, April 5, 1997.

11. Earle Eldridge, "Car Buyers Turn to Consumer Reports," *USA Today*, March 18, 1997.

12. Connie Koenenn, "Consumer Reports: A Bible of the '90s," *The Record* (New Jersey), December 31, 1994.

13. "Suzuki Blasts Back at Criticism of Handling of Sporty Samurai," *Houston Chronicle*, June 10, 1988. In a joint press release issued in July 2004, Consumers Union and Suzuki announced the settlement and dismissal of the lawsuit.

14. Jerry Dubrowski, "Car Trade Magazines Carry a Lot of Clout," Reuters News, August 3, 1993.

15. "Samurai Sales Down in June," *The Dallas Morning News*, July 6, 1988.

16. Pete Mulhern, interview with author, August 5, 2004.

17. "How Much Car for $3990?" *Consumer Reports* 51:2 (February 1986): 84.

18. The reception was held at the Royal Sonesta Hotel on Bourbon Street. See "NADA Convention: Receptions," *Automotive News*, February 10, 1986

19. "How Much Car for $3990?" 86.

20. Ibid., 84.

21. Pete Mulhern, interview with author, August 5, 2004.

22. Robert D. Knoll, interview with author, June 21, 2007.

23. "How Much Car for $3990?" 86.

24. Tony Ciminera, interview with author, June 14, 2004.

25. Pete Mulhern, interview with author, August 5, 2004.

26. Dan Jedlicka, "Iacocca Tells 'Vice' Story," *Chicago Sun-Times*, April 10, 1986.

27. "NHTSA Orders Recall of Yugos," *Automotive News*, February 17, 1986.

28. Amy Harmon, "Crash-testing Pits Science and Politics," *Chicago Sun-Times*, January 19, 1992.

29. Jim Daw, "U.S. Agency Tests Cars at Smash Palace," *The Toronto Star*, October 4, 1986.

30. Ibid.

31. "Federal Safety Report—Yugo GV Does Poorly in Crash Tests," *San Francisco Chronicle*, March 13, 1986.

32. "Yugo Results Poor in Crash Tests," *The Washington Post*, March 13, 1986.

33. "Yugo Scores Poorly in Safety Agency's 35-MPH Crash Test," *The Wall Street Journal*, March 17, 1986; "No Go for Yugo in Crash Testing," *Sun-Sentinel*, March 17, 1986; "Yugo Worst in Crash Safety Test, Study Finds," *Chicago Tribune*, March 13, 1986.

34. "How the Cars Fared in Crash Tests," *The Charlotte Observer*, August 8, 1986.

35. Ibid.
36. John R. White, "Whose Crash Data Are Correct?" *The Boston Globe*, November 25, 1989.
37. Jim Daw, "U.S. Agency Tests Cars at Smash Palace."
38. "Yugo Scores Poorly in Safety Agency's 35-mph Crash Test."
39. "Low Cost Imports Fare Badly in Test," *Newsday*, August 9, 1986.
40. Bill Adair, "Is Your Car Safe? Here Are Real Figures," *St. Petersburg Times*, April 27, 1991.
41. Ibid.
42. Al Haas, "For Yugo, a Year of Slow Sales and Stinging Reviews," *The Philadelphia Inquirer*, August 17, 1986.
43. Karl Vick, "TV Twists of Fate," *St. Petersburg Times*, August 27, 1986.
44. Gail Shister, "Tom Brokaw Breaks CBS Winning Streak," *The Philadelphia Inquirer*, June 4, 1986.
45. "Letters," *Ward's AutoWorld* 23:2 (February 1986): 18.
46. Jonathan Freedman, "The American Gas-Guzzler Is Still the One," *The San Diego Union-Tribune*, November 24, 1986.
47. "Gas-Guzzler Sales Down 30%," *San Francisco Chronicle*, May 7, 1986.
48. Pete Mulhern, interview with author, August 5, 2004.
49. Mike Royko, "This Car Is Just a Little Creep," *Chicago Tribune*, August 29, 1985.
50. "Naderites' Warning: Small Cars Kill," *The Wall Street Journal*, November 1, 1991.
51. Bill Braucher, "Yugoslavians Put Tiny Dent in U.S. Market," *The Miami Herald*, October 8, 1985.
52. "Yugo America Inc. Announces That It Has Sold Its 10,000th Car," PR Newswire, April 7, 1986.
53. "Yugos for California," *San Francisco Chronicle*, July 9, 1986.
54. "Yugo to Make Its California Debut at L'Ermitage, Beverly Hills," PR Newswire, July 14, 1986; "Yugo GV to Make Northern California Debut," PR Newswire, July 15, 1986.
55. John Schneidawind, "Cheapest Car in Town Aims to Sell 10,000 Cars in California," *San Jose Mercury News*, July 19, 1986.
56. Nelson Antosh, "Stop at the Cut—Barbours Cut Terminal Is Yugo's 2nd Entry Port," *Houston Chronicle*, May 12, 1986.
57. Ira Edelson, interview with author, May 27, 2004.
58. "Group Rates Cars on Costs of Crash Repairs," *The New York Times*, May 11, 1986.
59. William Allan, "Save by Shopping for Insurance—Structure, Size of Auto Will Vary Rates," *The Seattle Times*, February 6, 1988.
60. "Differences in Insurance Premiums Based Partly on Type of Vehicle," *The Washington Post*, December 12, 1988; "State Farm Announces Premium Rates for Car Damage and Auto Theft," PR Newswire, December 20, 1988.

13: The Proton Saga Saga

1. Chris Sherwell, "Malaysia Faces Crisis of Maturity," *Financial Times*, March 29, 1986.

2. Jomo K. S. ed., and Chris Edwards, "Malaysian Industrialisation in Historical Perspective," in Jomo K. S., ed., *Industrialising Malaysia: Policy, Performance, Prospects* (New York: Routledge, 1993), 28–29.

3. Kit G. Machado, "Japanese Transnational Corporations in Malaysia's State Sponsored Heavy Industrialization Drive: The HICOM Automobile and Steel Projects," *Pacific Affairs* 62:4 (Winter 1989–90): 509.

4. Wong Sulong, "Mitsubishi in Pounds 163m Deal to Make Malaysian Cars," *Financial Times*, May 14, 1983.

5. Marlane Guelden, "Malaysian Auto Is Caught Between Success, Failure," *Automotive News*, June 16, 1986.

6. R. S. Milne and Diane K. Mauzy, *Malaysian Politics Under Mahathir* (New York: Routledge, 2002), 65.

7. Andrew Tank, "The Saga of Proton: Will Malaysian Automobile Make It on the World Stage?" *Automotive News*, August 4, 1986.

8. Ibid.

9. Bryan Johnson, "Malay Security Law Crushes Opposition," *The Globe and Mail* (Toronto), March 20, 1981.

10. "Two Australians Hanged in Malaysia Drug Case," *The Seattle Times*, July 7, 1986.

11. Jonathan Mantle, *Car Wars: Fifty Years of Backstabbing, Infighting, and Industrial Espionage in the International Market* (New York: Arcade Publishing, 1997), 152.

12. Marlane Guelden, "Malaysian Auto Is Caught Between Success, Failure."

13. "The Malaysian *Business Times* Reviews the Local Motor Industry in 1985," *Business Times*, December 28, 1985.

14. Marlane Guelden, "Malaysian Auto Is Caught Between Success, Failure."

15. Edith Terry, *How Asia Got Rich: Japan, China, and the Asian Economic Miracle* (Armonk, NY: M. E. Sharpe, 2002), 175.

16. Andrew Tank, "The Saga of Proton: Will Malaysian Automobile Make It on the World Stage?"

17. "At Least Two Japanese Motor Vehicle Manufacturers Have Temporarily Ceased Production in Malaysia," Textline Multiple Source Collection, November 21, 1986.

18. Marlane Guelden, "Malaysian Auto Is Caught Between Success, Failure."

19. Kit G. Machado, "Japanese Transnational Corporations in Malaysia's State Sponsored Heavy Industrialization Drive," 522.

20. Chrysler also sold the Mitsubishi-made Starion sports car in America as the Dodge and Plymouth Conquest.

21. Marlane Guelden, "Malaysian Auto Is Caught Between Success, Failure."

22. Kit G. Machado, "Proton and Malaysia's Motor Vehicle Industry," in K. S. Jomo, ed., *Japan and Malaysian Development: In the Shadow of the Rising Sun* (New York: Routledge, 1994), 321.

23. Friedemann Bartu, *The Ugly Japanese: Nippon's Economic Empire in Asia* (New York: Longman, 1992), 76.

24. Tony Ciminera, interview with author, June 14, 2004.

25. Ibid.

26. In 1988, Yugo America's parent company, Global Motors, went bankrupt and left Kissinger Associates with over $240,000 in unpaid bills. The contract between Bricklin Industries and Kissinger Associates was included in Yugo America's

Chapter 11 bankruptcy file housed at the National Archives repository in Lee's Summit, Missouri. See Global Motors bankruptcy proceedings, U.S. Bankruptcy Court, District of New Jersey, Case Number 89-00678C.

27. Friedemann Bartu, *The Ugly Japanese*, 74.
28. Quoted in Walter Isaacson, *Kissinger: A Biography* (New York: Simon & Schuster Paperbacks, 2005), 743.
29. Tony Ciminera, interview with author, June 14, 2004.
30. Charles Siler, "Hyundai Motors Sets Formidable Sales Record for Rookie Importers," *The Orange County Register*, January 7, 1987.
31. "Best Selling Cars and Trucks for 1993," Reuters News, January 4, 1994.
32. "Bricklin Industries Inc. Forms Global Motors Inc. as Parent Company of Yugo America Inc. and Proton America Inc.," PR Newswire, September 26, 1987.
33. John Holusha, "New Imports Dazzle Dealers," *The New York Times*, February 7, 1987.
34. Ibid.
35. The $60 royalty figure was attested to by Marcel Kole, Ira Edelson's successor as Yugo America CFO. On November 21, 1989, Kole was deposed as part of Global Motors' Chapter 11 bankruptcy proceedings. See Global Motors bankruptcy proceedings, U.S. Bankruptcy Court, District of New Jersey, Case Number 89-00678C.
36. The royalty figure for Per Arneberg and Fram Shipping was given by Zastava manager Toma Savic. Toma Savic, interview with author, July 28, 2006. The royalty figure for the Pepe brothers was estimated by the author.
37. Quote from Marcel Kole deposition, Global Motors bankruptcy proceedings.
38. Ira Edelson, interview with author, May 21, 2007.
39. Friedemann Bartu, *The Ugly Japanese*, 76–77.
40. Raphael Pura, "Malaysia's Ambition to Market Car in U.S. Faces Snags," *The Wall Street Journal*, January 30, 1987.
41. Friedemann Bartu, *The Ugly Japanese*, 78.
42. Raphael Pura, "Malaysia's Ambition to Market Car in U.S. Faces Snags."

14: Thirty-five Hundredths of a Percent

1. Toma Savic, interview with author, July 28, 2006.
2. "Import Briefs," *Journal of Commerce*, February 24, 1987.
3. "Yugo America Inc. Reports Record Sales for February 1987," PR Newswire, March 4, 1987.
4. Amal Kumar Naj, "U.S. Car Sales Stayed Weak in Late May," *The Wall Street Journal*, June 4, 1987.
5. "Yugo America Inc. Imports Its 50,000th Yugo GV," PR Newswire, February 10, 1987.
6. "Yugo to Hold Line on Prices but Nissan Plans Increases," *Newsday*, October 21, 1986.
7. L. Eric Elie, "Hertz Corp. Rolls Out Facts and Figures on the Used Car Market," *The Atlanta Journal-Constitution*, June 8, 1987.
8. Philip H. Dougherty, "Yugo Likes Its New Campaign," *The New York Times*, December 9, 1986.

9. Gordon Martin, "How Do 1986 Cars Compare for Consumer Satisfaction?" *San Francisco Chronicle*, August 20, 1987. In both 1986 and 1987, the Yugo was also number one in complaints in the Massachusetts Consumer Affairs Office.

10. John A. Russell, "Ouster of Yugo's Ad Agency Sparks War of Words," *Automotive News*, July 7, 1986. See also Philip H. Dougherty, "Yugo America Shifts to Fledgling Agency," *The New York Times*, July 1, 1986.

11. John A. Russell, "Ouster of Yugo's Ad Agency Sparks War of Words."

12. Ibid.

13. All 114 Yugo commercials airing from July 1986 to March 1988 are available, for a rental fee, at the Vanderbilt University Television News Archive in Nashville, Tennessee.

14. Kathryn Baker, "Some Good News for CBS Ratings," *The Record* (New Jersey), February 4, 1987.

15. Philip H. Dougherty, "Yugo Likes Its New Campaign."

16. Testimony of Marcel Kole, Global Motors bankruptcy proceedings, U.S. Bankruptcy Court, District of New Jersey, Case Number 89-00678C.

17. Ibid.

18. Total U.S. passenger vehicle sales were 11,442,725 in 1986. See Janet Braunstein, "Auto Sales Set Record During 1986," *The Orange County Register*, January 8, 1987.

19. John McMillan, "Economic Downswing Clearly Defined," *The State-Times* (Baton Rouge), March 16, 1987.

20. Cited in "Yugo Automobile Becomes Definitive Term in Writers' and Speakers' Lexicons Since Its United States Launch in 1985," PR Newswire, May 18, 1987.

21. Gene Wojciechowski, "The Little Big Man: Giants' Morris Overcomes His Lack of Size with an Abundance of Heart," *The Dallas Morning News*, January 24, 1987.

22. "Adobe" text taken from *Saturday Night Live* transcripts, www.snltranscripts .jt.org (site accessed April 26, 2009).

23. Yugo scene in *Dragnet*, directed by Tom Mankiewicz (1987; DVD: Universal City, CA: Universal Studios, 1998).

24. Frank Swertlow, "L.A. Life," *Daily News* (Los Angeles), May 31, 1990.

25. George J. Tanber, "Yugos Begin American Comeback," *Las Vegas Review-Journal*, January 28, 1991.

26. "L.A. Life," *Daily News* (Los Angeles), November 7, 1991.

27. Nathan Cobb, "Nice Guys Finish First," *The Boston Globe Magazine*, September 15, 1991, 16.

28. Robert J. Hawkins, "Leno Live: 90 Solid Minutes of Laughs," *The San Diego Union-Tribune*, May 31, 1991.

29. For a complete catalog of David Letterman's "Top Ten Lists" from NBC and his "Late Show Top Ten Lists" from CBS, visit www.mudslide.net/TopTen (site accessed April 28, 2009).

30. "Tipoff Gates Reveals He Fixed Ticket for Lasorda," *Daily News* (Los Angeles), June 30, 1991.

31. Tony Kornheiser, "Baseball in '87! They Said It Would Never Happen. They Were Wrong," *The Washington Post Magazine*, March 1, 1987, 20.

32. Ibid.

33. Tony Kornheiser, "Senators Walk Everybody but O's Bat Boy, Win 8–6 in Home Opener," *The Washington Post Magazine*, April 19, 1987, 30.

34. Tony Kornheiser, "Senators' Rebellion Explodes into Guerilla War Against Tang," *The Washington Post Magazine*, September 20, 1987, 62.

35. "Take My Wife for Example," *Moonlighting*, season 5, episode 60 (1985; DVD: Santa Monica, CA: Lion's Gate, 2007).

36. "Yugo Automobile Becomes Definitive Term in Writers' and Speakers' Lexicons Since Its United States Launch in 1985."

37. James R. Healey, "Free Yugo Is a No-Go," *USA Today*, April 20, 1987.

38. Al Haas, "Dead Giveaway: Take My Yugo—Please!" *The Philadelphia Inquirer*, April 15, 1987.

39. James R. Healey, "Free Yugo Is a No-Go."

40. Michael Lamm, "PM Owners Report: Yugo GV," *Popular Mechanics* 164:6 (June 1987): 147.

41. Ibid., 148.

42. Pete Mulhern, interview with author, August 5, 2004.

43. Richard Roeper, "Some Random Observations from a Bemused Road Warrior," *Chicago Sun-Times*, June 28, 1987.

44. Lewis Mumford, *The Highway and the City* (New York: New American Library, 1964), 245.

45. Dina Heredia, "Dealer Sees BMW Fans Go from Buffs to Yuppies; Franchise Tops Nation in Sales of Status Symbol," *The Orange County Register*, July 28, 1988.

46. Dan Jedlicka, "Car Buyers Looking for Luxury," *Chicago Sun-Times*, August 8, 1988.

47. Mark Maremont et al., "Europe's Long, Smooth Rise in Luxury Cars Is Over," *BusinessWeek*, March 7, 1988.

48. "Jaguar Output Hits Record in '86 with 41,437 Cars," *The Toronto Star*, January 3, 1987.

49. Warren Brown, "Toyota Ready to Rev Up Luxury Car Rivalry," *The Washington Post*, July 26, 1987.

50. Gil Troy, *Morning in America: How Ronald Reagan Invented the 1980s* (Princeton: Princeton University Press, 2005), 119.

51. Ibid.

52. Pam Lambert, "Television: Star Treacle," *The Wall Street Journal*, September 9, 1985.

53. Ira Berkow, "Trump Building the Generals in His Own Style," *The New York Times*, January 1, 1984.

54. Quoted in Gil Troy, *Morning in America*, 218.

55. Richard D. Stevenson, "Bumper Crop of Brand Names," *The New York Times*, November 12, 1986.

56. Sally Squires, "Is Bottled Water Worth It?" *The Washington Post*, January 22, 1986.

57. Myron Magnet, "The Money Society: Money Seems to Be the Only Thing That Counts These Days," *Fortune*, July 6, 1987, 26. Quoted in Robert M. Collins, *Transforming America: Politics and Culture in the Reagan Years* (New York: Columbia University Press, 2007), 157.

58. Katherine Bishop, "Status on a Budget: California Company Ringing Registers with Fake Car Phone," *St. Petersburg Times*, April 24, 1988.

59. Paul Schwartzman, "Trendy and Hot: Hood Ornaments," *The Record* (New Jersey), May 4, 1987.

60. "Status Symbols," *USA Today*, November 15, 1988.
61. Brock Yates, "In Search of the Car That, Uh, Improves You," *The Washington Post*, February 14, 1988.
62. Nanette Asimov, "The Word on High School Cool," *San Francisco Chronicle*, May 9, 1988.

15: Mabon In, Bricklin Out
1. "Yugo Celebrates Second Anniversary," PR Newswire, August 31, 1987.
2. "This Week's Historic; Yugo Breaks Through," *USA Today*, October 21, 1987.
3. Rich Ceppos, "Yugo GVX: Adventures in Capitalist Hot Rodding," *Car and Driver* 34:5 (November 1988): 159.
4. Ibid., 160.
5. Jack R. Nerad, "Hyundai Excel GS vs. Yugo GVX," *Motor Trend* (December 1988): 65.
6. Ira Edelson, interview with author, May 21, 2007.
7. Ibid.
8. Mark Colodny, "Kravis Lassoes Bricklin's Spread," *Fortune* 123:11 (June 3, 1991): 212.
9. Jon Van Housen, "Bricklin 'Disneyland' Removed; Kravis' $5 Million Transformation Includes Log Home, Guest Houses," *The Denver Post*, May 22, 1992.
10. Dee Weiss, interview with author, May 30, 2007.
11. Ellen Haddow, "A Town Worries That Its Benefactor Is Now Broke," *The Boston Globe*, April 19, 1988.
12. Ira Edelson, interview with author, May 27, 2004.
13. Warren Brown, "Bricklin Exits the Auto Industry—Again," *The Washington Post*, April 20, 1988.
14. The financial terms of the deal were provided by Yugo America's chief financial officer, Ira Edelson.
15. In fact, each Yugo principal received a consulting contract. Bricklin's was a five-year contract worth $250,000 for the first year, $300,000 for years two and three, and $350,000 for years four and five. Bill Prior received a five-year contract worth $375,000 per annum; Dan Prior, three years, $235,000 per annum; Tony Cimi-nera, three years, $200,000 per annum; Ira Edelson, one year, $120,000; Ron Edel-son, one year, $120,000. These figures appear in Global Motors bankruptcy proceedings, U.S. Bankruptcy Court, District of New Jersey, Case Number 89-00678C.
16. Ira Edelson, interview with author, May 21, 2007.
17. Ibid.
18. Larry Tye, "California S&L's Fall from Grace Is a Classic Case," *The Boston Globe*, July 22, 1990.
19. Stephen Pizzo, Mary Fricker, and Paul Muolo, *Inside Job: The Looting of America's Savings and Loans* (New York: HarperPerennial, 1991), 23.
20. Catherine England, "Lessons from the Savings and Loan Debacle: The Case for Further Financial Deregulation," *Regulation* 15:3 (Summer 1992): 37.
21. "US S&Ls Record Loss of $4.91 Billion in 1981," *The Globe and Mail* (Toronto), January 30, 1982.

22. John Kenneth Galbraith, *The Culture of Contentment* (New York: Houghton Mifflin Co., 1992), 61.

23. Stephen Pizzo, Mary Fricker, and Paul Muolo, *Inside Job*, 27.

24. "Imperial Junk Bonds Ranked 2nd in Nation," *The San Diego Union-Tribune*, July 19, 1989.

25. "Mabon, Nugent Relocating Headquarters to One Liberty Plaza," PR Newswire, February 17, 1989.

26. Pravin Banker, interview with author, May 31, 2007.

27. "Mabon Nugent Adds Three to Investment Banking," *Securities Week*, June 22, 1987, 10.

28. Zoran Basaraba, interview with author, June 23, 2004.

29. The plans were announced in June and August 1988. See "Yugo America Offers Discounts Up to 17% on Its Major Models," *The Wall Street Journal*, June 30, 1988; and Jacob M. Schlesinger, "Yugo America Inc. Unveils a Program to Ease Financing," *The Wall Street Journal*, August 2, 1988.

30. Stephen Duthie, "Car Exports to U.S. by Malaysia Set Back by Japan's Takeover," *The Wall Street Journal*, September 13, 1988.

31. A draft of the Global Motors–Perusahaan contract can be found in Global Motors bankruptcy proceedings, U.S. Bankruptcy Court, District of New Jersey, Case Number 89-00678C. Dated October 1987, the contract is sixty-five pages long and makes no mention of Mitsubishi.

32. Ira Edelson, interview with author, May 21, 2007.

33. "Owner of Big Stake in Yugo's Marketer Seeks to Sell Holding," *The Wall Street Journal*, December 23, 1988.

34. Victor E. Sasson, "Cash, Court Halt Yugo's Demise," *The Record* (New Jersey), February 15, 1989.

35. James R. Healey, "Yugo Won't Go; Dealers in Limbo," *USA Today*, January 27, 1989.

36. Kim Norris, "Mabon, Nugent Reportedly Seeking a Buyer Amid Internal Strife," *Securities Week*, November 28, 1988, 1. See also "Mabon, Nugent Relocating Headquarters to One Liberty Plaza."

37. "International Capital Markets: Italian Group Buys Majority of US Broker," *Financial Times*, April 10, 1991.

38. John Ikeda, "Imperial Traces Loss to Several Big Loans," *The San Diego Union-Tribune*, January 9, 1989.

39. Richard W. Stevenson, "California Saving Unit Is Seized," *The New York Times*, February 24, 1990. All told, Imperial's collapse cost the U.S. government $1.6 billion, which meant that (like it or not) every tax-paying American paid for at least a tiny part of the Yugo.

40. "Citibank Sues Bricklin over Credit-Card Balance," *The Denver Post*, August 29, 1989.

41. "IRS Sells Its Share of Bricklin Ranch," *The Gazette* (Colorado Springs), January 18, 1989.

42. Jon Van Housen, "Bricklin 'Disneyland' Removed."

43. "Bricklin Ranch Sold to Financier," *Rocky Mountain News*, April 23, 1991.

44. Frederick Standish, "Jazzy Video Show a Feature of Proposed 1,000-Dealer Network," Associated Press, January 23, 1989.

45. Ibid.
46. "Ward's Wrap Up," *Ward's AutoWorld*, 25:2 (February 1989): 2.
47. "Judge Orders Bricklin to Pay $17 Million for Contract Breach," *The Wall Street Journal*, June 11, 1991.
48. "Yugo Importer Bricklin Files for Bankruptcy Liquidation," Associated Press, August 22, 1991.
49. Victor E. Sasson, "In Yugo Story, It's Chapter 11 Yugoslav Maker to Take Over," *The Record* (New Jersey), January 31, 1989.
50. Victor E. Sasson, "Yugo Importer Files Reorganization Plan—Offers 9 Cents on Dollar," *The Record* (New Jersey), September 3, 1989.
51. Yugo America reorganization figures were from an internal company spreadsheet provided by Toma Savic. Document in possession of author. The figures reported in the press at the time varied widely and were significantly less than the detailed totals provided by Savic.
52. Stephanie Stokes and Marilee Loboda Braue, "New Firm at Helm of Yugo Reorganization Plan Approved," *The Record* (New Jersey), December 21, 1989.

16: "The Yugo Is a No-Go"

1. Zoran Basaraba, interview with author, June 23, 2004.
2. Ibid.
3. "Global Motors' Yugo Unit Is to Unveil Survival Plan," *The Wall Street Journal*, June 30, 1989.
4. Toma Savic, interview with author, July 28, 2006.
5. Paul Ingrassia, "Yugo Minicar's Importer in Chapter 11; Infusion by Manufacturer Is Expected," *The Wall Street Journal*, January 31, 1989.
6. "Authorized Yugo Dealers Retain Miami Attorney," PR Newswire, February 28, 1989.
7. Toma Savic, interview with author, July 28, 2006.
8. Andrew Blum, "Group Says Yugo Is Little Car That Can't," *The National Law Journal*, June 12, 1989.
9. Robert Hanley, "Imperial Sues Yugo Distributor," *The San Diego Union-Tribune*, February 9, 1989.
10. Toma Savic, interview with author, July 28, 2006.
11. Tom Hundley, "Accident Kills 1 but It Was Deja Vu for Other Drivers," *Chicago Tribune*, October 3, 1989.
12. "Bridge Crash Faces Review Mediators to Weigh Settlement," *Detroit Free Press*, December 1, 1991.
13. See Richard Sisson et al., eds., *The American Midwest: An Interpretive Encyclopedia* (Bloomington: Indiana University Press, 2007), 21. For the Yugo's Wikipedia entry, see en.wikipedia.org/wiki/Yugo (site accessed May 27, 2008).
14. The Yugo show idea appeared on MythBusters' "Show Ideas" message board.
15. David Hacker and Robert Musial, "Woman May Be Bridge Victim; Royal Oak Resident, 31, Missing on Trip to UP," *Detroit Free Press*, September 27, 1989.
16. Bart Stupak, *Special Subcommittee Report on Mackinac Bridge Safety* (Lansing, MI: House Transportation Subcommittee, 1990), 7.
17. "Bridge Victim's Lawyer Calls Car, Span Unsafe; State, Mackinac Operator, Yugo Face Suits," *Detroit Free Press*, November 8, 1989.

18. Hugh McDiarmid Jr., "Mother of 1989 Victim Says State Should Wake Up," *Detroit Free Press*, March 4, 1997.

19. "Bridge Victim's Lawyer Calls Car, Span Unsafe; State, Mackinac Operator, Yugo Face Suits."

20. Ibid.

21. "Yugo Reorganization Plan May Be Cleared in a Month," *The Wall Street Journal*, November 14, 1989.

22. Daniel J. Wakin, "Yugo America Offers Dealer-Discounts to Spur Sales," *The Record* (New Jersey), March 29, 1989; Stephanie Stokes, "Yugo America Ready to Shift into Drive," *The Record* (New Jersey), May 18, 1990.

23. Victor E. Sasson, "It's Show Time at Yugo: Convertible Is Expected to Finally Make Its Debut," *The Record* (New Jersey), August 3, 1989.

24. Denise Couture, "At Yugo America, Determination," *The Record* (New Jersey), March 26, 1989; Jim Henry, "Yugo Trying to Shake Off Reputation for Poor Quality, Bankruptcy Stigma," *The Atlanta Journal-Constitution*, October 5, 1990.

25. Mark Alpert, "Yugo Tries Again," *Fortune* 122:10 (October 22, 1990): 12; "Lemons 'n' Losers: Cars That Bombed in the 1980s," *USA Today*, November 29, 1989; Yardena Arar, "Coast to Coast on a Wing and a Yugo," *Daily News* (Los Angeles), November 29, 1989.

26. Tom and Ray Magliozzi, "For Now, Keep Your Yugo and Your Sense of Humor," *The Dallas Morning News*, July 3, 1990.

27. David Leon Moore, "Imports Find Rewarding Life in NBA," *USA Today*, April 30, 1990.

28. Brian Hanley, "Bulls Hoping Kukoc Will Be Worth Wait," *Chicago Sun-Times*, June 28, 1990.

29. Kevin Lyttle, "Lowly Americans Prove to Be Yugo of Soccer Teams," *Austin American-Statesman*, June 12, 1990.

30. "LSU's 'Paper Tigers' Stumble to Top Ranking," *The Advocate* (Baton Rogue), October 11, 1989.

31. Bill Flick, "He's Really 'Bowled' Over by Corporate Sponsorship," *The Pantagraph* (Bloomington, IL), January 7, 1990.

32. Stephanie Stokes, "Yugo America Ready to Shift into Drive."

33. Doron P. Levin, "Yugo's Woes: Unsold Cars Piling Up," *Daily Breeze* (Torrance, CA), December 4, 1988.

34. Oddly enough, Group Lotus is today owned by Perusahaan Otomobil Nasional, the maker of the Proton.

35. "Lotus Esprit Turbo," *Chicago Sun-Times*, May 17, 1989.

36. Erik Brady, "Camacho Gets Cut When Car Hits Tree," *USA Today*, March 16, 1989.

37. "Lemons 'n' Losers: Cars That Bombed in the 1980s."

38. Janet Braunstein, "Little Yugo Revs for Comeback," *The Atlanta Journal-Constitution*, April 12, 1991.

39. Nancy Millman, "Bumper to Bumper, New Car Campaigns Try Different Routes," *Chicago Sun-Times*, October 3, 1990.

40. Thomas R. King, "Yugo Taps Agency to Reverse Bad Image," *The Wall Street Journal*, August 24, 1990.

41. Stuart Elliott, "'91 Auto Ads Put to the Test," *USA Today*, October 26, 1990.

42. "On the Road Again: He's the Comeback Kid; Yugo Co-founder Taking Another Shot," *The Record* (New Jersey), April 30, 1991.

43. Stephanie Stokes, "Yugo America Ready to Shift into Drive."
44. "U.S. auto sales worst since '83," *The Pantagraph* (Bloomington, IL), January 5, 1991.
45. Kevin Done, "Rover to Quit US Market after Decline in Car Sales," *Financial Times*, August 10, 1991. See also, "French Automaker Decides to Quit Selling Cars in U.S.," *The Pantagraph* (Bloomington, IL), August 8, 1991.
46. Kristine Stiven Breese, "Daihatsu Struggles to Make Itself Known: Limited Availability, Vague Image Hurt Sales," *The Atlanta Journal-Constitution*, April 27, 1991.
47. Richard Walker, "Yugo Car Prospects Bleak—Yugoslavian Official," *Akron Beacon Journal*, September 6, 1990.
48. Louis Sell, *Slobodan Milosevic and the Destruction of Yugoslavia* (Durham, NC: Duke University Press, 2002), 102.
49. Paul A. Eisenstein, "Yugo Is Back, but for How Long?" *The Washington Times*, December 6, 1991.
50. Barbara Wendling, interview with author, June 12, 2007.
51. Charles A. Radin, "Like Its Country, Yugo Risks Losing Key Parts," *The Boston Globe*, November 30, 1991. Zastava's suppliers are listed in *Guide to Yugo* (Kragujevac: Zastava-Yugo Car Factory Export Bureau, 1988).
52. Michael Palairet, "The Rise and Fall of Yugoslav Socialism: A Case Study of the Yugo Automobile Enterprise, 1954–92," in David F. Good, ed., *Economic Transformations in East and Central Europe* (New York: Routledge, 1994), 107.
53. "On the Road Again: He's the Comeback Kid; Yugo Co-founder Taking Another Shot."
54. Ibid.
55. "New Boss at Yugo Is Determined to Get Business Rolling Again," *The Atlanta Journal-Constitution*, July 5, 1991.
56. Frederick Standish, "Yugoslavian Unrest Little Bother to Yugo," Associated Press, July 12, 1991.
57. Ibid.
58. Jeff Danziger, "Why Yugo Owners Are Not Surprised by Recent Events," *The Christian Science Monitor*, July 9, 1991.
59. "Bosnia," *TV Nation* (1994; VHS: Columbia TriStar, 1997).
60. "Prior Leaves Yugo . . . Again," *Automotive News*, November 25, 1991.
61. Dan Jedlicka, "No More Yugos for America," *Chicago Sun-Times*, April 21, 1992.
62. Jim Mateja, "Yugo Backs Out of U.S. as Civil War Takes Toll," *Chicago Tribune*, April 21, 1992.
63. Ibid.
64. Jim Henry, "Yugo Dealers Left Stranded," *Automotive News*, May 1, 1992.
65. Jim Mateja, "Yugo Backs Out of U.S. as Civil War Takes Toll."
66. Ibid.
67. Jim Henry, "Yugo Dealers Left Stranded."

17: "ZMW, Get It?"

1. Andrew Katell and Walter R. Mears, "Yugoslav Assets Targeted—Bush Orders Freeze on Holdings in U.S.," *Star-Telegram* (Fort Worth), May 31, 1992.

2. "U.S. Widens, Tightens Squeeze on Yugoslavia," *Dayton Daily News*, July 7, 1992.

3. For one such list, see "Federal Republic of Yugoslavia Sanctions," *Federal Register* 60:74 (April 18, 1995): 19448–62.

4. Barbara Demick, "Bosnia Fallout Scars a Company in Bucks," *The Philadelphia Inquirer*, May 24, 1993.

5. William E. Thompson, "Rusting at Anchor—*Durmitor*: The Stranded Ship Has Become a Five-Year Fixture in the Harbor," *The Sun* (Baltimore), March 26, 1997.

6. James H. Rubin, "U.S. Indicts Bobby Fischer for Chess Match," *San Francisco Chronicle*, December 16, 1992.

7. Michael York and Joseph McLellan, "Chess Star Indicted for Ignoring Sanctions," *The Washington Post*, December 16, 1992.

8. Toma Savic, interview with author, July 28, 2006. Savic sent a letter of complaint to Zastava concerning CPAI's activities on December 25, 1994. That letter is in the possession of the author.

9. Stephanie Stokes, "Requiem for a Lightweight—Yugo Going, Going, Gone," *The Record* (New Jersey), September 16, 1992.

10. Dusan Stojanovic, "War Is Fatal Blow: Closed Shop, Unemployment, and Despair for Yugo Employees," *The Seattle Times*, November 20, 1992.

11. Roger Cohen, "A Defunct Car, Like Its Homeland, Was the Sum of Its Parts," *The New York Times*, October 18, 1992.

12. Senate Foreign Relations Committee, Hearing of the Senate Foreign Relations Committee: Confirmation of Deputy Secretary of State, 101st Cong., 1st Sess., March 16, 1989, 56.

13. "Senate Panel Vote—Eagleburger OKd for State Dept. Job," *San Francisco Chronicle*, March 17, 1989.

14. Jack Anderson, "Eagleburger and Yugoslavia," *San Francisco Chronicle*, February 21, 1989.

15. "Eagleburger Wins Panel's Approval," *The Boston Globe*, March 17, 1989.

16. David Binder, "Eagleburger Anguishes over Yugoslav Upheaval," *The New York Times*, June 19, 1992.

17. Saul Friedman, "Bush Aides Leaned Toward Serb Leadership," *Newsday*, August 10, 1992.

18. Ibid.

19. The "General Framework Agreement for Peace in Bosnia and Herzegovina" was negotiated in November 1995 at the Wright-Patterson Air Force Base near Dayton, Ohio. It was formally signed in Paris on December 14, 1995.

20. Chris Hedges, "Isolated and Corrupt, Serbia's Economy Stagnates," *The New York Times*, July 9, 1996.

21. "When All Else Fails, Milosevic Tries Peace," *The Miami Herald*, August 22, 1996.

22. Misha Savic, " 'Yugo' Town Has Key Role in Opposition," *The Miami Herald*, December 7, 1996.

23. Chris Hedges, "Isolated and Corrupt, Serbia's Economy Stagnates."

24. "Yugo Maker Stalls on Communism Fear," *The Press of Atlantic City*, April 10, 1996.

25. Bill Schiller, " 'Detroit of Balkans' Struggles to Survive," *The Toronto Star*, February 16, 1997.

26. Chris Hedges, "Serbian Town Finds the Cost of Democracy Is Lost Jobs," *New York Times*, December 13, 1996.
27. Tom Hundley, "Whether NATO Allies Will Agree to Strike Yugoslavia Is Unclear," *The Seattle Times*, September 25, 1998.
28. Tom Walker, "NATO Missiles Destroy Car Plant," *The Globe and Mail* (Toronto), April 10, 1999.
29. Uli Schmetzer, "NATO Bombs Deal Fatal Blow to Once-Proud Automaker," *Chicago Tribune*, June 16, 1999.
30. Tom Walker, "NATO Missiles Destroy Car Plant."
31. "Foot Down," *Financial Times*, February 22, 1999.
32. "Serbian Phone Deal by Italians and Greeks," *The New York Times*, June 10, 1997.
33. "Yugoslavia's Currency Under Pressure Again," Beta News Agency (Belgrade), July 4, 1998.
34. Peter Klebnikov, "The Serbs' New Quest: Western Investment," *BusinessWeek*, September 20, 1999, 4.
35. Uli Schmetzer, "NATO Bombs Deal Fatal Blow to Once-Proud Automaker."
36. "Milosevic Claims '99 Was Glorious Year," *Contra Costa Times* (California), January 2, 2000.
37. Lori Montgomery, "Milosevic Touts Sham Recovery in Yugoslavia," *The Seattle Times*, October 26, 1999.
38. Steven Erlander, "The Yugo, Wartime Survivor, Faces Open Market," *The New York Times*, January 5, 2001.
39. Ibid.
40. "France's Renault Takes over 51 Per Cent of Romanian Car Firm," Rompres News Agency (Bucharest), September 30, 1999.
41. Milovan Mracevich, "Remember the Yugo?" *Transitions Online*, November 11, 2002, www.tol.cz (site accessed on January 29, 2009).
42. Ibid.
43. Ibid.
44. The *Forbes* report (entitled "Yugo Redux") was written by Doug Donovan and appeared on the Forbes.com website on April 23, 2002. www.forbes.com/2002/04/23/0423yugo.html (site accessed on June 20, 2008).
45. Ira Edelson, interview with author, May 27, 2004.
46. Walter Hamilton, "Charging Ahead—Company Drives to Mass Produce Electric Vehicles," *Daily News* (Los Angeles), June 6, 1993.
47. Damon Darlin, "Bikes by Bricklin," *Forbes* 156:1 (July 3, 1995): 78.
48. Ibid.
49. Dick Marlowe, "Despite Misfires, Bricklin Keeps Ideas Moving," *Sun-Sentinel*, June 16, 1995.
50. "Entrepreneurs Plug New Electric Bikes," *Sun-Sentinel*, June 18, 1996.
51. Dick Marlowe, "Despite Misfires, Bricklin Keeps Ideas Moving."
52. Mark Rechtin, "Bricklin Project Dies, but He Touts New One," *Automotive News*, September 22, 1997.
53. Ben Sullivan, "Bricklin Resumes Pursuit of Electric Bike Venture," *Los Angeles Business Journal*, April 7, 1997, 13.
54. Mark Rechtin, "Bricklin Project Dies, but He Touts New One."
55. Doug Donovan, "Will the Wheels Stay On?" *Forbes* 170:1 (July 8, 2002): 155.

56. "From Yugo to ZMW—Boone Grad at the Wheel," *Sun-Sentinel*, May 2, 2002.
57. Ibid.
58. Ira Edelson, interview with author, May 27, 2004.
59. Greg Williams, "Bricklin's Vision for Vehicles Electrifying," *Calgary Herald*, February 8, 2008.
60. Michael Murphy, "Serbia: Fiat to Enter JV with Serbian Government," *Automotive World*, April 29, 2008.

Epilogue

1. Dusan Stojanovic, "Serbia Bids Farewell to Yugo," Associated Press, November 19, 2008.
2. "End of Road Comes for Serbia's Zastava Car," SeeNews, November 20, 2008.
3. Yugonostalgia is a well-documented phenomenon. It is the subject of numerous academic treatises, and has even been featured in a segment of National Public Radio's *All Things Considered*. See Nicole Lindstrom, "Yugonostalgia: Restorative and Reflective Nostalgia in Former Yugoslavia," *East Central Europe* 32:1–2 (July 2006): 231–42.
4. Zabranjeno Pusenje, "Jugo 45" (Agent Tajne Sile, 1999). Translation by Magdalena Markovinovic.
5. "Movie trailer," *Drowning Mona*, directed by Nick Gomez (2000; DVD: Culver City, CA: Sony Pictures, 2000).
6. Doron Levin, "Bricklin Again Rises from Past Debacles—His Latest Chase for Success: Selling the Yugo," *The Wall Street Journal*, May 16, 1986.
7. B92.net, "Yugo Production to Continue in Congo," www.b92.net/eng/news/business-article.php?yyyy=2008&mm=10&dd=28&nav_id=54563 (site accessed February 14, 2009).

Acknowledgments

I owe a great deal of gratitude to several dozen people who helped me with this book. First, I wish to thank those who gave generously of their time and who allowed me to interview them, including Ira Edelson, Tony Ciminera, Malcolm Bricklin, Roger Berry, Toma Savic, Miroslav Kefurt, Marcel Kole, the late Pete Mulhern, Dave Benton, Zoran Basaraba, Barbara Wendling, Veljko Rujanovic, Andrej Kirylak, Bob Randall, Zdravka Damjanic, Karl Ludvigsen, Fulvio Dobrich, Maggie Mudd, Borka Konte, Bill Fahringer, Dee Weiss, Ray Burns, Lloyd George, Russell Prickett, Patrick Nichols, the late Ambassador John Scanlan, Pravin Banker, Bob Knoll, John Yardley, Christina Ford, Andrew DeTablan, Ron Jellis, and Jay Pierce. I'd also like to thank Dario Vitez, Tom Magliery, Wendy Wintman, and Charlie Russell for kindly providing me with permissions; Adam Periskic, Slavica Periskic, and Magdalena Markovinovic for help with translations; Thomas LeBien of Hill and Wang for taking a big chance on a screwy book; Halina Stephan of the Center for Slavic and East European Studies at the Ohio State University for being a good boss and an even better friend; John Treadway and Charles Jelavich for being true mentors; and all of my friends and colleagues from Punta Gorda, Wake, IU, OSU, and Bridgewater College for their kindness and support. And last but certainly not least, I'd like to thank my parents; my friend Al Jean; my sister, Kelly (who is also the best researcher I know); my brother-in-law, Trey; my beautiful nieces and nephews; the Dixon family; the Zivkovic family; the Periskic family; the extended Vuic family; the Mitchell family; my Maimed Aunt and my Uncle Patrick; Drs. Fogarty, Honeycutt, and Overway (my fo' shizzles); Robbie

Mataric; Luke Wock-a-nesky; John Ashbrook; Jody Prestia; Randy, Dorothy, Mimi, Marquis, and Marqual; and my beautiful wife and best friend, Kara (who, incidentally, will *not* let me buy a Yugo).

Index

General Agreement on Tariffs and Trade
(GATT), 89–90
General Motors, 18–19, 53, 75; annual
model changes, 62, 63; econo-box
market, 108–109, 112, 120; price
stairways, 62–63
General Vehicle Inc., 31–33, 35
Genex, 12, 46, 69–72, 94, 99, 186, 199
Germany, 7, 53, 55, 64; cars, 11, 67,
102–103, 121; Nazi, 53, 54–56; World
War I, 52; World War II, 54–56
Global Motors, 115, 158–59, 178–83, 189,
236*n*26; Proton deal, 178–83, 241*n*31
Goodway Printing, 28–29, 41
Great Britain, 8, 11, 52, 155; cars, 43,
68–69; press, 68–69; Yugo in, 43, 67,
68–69, 224*n*22, 231*n*37
Greece, 54, 67, 97; cars, 115
Greenwald, Gerald, 112
GTE, 93

Halperin, Jonas, 44, 50, 88, 97, 102,
159–60
Hammer, Armand, 44–47
Handyman America Inc., 21–23, 219*n*4
Harkin, Tom, 92
Hatfield, Richard, 32, 35, 36, 38
Heavy Industries Corporation of
Malaysia (HICOM), 151–54
Helms, Jesse, 201, 202
Hertel, Dennis, 88, 89, 97
Hertz Corporation, 18
Hitler, Adolf, 54–55, 93
Honda, 10–11, 19, 25, 90, 95, 120
Honda Accord, 19, 195
Honda Accord LX, 19
Honda Civic, 19, 68, 107, 120, 122,
218*n*54
Honda Civic CRX, 104
Honda 600, 10–11
Hyundai, 20, 115–22, 205; as Yugo
competition, 115–22
Hyundai Engineering and Construction
Company, 115–16
Hyundai Excel, 107, 108, 109, 117–20,
144, 145, 146, 158, 164

Hyundai Motor America, 118
Hyundai Pony, 20, 117, 119

icon, Yugo as, 5–6, 8
Imperial Savings and Loan, 178, 186,
189, 241*n*39; Mabon, Nugent–Global
Motors deal, 178–83, 241*n*31
Independent, 119
Innocenti, 23–24
insurance, 149; collision rates, 149–50
Insurance Institute for Highway Safety
(IIHS), 6–7, 146, 149–50; crash tests,
149–50
International Automobile Importers
(IAI), 21, 39–50, 69–72, 75, 102; failed
operation, 48–49; Occidental-Zastava
trade/barter agreement, 44–47, 69–72;
Yugo America and, 75, 95; Zastava
and, 44–47, 69–72, 75, 95, 115
International Trade Commission (ITC),
90, 97
Intreprinderea de Autoturisme Pitesti,
113–14
Investbanka, 94
Isuzu, 95
Isuzu I-Mark, 144, 145
Italdesign, 119
Italy, 21, 39, 42, 52, 55, 66; cars, 21,
39–43, 57–59; importation of cars to
America, 39–43
Ivcec, Petar, 126
Iwabuchi, Kenji, 182

Jaguar, 43, 87, 164, 171
Jamiesson, Max, 118
Japan, 18–19, 24, 88, 107, 124; car parts
industry, 152, 153, 156; econo-box
car market, 18–19, 107–109, 118, 119,
120, 121, 122; importation of cars to
America, 19, 24–29, 90, 107; upscale
car models, 19; VER quotas, 19, 156
J. D. Power and Associates, 6, 121, 164
Jeep, 57
jokes, Yugo, 5, 142, 167–68, 193, 197, 212
Jovanovic, Gvozden, 206

Jugo, 67–68
Jugobanka, 199
Jugo Florida, 68
"Jugo 45" (song), 212
Jugo Koral, 68
Jugo Skala, 68
junk bonds, 180, 183–84, 185

Kaiser-Fraser Corporation, 220*n*2
Kefurt, Miroslav, 9–20, 47–50, 113;
  Bricklin and, 47–49; idea for Yugo
  sales in America, 9–20; Yugo 45
  distribution in California, 12–16,
  47–48
Kelley Blue Book, 135
Kia, 121
Kissinger, Henry, 91, 94, 157, 160, 161,
  181, 201
Kissinger Associates, 91–94, 157, 160,
  202, 227*n*17, 236*n*26
Knepper, Mark, 101
Knoll, Bob, 139, 140, 142
Knudsen, S. E. "Bunky," 27
Koffman family, 29, 38
Kole, Marcel, 166, 185, 188, 237*n*35
Korea, 20, 88; cars, 20, 115–22
Kornheiser, Tony, 168
Kosovo, 64, 123, 195, 196, 204
Kostic, Budimir, 94
Kragujevac, Serbia, 11–12, 13, 49,
  51–57, 95, 99, 203; arms factory, 52,
  53–55; World War II, 53–56; Yugo
  production, 77–83, 95–100; Zastava
  factory, 11–13, 49, 57, 58–59, 66–72,
  77–83, 95–100, 112, 123, 160, 217*n*11
Kravis, Henry, 184
Krstic, Milos, 94
Kucan, Milan, 195

Lada, 7, 58, 61, 66, 115
Lambert, Dale, and Bernhard, 165
Lamborghini Countach 5000, 83
Lambretta scooters, 23–24
Lamm, Harvey, 25–27
Landegger, Celia, 4

Lautenberg, Frank, 92
Lemon Indexes, 7
Leno, Jay, 5, 167, 197
Letterman, David, 167–68
Ligero, 115
Lincah Gama, 115, 158
Lincoln Town Car, 105, 106
loan against imports, 131–32
loans, car, 105–107
Loomis, Fred, 169
Los Angeles, 9, 47; 1984 AutoExpo, 9,
  16–17, 20, 47; 1984 Olympics, 13–15;
  Yugo in, 13–17
Los Angeles *Daily News*, 4, 167
Los Angeles Times, 16
Lotus Performance Cars, 193–94,
  243*n*34
luxury cars, 39, 171, 193

Mabon, Nugent & Company, 178–83,
  189; Imperial–Global Motors deal,
  178–83, 241*n*31
Macedonia, 64, 91, 195, 204, 211; Skopje
  earthquake, 91–92
Magliozzi, Tom and Ray, 192
Mahathir bin Mohamad, 151–61, 181
Mahindra, 115
Malaysia, 7, 151–52; cars, 7, 115, 151–61,
  163; economy, 154; industrialization,
  151–54
Manufacturers Hanover Trust, 130;
  Yugo America loan, 130–34, 148, 149,
  160, 183, 233*n*38
Markovic, Ante, 195, 196
Maryland, 159
Maserati, 87
Mateja, Jim, 109
materialism, of 1980s, 170–73, 212
Mazda, 95, 152
Mazda 323, 107, 144
McDonald's, 12, 13, 93
McDonnell Douglas, 45
media, 4–5, 65, 96, 113, 121, 126; on
  Bricklin SV-1, 33, 35; on Yugo, 4–5, 8,
  16–17, 50, 68–69, 75–76, 84, 87, 88, 90,
  101–104, 106, 125, 133–35, 140–50,

Printed in the USA
CPSIA information can be obtained
at www.ICGtesting.com
LVHW010331150724
785510LV00001B/45

9 780809 098958